KETO CHAFFLE
RECIPES
COOKBOOK

500 Mouth-Watering, Quick & Easy Ketogenic Low-Carb Waffles to Lose Weight with Taste

By Jennifer Swayze

© Copyright 2021 by Jennifer Swayze - All rights reserved.

TABLE OF CONTENTS

JENNIFER SWAYZE

CHAPTER 6:SWEET CHAFFLE ROLL RECIPES ...139

CHAPTER 5:   PIZZA CHAFFLE RECIPES 128

INTRODUCTION

Welcome to the mouth-watering world of Keto Chaffles, the easy low-carb waffles that became a must-have for all Ketogenic diet followers thanks to their simplicity.

A chaffle, or cheddar waffle, is just a waffle made of cheese and eggs. It can be easily prepared at home and it's suitable for your breakfast, lunch, snack or dessert.

Chaffles are a fantastic alternative to waffles as they are high-fat, high-protein, and low-carbohydrates: they won't spike your insulin levels, causing the accumulation of fat. They are ketogenic healthy foods that respect the Keto diet recommendations.

Thanks to the easy base ingredients and to the limitless number of possible recipes that can be prepared, you will certainly find one to love! You can start from the fundamental recipe for a chaffle and create your own one: sweet or savory, a cake or a sandwich, as you prefer!

The purpose of this book is to introduce you into the making process of chaffles and to provide some useful tips and information but, most of all, you will find 500 quick recipes to taste with your family.

All the suggested ingredients are keto-friendly foods: you will enjoy only low-carb recipes that will enable you to maintain ketosis and to easily lose weight without sacrificing taste.

So, are you ready to get started? Chaffles are waiting to be enjoyed!

CHAPTER 1:   WHAT IS A CHAFFLE?

The name chaffle comes from Cheese + Waffle = Chaffle. A basic chaffle is just made of two ingredients: 1 egg and ½ cup of shredded cheese. It's simply a waffle but made with cheese and this is great if you are following a keto diet as you can eat low carb without sacrificing flavor.

You can change the type of cheese to use, changing in this way the taste of the chaffle.

Keto chaffles are a great alternative for bread and they can be used to prepare tasty sandwiches while staying in ketosis. Chaffles are delicious: it may seem strange, but you can be sure that they don't taste like burnt egg!

The Chaffle Maker

To prepare chaffles you can use a regular waffle maker or a special chaffle maker. There are several brands available and they come with different settings, different cooking times and non-stick versions.

The mini chaffle maker is very practical to prepare one chaffle and I really love it!

You can anyway prepare delicious chaffles also without a waffle maker. You just need a nonstick saucepan. Grease and hot the pan before pouring the batter: let cook until golden brown and use a spatula to gently flip it.

Practical Chaffle Tips

The basic chaffle recipe is so easy but there are a few tips to follow for a perfect result:

1. Preheat the chaffle maker so the batter will start cooking when hits the pan;
2. Sprinkle some extra cheese in the waffle iron before adding the batter if you wish to obtain a crispy chaffle;
3. Use finely shredded cheese for the batter;
4. If using the cream cheese, gently melt or soften it, to easily stir it into the batter;
5. If using coconut flour, let the batter sit for 2-3 minutes to thicken;
6. Don't open the chaffle maker too early. It's best to cook most of the chaffle recipes for a minimum of 4 minutes; you will know the chaffle is ready when steam is no longer coming out the sides;
7. To reduce the eggy taste, let chaffle cool completely and use egg whites instead of whole eggs;

How to Serve Chaffles

There are several approaches to serve chaffles and you can make many variations according to the kind of meal you are making chaffles for. Here are some ideas:

- Plain Chaffle: chaffle is delicious all alone and you can serve it close by avocado, bacon, sour cream or your favorite keto sauce;
- Chaffle Sandwich: you can prepare two chaffles and use them as bread. Per the filling, you can choose the ones of your favorite keto sandwiches;
- Sweet Chaffle: there are many sweet chaffle varieties you can taste for breakfast or dessert. Top your chaffle with berries, keto syrup or keto whipped cream.

For a different flavor, you can try various type of cheese in the base. This will produce somewhat various surfaces; you just have to find your top choice.

Can Chaffles Be Frozen?

Yes, sure! You can freeze chaffles for 20-30 days. Just be sure to keep them in a freezer bag and in case you are freezing more than one, place a parchment paper piece between them.

You can reheat chaffles in the toaster oven, saucepan, toaster or conventional oven.

Toaster is my favorite choice, as easiest and fastest.

How to Clean the Waffle Maker

- Clean the chaffle maker as soon as it is cool enough;

- Use a paper towel for wiping away the crumbs;

- Wipe the exterior with the paper towel;

- Wash the cooking plates with soap in warm water;

You can find several dishwashing gadgets that can get between the grooves if needed.

CHAPTER 2:   BASIC CHAFFLE RECIPES

Classic Chaffle

Prep Time: 5 minutes
Cook Time: 8 minutes
Servings: 2 chaffles

Ingredients:
1 large egg, beaten
½ cup of cheese

Instructions:
Heat up the mini waffle maker.
Add cheese and egg to a small mixing bowl and combine well.

Pour half of the batter into the waffle maker and cook for 4 minutes until golden brown. Repeat with the rest of the batter to make another chaffle.
Let cool for 3 minutes to let chaffles get crispy.
Serve and enjoy!

Almond Flour Chaffle

Prep Time: 5 minutes
Cook Time: 8 minutes
Servings: 2 chaffles

Ingredients:
1 large egg, beaten

½ cup of cheese
2 tbsp. almond flour

Instructions:
Heat up the mini waffle maker.
Add the cheese, almond flour, and egg to a small mixing bowl and combine well.
Pour half of the batter into the waffle maker and cook for 4 minutes until golden brown. Repeat with the rest of the batter to make another chaffle.
Let cool for 3 minutes to let chaffles get crispy.
Serve and enjoy!

Almond Flour Chaffle with Mozzarella

Prep Time: 5 minutes
Cook Time: 8 minutes
Servings: 2 chaffles

Ingredients:
1 large egg, beaten
½ cup of mozzarella cheese, shredded
2 tbsp almond flour
¼ tsp baking powder

Instructions:
Heat up the mini waffle maker.
Add all the ingredients to a small mixing bowl and combine well.
Pour half of the batter into the waffle maker and cook for 4 minutes until brown. Repeat with the rest of the batter to make another chaffle.
Let cool for 3 minutes to let chaffles get crispy.
Serve and enjoy!

Coconut Flour Chaffle

Prep Time: 5 minutes
Cook Time: 8 minutes
Servings: 2 chaffles

Ingredients:
1 large egg, beaten
½ cup mozzarella cheese, grated
1 tsp coconut flour
1 tsp water
¼ tsp baking powder

Instructions:
Heat up the mini waffle maker.
Add all the ingredients to a small mixing bowl and combine well.
Pour half of the batter into the waffle maker and cook for 4 minutes until brown. Repeat with the rest of the batter to make another chaffle.
Let cool for 3 minutes to let chaffles get crispy.
Serve and enjoy!

Cheddar Chaffle

Prep Time: 5 minutes
Cook Time: 8 minutes
Servings: 2 chaffles

Ingredients:
1 large egg, beaten
½ cup shredded cheddar cheese

Instructions:
Heat up the waffle maker.
Add egg and shredded cheese to a small mixing bowl and combine well.
Pour half of the batter into the waffle maker and cook for 4 minutes until golden brown. Repeat with the rest of the batter to make another chaffle.
Let cool for 3 minutes to let chaffles get crispy.
Serve and enjoy!

Fontina Cheese Chaffle

Prep Time: 5 minutes
Cook Time: 8 minutes
Servings: 2 chaffles

Ingredients:
1 large egg, beaten
½ cup of fontina cheese, shredded

Instructions:
Heat up the mini waffle maker.
Add cheese and egg to a small mixing bowl and combine well.
Pour half of the batter into the waffle maker and cook for 4 minutes until golden brown. Repeat with the rest of the batter to make another chaffle.
Let cool for 3 minutes to let chaffles get crispy.

Serve and enjoy!

Herbs Chaffle

Prep Time: 5 minutes
Cook Time: 8 minutes
Servings: 2 chaffles

Ingredients:
1 egg, beaten
½ cup shredded cheddar cheese
1 tsp fresh basil
½ tsp dried oregano
½ tsp dried thyme

Instructions:
Heat up the waffle maker.
Add all the ingredients to a small mixing bowl and combine well.
Pour half of the batter into the waffle maker and cook for 4 minutes until golden brown. Repeat with the rest of the batter to make another chaffle.
Serve with sour cream and enjoy!

Mozzarella Chaffle

Prep Time: 5 minutes
Cook Time: 8 minutes
Servings: 2 chaffles

Ingredients:
1 large egg, beaten
½ cup shredded mozzarella cheese
A pinch of salt

Instructions:
Heat up the waffle maker.
Add egg, shredded mozzarella cheese and a pinch of salt to a small mixing bowl and combine well.
Pour half of the batter into the waffle maker and cook for 4 minutes. Repeat with the rest of the batter to make another chaffle.
Let cool for 3 minutes to let chaffles get crispy.
Serve and enjoy!

Chaffle with Garlic

Prep Time: 5 minutes
Cook Time: 8 minutes
Servings: 2 chaffles

Ingredients:
1 egg, beaten
½ cup shredded mozzarella cheese
¼ tsp garlic powder

Instructions:
Heat up the waffle maker.
Add egg, shredded mozzarella cheese and garlic powder to a small mixing bowl and combine well.
Pour half of the batter into the waffle maker and cook for 4 minutes. Repeat with the rest of the batter to make another chaffle.
Let cool for 3 minutes to let chaffles get crispy.
Serve and enjoy!

Chaffle with Garlic and Parsley

Prep Time: 5 minutes
Cook Time: 8 minutes
Servings: 2 chaffles

Ingredients:
1 egg, beaten
½ cup shredded mozzarella cheese
1 tsp coconut flour
¼ tsp baking powder
½ tsp garlic powder
½ tsp fresh parsley, minced

Instructions:
Heat up the waffle maker.
Add all the ingredients to a small mixing bowl and combine well.
Pour half of the batter into the waffle maker and cook for 4 minutes until golden brown. Repeat with the rest of the batter to make another chaffle.
Let cool for 3 minutes to let chaffles get crispy.
Serve and enjoy!

Parsley Chaffle

Prep Time: 5 minutes
Cook Time: 8 minutes
Servings: 2 chaffles

Ingredients:
1 egg, beaten
½ cup shredded mozzarella cheese
½ tbsp fresh parsley, finely chopped

Instructions:
Heat up the waffle maker.
Add egg, shredded mozzarella cheese and parsley to a small mixing bowl and combine well.
Pour half of the batter into the waffle maker and cook for 4 minutes until brown. Repeat with the rest of the batter to make another chaffle.
Serve and enjoy!

Fresh Basil Chaffle

Prep Time: 5 minutes
Cook Time: 8 minutes
Servings: 2 chaffles

Ingredients:
1 egg, beaten
½ cup shredded cheddar cheese
½ tbsp fresh basil, finely chopped

Instructions:
Heat up the waffle maker.
Add egg, shredded cheddar cheese, and basil to a small mixing bowl and combine well.
Pour half of the batter into the waffle maker and cook for 4 minutes until brown. Repeat with the rest of the batter to make another chaffle.
Serve with a slice of tomato and keto mayonnaise and enjoy!

Provolone Cheese Chaffle

Prep Time: 5 minutes
Cook Time: 8 minutes
Servings: 2 chaffles

Ingredients:
1 egg, beaten
½ cup shredded Provolone cheese

Instructions:
Heat up the waffle maker.
Add egg and shredded cheese to a small mixing bowl and combine well.
Pour half of the batter into the waffle maker and cook for 4 minutes until brown. Repeat with the rest of the batter to make another chaffle.
Let cool for 3 minutes to let chaffles get crispy.
Serve and enjoy!

Cheesy Chaffle

Prep Time: 5 minutes
Cook Time: 8 minutes
Servings: 2 chaffles

Ingredients:
1 large egg, beaten
½ cup shredded Cheddar cheese
½ tsp ground flaxseed
¼ tsp baking powder
2 tbsp shredded Parmesan cheese

Instructions:
Heat up the mini waffle maker.
Add all the ingredients except Parmesan cheese to a small mixing bowl and stir until well combined.
Pour half of the Parmesan cheese in the preheated waffle maker.
Pour half of the batter into the waffle maker, top with the remaining Parmesan cheese and cook for 4 minutes until brown. Repeat with the remaining batter/cheese to prepare another chaffle.
Let cool for 3 minutes to let chaffles get crispy.
Serve and enjoy!

Parmesan Cheese Chaffle

Prep Time: 5 minutes
Cook Time: 8 minutes
Servings: 2 chaffles

Ingredients:
1 large egg, beaten

½ cup Parmesan cheese, finely grated
A pinch of salt and pepper

Instructions:
Heat up the waffle maker.
Add all the ingredients to a small mixing bowl and combine well.
Pour half of the batter into the waffle maker and cook for 4 minutes until golden brown. Repeat with the rest of the batter to make another chaffle.
Let cool for 3 minutes to let chaffles get crispy.
Serve and enjoy!

Swiss Cheese Chaffle

Prep Time: 5 minutes
Cook Time: 8 minutes
Servings: 2 chaffles
Ingredients:
1 large egg, beaten
½ cup of Swiss cheese, shredded
1 tbsp almond flour

Instructions:
Heat up the waffle maker.
Add the cheese, almond flour, and egg to a small mixing bowl and combine well.
Pour half of the batter into the waffle maker and cook for 4 minutes until golden brown. Repeat with the rest of the batter to make another chaffle.
Let cool for 3 minutes to let chaffles get crispy.
Serve and enjoy!

Bread Chaffle

Prep Time: 4 minutes
Cook Time: 8 minutes
Servings: 2 chaffles

Ingredients:
1 egg
2 tbsp almond flour
1 tbsp mayonnaise
¼ tsp baking powder
1 tsp water

Instructions:
Heat up the waffle maker.

In a small bowl, whisk the egg until beaten.
Mix almond flour, mayonnaise, baking powder, and water in a mixing bowl.
Combine egg and flour mixture.
Pour half of the batter into the waffle maker and cook for 4 minutes. Repeat with the rest of the batter to make another chaffle.
Serve and enjoy!

Delicious Bread Chaffle

Prep Time: 4 minutes
Cook Time: 16 minutes
Servings: 4 chaffles
Ingredients:
2 eggs white, beaten
4 tbsp almond flour
1 tbsp mayonnaise
¼ tsp baking powder
1 tsp poppy seeds, chopped
1 tsp water
Salt to taste

Instructions:
Heat up the waffle maker.
Add all the ingredients to a small mixing bowl and stir until well combined.
Pour ¼ of the batter into the waffle maker and cook for 4 minutes until golden brown. Repeat with the rest of the batter to make the other chaffles.
Serve and enjoy!

Dairy free Chaffle

Prep Time: 2 minutes
Cook Time: 12 minutes
Servings: 3 chaffles

Ingredients:
1 tbsp coconut flour
1 tbsp beef gelatin powder
2 eggs
1 tbsp mayonnaise
A pinch of salt

Instructions:
Heat up the mini waffle maker.

Mix the coconut flour, beef gelatin and salt in a small mixing bowl.

Whisk in the eggs and mayonnaise.

Pour 1/3 of the batter into the waffle maker and cook for 4 minutes. Repeat with the rest of the batter to make other 2 chaffles.

Serve and enjoy!

Rosemary Chaffle

Prep Time: 5 minutes
Cook Time: 8 minutes
Servings: 2 chaffles
Ingredients:
1 egg, beaten
½ cup shredded cheddar cheese
½ tbsp fresh rosemary, finely chopped

Instructions:
Heat up the waffle maker.

Add egg, shredded cheddar cheese, and rosemary to a small mixing bowl and combine well.

Pour half of the batter into the waffle maker and cook for 4 minutes until brown. Repeat with the rest of the batter to make another chaffle.

Serve with your favorite keto dressing and enjoy!

Fresh Dill Chaffle

Prep Time: 5 minutes
Cook Time: 8 minutes
Servings: 2 chaffles

Ingredients:
1 egg, beaten
½ cup shredded cheddar cheese
½ tbsp fresh dill, finely chopped

Instructions:
Heat up the waffle maker.

Add egg, shredded cheddar cheese, and dill to a small mixing bowl and combine well.

Pour half of the batter into the waffle maker and cook for 4 minutes until brown. Repeat with the rest of the batter to make another chaffle.

Serve with your favorite keto dressing and enjoy!

Fresh Coriander Chaffle

Prep Time: 5 minutes
Cook Time: 8 minutes
Servings: 2 chaffles

Ingredients:
1 egg, beaten
½ cup shredded mozzarella cheese
1 tsp coconut flour
¼ tsp baking powder
½ tsp fresh coriander, minced

Instructions:
Heat up the waffle maker.

Add all the ingredients to a small mixing bowl and combine well.

Pour half of the batter into the waffle maker and cook for 4 minutes until golden brown. Repeat with the rest of the batter to make another chaffle.

Let cool for 3 minutes to let chaffles get crispy.

Serve and enjoy!

Cornbread Chaffle

Prep Time: 5 minutes
Cook Time: 8 minutes
Servings: 2 chaffles

Ingredients:
1 egg, beaten
½ cup shredded cheddar cheese
¼ tsp corn bread extract
¼ tsp baking powder
A pinch of salt and pepper

Instructions:
Heat up the waffle maker.

Add all the ingredients to a small mixing bowl and stir until well combined.

Pour half of the batter into the waffle maker and cook for 4 minutes until brown. Repeat with the rest of the batter to make another chaffle.

Let cool for 3 minutes to let chaffles get crispy.

Serve and enjoy!

Soft Chaffle

Prep Time: 5 minutes
Cook Time: 16 minutes
Servings: 4 chaffles

Ingredients:
¼ cup almond flour
½ cup mozzarella cheese, shredded
1 egg, beaten
1 large egg white
2 tbsp cream cheese
1 tbsp sweetener
½ tsp baking powder
¼ tsp vanilla extract
2 tbsp coconut flour

Instructions:
Heat up the mini waffle maker.
Add all the ingredients to a small mixing bowl and combine well.
Pour ¼ of the batter into your waffle maker and cook for 4 minutes until golden brown. Then cook the remaining batter to prepare the other chaffles.
Serve and enjoy!

Savory Chaffle

Prep Time: 5 minutes
Cook Time: 16 minutes
Servings: 4 chaffles

Ingredients:
4 eggs, beaten
1 cup shredded Provolone cheese
1 cup Mozzarella cheese, shredded
½ cup almond flour
2 tbsp coconut flour
2 tsp baking powder
A pinch of salt and pepper

Instructions:
Heat up the waffle maker.
Add all the ingredients to a small mixing bowl and combine well.
Pour ¼ of the batter into the waffle maker and cook for 4 minutes until brown. Repeat with the rest of the batter to prepare the other chaffles.

Let cool for 3 minutes to let chaffles get crispy. Serve and enjoy!

Egg-free Chaffle

Prep Time: 5 minutes
Cook Time: 4 minutes
Servings: 1 chaffle

Ingredients:
2 tbsp mozzarella cheese, shredded
1 tbsp cream cheese
1 tbsp psyllium husk powder

Instructions:
Heat up the waffle maker.
Add all the ingredients to a small mixing bowl and combine well.
Pour the batter into the waffle maker and cook for 4 minutes until brown.
Let cool for 3 minutes to let chaffles get crispy. Serve and enjoy!

Traditional Chaffle

Prep Time: 5 minutes
Cook Time: 8 minutes
Servings: 2 chaffles

Ingredients:
1 egg, beaten
½ cup of mozzarella cheese, shredded
2 tbsp almond flour
¼ tsp baking powder
½ psyllium husk powder

Instructions:
Heat up the waffle maker.
Add all the ingredients to a small mixing bowl and stir until well combined.
Pour half of the batter into the waffle maker and cook for 4 minutes until golden brown. Repeat with the rest of the batter to make another chaffle.
Let cool for 3 minutes to let chaffles get crispy.
Serve and enjoy!

Breakfast Chaffle

Prep Time: 5 minutes
Cook Time: 8 minutes
Servings: 2 chaffles

Ingredients:
1 large egg, beaten
½ cup cheddar cheese, shredded
¼ cup almond flour
¼ cup heavy cream

Instructions:
Heat up the waffle maker.
Add all the ingredients to a small mixing bowl and stir until well combined.
Pour half of the batter into the waffle maker and cook for 4 minutes until golden brown. Repeat with the rest of the batter to make another chaffle.
Let cool for 3 minutes to let chaffles get crispy.
Serve with maple syrup and berries and enjoy!

Curry Chaffle

Prep Time: 5 minutes
Cook Time: 8 minutes
Servings: 2 chaffles
Ingredients:
1 egg, beaten
½ cup shredded mozzarella cheese
½ tsp curry powder
½ tsp fresh basil, finely chopped

Instructions:
Heat up the waffle maker.
Add egg, shredded mozzarella cheese, curry powder and basil to a small mixing bowl and combine well.
Pour half of the batter into the waffle maker and cook for 4 minutes until brown. Repeat with the rest of the batter to make another chaffle.
Serve and enjoy!

Blue Cheese Chaffle

Prep Time: 5 minutes
Cook Time: 8 minutes
Servings: 2 chaffles

Ingredients:
1 large egg, beaten
½ cup Blue cheese, shredded
1 tsp sweetener

Instructions:
Heat up the waffle maker.
Add all the ingredients to a small mixing bowl and stir until well combined.
Pour half of the batter into the waffle maker and cook for 4 minutes until golden brown. Repeat with the rest of the batter to make another chaffle.
Let cool for 3 minutes to let chaffles get crispy.
Serve and enjoy!

Chives Chaffle

Prep Time: 5 minutes
Cook Time: 8 minutes
Servings: 2 chaffles

Ingredients:
1 large egg, beaten
½ cup of mozzarella cheese, shredded
2 tbsp almond flour
¼ tsp baking powder
1 tbsp chopped fresh chives

Instructions:
Heat up the waffle maker.
Add all the ingredients to a small mixing bowl and combine well.
Pour half of the batter into the waffle maker and cook for 4 minutes until brown. Repeat with the rest of the batter to make another chaffle.
Let cool for 3 minutes to let chaffles get crispy.
Serve and enjoy!

Ricotta Chaffle

Prep Time: 5 minutes
Cook Time: 8 minutes
Servings: 2 chaffles

Ingredients:
1 large egg, beaten
½ cup skim ricotta cheese
2 tbsp almond flour

½ tsp baking powder

Instructions:
Heat up the waffle maker.
Add all the ingredients to a small mixing bowl and stir until well combined.
Pour half of the batter into the waffle maker and cook for 4 minutes until golden brown. Repeat with the rest of the batter to make another chaffle.
Let cool for 3 minutes to let chaffles get crispy.
Serve and enjoy!

CHAPTER 3:   SWEET CHAFFLES RECIPES

Vanilla Chaffle

Prep Time: 5 minutes
Cook Time: 8 minutes
Servings: 2 chaffles

Ingredients for chaffles:
1 tbsp almond flour
½ cup mozzarella cheese
1 egg, beaten
1 tbsp sweetener
½ tsp vanilla extract

Instructions:
Heat up the waffle maker.
Add all the ingredients to a small mixing bowl and combine well.

Pour ½ of the batter into your waffle maker and cook for 4 minutes. Then cook the remaining batter to make another chaffle.
Top the chaffles with keto whipped cream or maple syrup.
Serve and enjoy!

Choco Chaffle

Prep Time: 5 minutes
Cook Time: 16 minutes
Servings: 4 chaffles

Ingredients:
2 eggs, beaten
2 tbsp heavy whipping cream

1 cup mozzarella cheese, shredded
1 tbsp dark cocoa, unsweetened
2 tsp coconut flour
½ tsp baking powder
½ tsp vanilla extract
½ tsp sweetener

Instructions:
Heat up the waffle maker.
Add all the ingredients to a small mixing bowl and stir until well combined.
Pour ¼ of the batter onto the bottom plate of the waffle maker.
Cook for approx. 4 minutes or until the chaffle is golden brown.
Repeat with the rest of the batter.
Serve with ice cream and enjoy!

Chaffle with Raspberries Syrup

Prep Time: 5 minutes
Cook Time: 8 minutes
Servings: 2 chaffles

Ingredients for chaffles:
1 egg, beaten
½ cup mozzarella cheese, shredded
1 tsp almond flour
1 tsp sour cream
A pinch of salt

Ingredients for raspberries syrup:
1 cup fresh raspberries
1 tsp vanilla extract
¼ cup sweetener
¼ cup water

Instructions for raspberries syrup:
In a saucepan over low heat add the raspberries, water, sweetener and vanilla extract.
Stir from time to time until you get a syrup.
Remove from heat, set aside and let cool.

Instructions for chaffles:
Heat up the waffle maker.
Add all the chaffles ingredients to a small mixing bowl and stir until well combined.

Pour half of the batter into the waffle maker and cook for 4 minutes until golden brown. Repeat with the rest of the batter to make another chaffle.
Let cool for 3 minutes to let chaffles get crispy.
Top the chaffles with raspberries syrup.
Serve and enjoy!

Peach Chaffle

Prep Time: 5 minutes
Cook Time: 8 minutes
Servings: 2 chaffles

Ingredients for chaffles:
1 tbsp almond flour
½ cup mozzarella cheese
1 egg, beaten
1 tbsp sweetener
½ teaspoon vanilla extract
Ingredients for topping:
1 ripe peach, sliced
1 tsp sweetener
1 tsp butter
1 tbsp whipped cream
1 tbsp unsweetened peach syrup

Instructions for peach topping:
Simmer the peach in butter for a few minutes and add a tsp of sweetener. Turn the heat off and set aside.
Instructions for chaffles:
Heat up the waffle maker.
Add all the ingredients to a small mixing bowl and combine well.
Pour ½ of the batter into your waffle maker and cook for 4 minutes until brown. Then cook the remaining batter to make another chaffle.
Top the chaffles with the butter poached peach slices, a dollop of whipped cream and a tbsp of unsweetened peach syrup.
Serve and enjoy!

Peach Chaffle with Chocolate Glaze

Prep Time: 5 minutes
Cook Time: 8 minutes
Servings: 2 chaffles

Ingredients for chaffles:
1 tbsp almond flour
½ cup mozzarella cheese, shredded
1 egg, beaten
1 tbsp sweetener
½ tsp vanilla extract

Ingredients for the chocolate icing:
¼ cup powdered erythritol
1 tbsp cocoa powder, unsweetened
1 tbsp almond milk
½ tsp vanilla extract
1 ripe peach, sliced for topping

Instructions for chocolate icing:
Add all the ingredients for the chocolate glaze, except peach, to a small bowl and combine well.

Instructions for chaffles:
Heat up the waffle maker.
Add all the ingredients to a small mixing bowl and combine well.
Pour ½ of the batter into your waffle maker and cook for 4 minutes until brown. Then cook the remaining batter to make another chaffle.
Top the chaffles with chocolate glaze and slices of peach.
Serve and enjoy!

Chaffle with Chocolate Chips & Custard

Prep Time: 5 minutes
Cook Time: 55 minutes
Servings: 2 chaffles

Ingredients for chaffles:
1 tbsp almond flour
½ cup mozzarella cheese
1 egg, beaten
1 tbsp sweetener
½ tsp vanilla extract

Ingredients for custard:
2 eggs
2 tbsp heavy cream
1 tbsp brown sugar substitute
½ tsp cinnamon powder
½ tsp vanilla extract

Ingredients for topping:
1 tbsp of unsweetened chocolate chips

Instructions for custard:
Preheat the oven at 350 °.
Place all ingredients in a small bowl and stir until well combined.
Pour the mixture in a baking tin and bake it for about 40-45 minutes.
Remove from heat and set aside to cool.

Instructions for chaffles:
Heat up the waffle maker.
Add all the chaffles ingredients to a small mixing bowl and combine well.
Pour ½ of the batter into your waffle maker and cook for 4 minutes until golden brown. Then cook the remaining batter to make another chaffle.
Top the chaffles with custard and sprinkle with chocolate chips.
Serve and enjoy!

Pecans Chaffle

Prep Time: 5 minutes
Cook Time: 8 minutes
Servings: 2 chaffles

Ingredients for chaffles:
1 tbsp almond flour
½ cup mozzarella cheese
1 egg, beaten
1 tbsp sweetener
½ tsp vanilla extract

Ingredients for topping:
1 tbsp whipped cream
1 tbsp unsweetened maple syrup
½ cup of chopped pecans

Instructions:
Heat up the waffle maker.
Add all the ingredients to a small mixing bowl and combine well.
Pour ½ of the batter into your waffle maker and cook for 4 minutes. Then cook the remaining batter to make another chaffle.
Top the chaffles with keto whipped cream, maple syrup and sprinkle with chopped pecans.
Serve and enjoy!

Greek Yogurt Chaffle

Prep Time: 5 minutes
Cook Time: 16 minutes
Servings: 4 chaffles

Ingredients:
2 tbsp almond flour
1 cup cheddar cheese, shredded
2 eggs, beaten
2 tbsp full-fat plain Greek yogurt
¼ tsp baking powder

Instructions:
Heat up the mini waffle maker.
Add all the ingredients to a small mixing bowl and stir until well combined.
Pour ¼ of the batter into the waffle maker and cook for 4 minutes until brown. Repeat with the rest of the batter to prepare the other chaffles.
Let cool for 3 minutes to let chaffles get crispy.
Serve and enjoy!

Yogurt and Nuts Chaffle

Prep Time: 5 minutes
Cook Time: 8 minutes
Servings: 2 chaffles

Ingredients:
2 tbsp almonds, chopped
½ cup mozzarella cheese, shredded
1 egg, beaten
1 tbsp yogurt
¼ tsp baking powder

Instructions:
Heat up the mini waffle maker.
Add all the ingredients to a small mixing bowl and stir until well combined.
Pour half of the batter into the waffle maker and cook for 4 minutes until brown. Repeat with the rest of the batter to prepare another chaffle.
Serve with sugar-free blackberry jam and enjoy!

Yogurt Chaffle

Prep Time: 5 minutes
Cook Time: 8 minutes
Servings: 2 chaffles

Ingredients:
½ tsp psyllium husk
½ cup mozzarella cheese, shredded
1 egg, beaten
1 tbsp yogurt
¼ tsp baking powder

Instructions:
Heat up the mini waffle maker.
Add all the ingredients to a small mixing bowl and stir until well combined.
Pour half of the batter into the waffle maker and cook for 4 minutes until brown. Repeat with the rest of the batter to prepare another chaffle.
Serve with sugar-free blackberry jam and enjoy!

Sweet Chaffle with Ice Cream

Prep Time: 5 minutes
Cook Time: 8 minutes
Servings: 2 chaffles

Ingredients for chaffles:
1 tbsp almond flour
½ cup mozzarella cheese
1 egg, beaten
1 tbsp sweetener
½ tsp vanilla extract

Instructions:
Heat up the waffle maker.
Add all the ingredients to a small mixing bowl and combine well.
Pour ½ of the batter into your waffle maker and cook for 4 minutes until golden brown. Then cook the remaining batter to make another chaffle.
Top the chaffles with vanilla ice cream and blackberries.
Serve and enjoy!

Raspberries and Yogurt Chaffle

Prep Time: 5 minutes
Cook Time: 8 minutes
Servings: 2 chaffles

Ingredients:
½ cup mozzarella cheese, shredded
1 egg, beaten
1 tbsp yogurt
1 tbsp raspberries, chopped
¼ tsp baking powder

Instructions:
Heat up the mini waffle maker.
Add all the ingredients to a small mixing bowl and stir until well combined.
Pour half of the batter into the waffle maker and cook for 4 minutes until brown. Repeat with the rest of the batter to prepare another chaffle.
Serve with keto whipped cream and enjoy!

Gingerbread Chaffle

Prep Time: 5 minutes
Cook Time: 8 minutes
Servings: 2 chaffles

Ingredients:
½ cup mozzarella cheese, shredded
1 egg, beaten
½ tsp baking powder
1 tsp sweetener
1/8 tsp cloves, chopped
2 tbsp almond flour
½ tsp ginger, chopped
¼ tsp nutmeg, chopped
½ tsp cinnamon, chopped

Instructions:
Heat up the waffle maker.
Add all the chaffles ingredients to a small mixing bowl and stir until well combined.
Pour half of the batter into the waffle maker and cook for 4 minutes until brown. Repeat with the rest of the batter to make another chaffle.
Serve and enjoy!

Coconut Chaffle

Prep Time: 5 minutes
Cook Time: 16 minutes
Servings: 4 chaffles

Ingredients for chaffles:
8 tbsp softened cream cheese
4 eggs, beaten
4 tbsp coconut flour
1 tsp baking powder
1 tbsp butter, melted
2 tsp vanilla
1 tbsp sweetener

Instructions:
Heat up the waffle maker.
Add all the ingredients to a small mixing bowl and combine well.
Pour ¼ of the batter into your waffle maker and cook for 4 minutes. Then cook the remaining batter to make the other chaffles.
Serve and enjoy!

Blueberry Jam Chaffle

Prep Time: 5 minutes
Cook Time: 24 minutes
Servings: 6 chaffles

Ingredients:
2 eggs, beaten
2 tbsp almond flour
½ tsp baking powder
1 tbsp blueberry jam, sugar-free
1 cup mozzarella cheese, shredded
1 tbsp cream cheese

Instructions:
Heat up the mini waffle maker.
Add all the chaffles ingredients to a small mixing bowl and stir until well combined.
Pour 1/6 of the batter into the waffle maker and cook for 4 minutes until brown. Repeat with the rest of the batter to prepare the other chaffles.
Let cool for 2-3 minutes to let chaffles get crispy.
Serve and enjoy!

Peanut Butter and Strawberry Jam Chaffle

Prep Time: 5 minutes
Cook Time: 24 minutes
Servings: 6 chaffles

Ingredients:
2 eggs, beaten
2 tbsp almond flour
½ tsp baking powder
1 tbsp strawberry jam, sugar-free
2 tbsp peanut butter
1 cup mozzarella cheese, shredded
1 tbsp cream cheese

Instructions:
Heat up the waffle maker.
Add all the chaffles ingredients to a small mixing bowl and stir until well combined.
Pour 1/6 of the batter into the waffle maker and cook for 4 minutes until brown. Repeat with the rest of the batter to prepare the other chaffles.
Let cool for 2-3 minutes to let chaffles get crispy.
Serve and enjoy!

Glazed Chaffles

Prep Time: 5 minutes
Cook Time: 12 minutes
Servings: 3 chaffles

Ingredients for chaffles:
½ cup mozzarella cheese, shredded
1/8 cup cream cheese
1 egg, beaten
2 tbsp unflavored whey protein isolate
2 tbsp swerve confectioners' sugar substitute
½ tsp baking powder
½ tsp vanilla extract
Ingredients for the glaze:
2 tbsp heavy whipping cream
4 tbsp swerve sugar substitute
½ tsp vanilla extract

Instructions:
Heat up the waffle maker.

Add all the chaffles ingredients to a small mixing bowl and mix well.
Pour 1/3 of the batter into the waffle maker and cook for 4 minutes until golden brown. Repeat with the rest of the batter to make other 2 chaffles.
Let cool for 3 minutes to let chaffles get crispy.
In a small mixing bowl beat the glaze ingredients.
Top every chaffles with the glaze.
Serve and enjoy!

Raspberry Chaffle

Prep Time: 5 minutes
Cook Time: 8 minutes
Servings: 2 chaffles

Ingredients:
1 tbsp almond flour
½ cup mozzarella cheese, shredded
1 egg, beaten
1 tablespoon sweetener
¼ cup raspberries puree
Keto whipped cream for topping

Instructions:
Heat up the waffle maker.
Add all the ingredients to a small mixing bowl and combine well.
Pour half of the batter into your waffle maker and cook for 4 minutes until brown. Then cook the remaining batter to prepare another chaffle.
Serve with keto whipped cream and enjoy!

White Chocolate Chaffles

Prep Time: 5 minutes
Cook Time: 16 minutes
Servings: 4 chaffles

Ingredients for chaffles:
2 eggs, beaten
1 tbsp butter, melted
1 tbsp softened cream cheese
2 tbsp unsweetened white chocolate chips
1 cup mozzarella cheese, shredded
2 tbsp sweetener
½ tsp baking powder

½ tsp instant coffee granules dissolved in 1 tablespoon hot water
½ tsp vanilla extract
A pinch of salt

Instructions:
Heat up the mini waffle maker.
Add all the chaffles ingredients to a small mixing bowl and mix well.
Pour ¼ of the batter into the waffle maker and cook for 4 minutes. Repeat with the rest of the batter to make 3 more chaffles.
Let cool for 3 minutes to let chaffles get crispy.
Serve and enjoy!

Lemon Chaffle

Prep Time: 5 minutes
Cook Time: 4 minutes
Servings: 1 chaffle

Ingredients:
1 tbsp heavy whipping cream
1 tbsp sweetener
1 tbsp coconut flour
1 egg
½ cup mozzarella cheese, shredded
½ tsp lemon extract
¼ tsp lemon zest

Instructions:
Heat up the waffle maker.
Mix all the ingredients in a small mixing bowl and blend until creamy.
Pour the batter into the waffle maker and cook for about 4 minutes until brown.
Serve and enjoy!

Lime Chaffle

Prep Time: 5 minutes
Cook Time: 4 minutes
Servings: 1 chaffle

Ingredients:
1 tbsp heavy whipping cream
1 tsp sweetener
1 tbsp almond flour

1 egg
½ cup mozzarella cheese, shredded
2 tsp cream cheese
¼ tsp baking powder
½ tsp lime juice
½ tsp lime zest

Instructions:
Heat up the waffle maker.
Mix all the ingredients in a small mixing bowl and blend until creamy.
Pour the batter into the waffle maker and cook for about 4 minutes until brown.
Serve and enjoy!

Blueberry Chaffle

Prep Time: 4 minutes
Cook Time: 20 minutes
Servings: 5 chaffles

Ingredients:
1 cup of mozzarella cheese
2 tbsp almond flour
2 tsp of sweetener
3 tbsp blueberries
1 tsp baking powder
2 eggs
1 tsp cinnamon

Instructions:
Heat up the Mini Waffle Maker.
Add the mozzarella cheese, baking powder, almond flour, eggs, cinnamon, sweetener, and blueberries in a medium mixing bowl. Mix well.
Spray the waffle maker with a cooking spray.
Add in about 1/5 a cup of blueberry keto batter and cook the chaffle for 4-5 minutes until it is crispy and brown. Repeat with the remaining batter to prepare the other chaffles.
Serve with a keto syrup.
Serve and enjoy!

Blueberry Compote Chaffle

Prep Time: 4 minutes
Cook Time: 16 minutes

Servings: 4 chaffles

Ingredients for chaffles:
1 cup of mozzarella cheese
2 tbsp almond flour
2 tsp of sweetener
3 tbsp blueberries
1 tsp baking powder
2 eggs
1 tsp cinnamon

Ingredients for topping:
½ cup blueberries
4 tsp blueberry unsweetened compote
4 tbsp dairy-free yogurt

Instructions:
Heat up the Mini Waffle Maker.
Add the mozzarella cheese, baking powder, almond flour, eggs, cinnamon, sweetener, and blueberries in a medium mixing bowl. Mix well.
Spray the waffle maker with a cooking spray.
Add in about ¼ a cup of blueberry keto batter and cook the chaffle for 4-5 minutes until it is crispy and brown. Repeat with the remaining batter to prepare the other chaffles.
Top with a tbsp of dairy-free yogurt and blueberry compote mixed with fresh blueberries.
Serve and enjoy!

Crispy Berries Mousse Chaffle

Prep Time: 5 minutes
Cook Time: 8 minutes
Servings: 2 chaffles

Ingredients for chaffles:
1 large egg, beaten
½ cup mozzarella cheese, grated
1 tsp coconut flour
1 tsp water
¼ tsp baking powder

Ingredients for mousse:
2 tbsp heavy whipping cream
1 tbsp fresh strawberries
1 tbsp fresh blueberries
½ tbsp pecans, minced
½ tsp lemon zest
½ tsp vanilla extract

Instructions for mousse:
In a bowl, whip all the mousse ingredients, except for pecans, until fluffy. Add pecans and mix well. Set aside.

Instructions for chaffles:
Heat up the mini waffle maker.
Add all the chaffles ingredients to a small mixing bowl and combine well.
Pour half of the batter into the waffle maker and cook for 4 minutes until brown. Repeat with the rest of the batter to make another chaffle.
Let cool for 3 minutes to let chaffles get crispy.
Top the chaffles with berries mousse.
Serve and enjoy!

Blackberries Chaffle

Prep Time: 4 minutes
Cook Time: 20 minutes
Servings: 5 chaffles

Ingredients:
1 cup of mozzarella cheese
2 tbsp almond flour
2 tsp of sweetener
3 tbsp blackberries
1 tsp baking powder
2 eggs
1 tsp cinnamon
2 tbsp heavy cream for the topping

Instructions:
Heat up the Mini Waffle Maker.
Add the mozzarella cheese, baking powder, almond flour, eggs, cinnamon, sweetener, and blackberries in a medium mixing bowl. Mix well.
Spray the waffle maker with a cooking spray.
Add in about 1/5 a cup of blackberry keto batter. Cook the chaffle for 4-5 minutes until it is crispy and brown. Repeat with the remaining batter to prepare the other chaffles.
Serve with heavy cream and enjoy!

Strawberry Chaffle and Maple Pecan Syrup

Prep Time: 4 minutes
Cook Time: 20 minutes
Servings: 5 chaffles

Ingredients for chaffles:
1 cup of mozzarella cheese
2 tbsp almond flour
2 tsp of sweetener
1 tsp baking powder
2 eggs
1 tsp cinnamon

Ingredients for topping:
3 tbsp sugar free milk chocolate chips
5 sliced fresh strawberries
3 tbsp sugar free maple pecan syrup

Instructions:
Heat up the Mini Waffle Maker.
Add the mozzarella cheese, baking powder, almond flour, eggs, cinnamon and sweetener in a medium mixing bowl. Mix well.
Spray the waffle maker with a cooking spray.
Add in about 1/5 a cup of the keto batter and cook the chaffle for 4-5 minutes until it is crispy and brown. Repeat with the remaining batter to prepare the other chaffles.
Top each chaffle with sugar fee maple pecan syrup, a sliced strawberry and sprinkle with milk chocolate chips.
Serve and enjoy!

Blackberries Chaffle and Milk Chocolate Chips

Prep Time: 4 minutes
Cook Time: 20 minutes
Servings: 4 chaffles

Ingredients for chaffles:
1 cup of mozzarella cheese
2 tbsp almond flour
2 tsp of sweetener
1 tsp baking powder
2 eggs
1 tsp cinnamon

Ingredients for topping:
2 tbsp sugar free milk chocolate chips
½ cup of fresh blackberries
2 tbsp sugar free maple pecan syrup

Instructions:
Heat up the Mini Waffle Maker.
Add the mozzarella cheese, baking powder, almond flour, eggs, cinnamon and sweetener in a medium mixing bowl. Mix well.
Spray the waffle maker with a cooking spray.
Add in about 1/4 a cup of the keto batter and cook the chaffle for 4-5 minutes until it is crispy and brown. Repeat with the remaining batter to prepare the other chaffles.
Top each chaffle with sugar fee maple pecan syrup and sprinkle with milk chocolate chips and blackberries.
Serve and enjoy!

Pumpkin and Chocolate Chaffle

Prep Time: 5 minutes
Cook Time: 12 minutes
Servings: 3 chaffles

Ingredients:
½ cup shredded mozzarella cheese
4 tsp pumpkin puree
1 egg, beaten
2 tbsp sweetener
¼ tsp pumpkin pie spice
4 tsp sugar free chocolate chips
1 tbsp almond flour

Instructions:
Heat up the waffle maker.
Mix all the chaffles ingredients in a small mixing bowl and stir until well combined.
Pour half of the batter into the waffle maker and cook for 4-5 minutes. Then cook the rest of the batter to make the other chaffles.
Serve with sweetener and enjoy!

Chocolate Chips Chaffle

Prep Time: 4 minutes
Cook Time: 8 minutes
Servings: 2 chaffles

Ingredients:
½ cup shredded mozzarella cheese
1 tbsp almond flour
1 egg
¼ tsp cinnamon
½ tbsp sweetener
2 tbsp low carb chocolate chips
Instructions:
Heat up the waffle maker.
Mix the mozzarella cheese, almond flour, egg, cinnamon, sweetener and chocolate chips in a small mixing bowl.
Add half of the batter into the waffle maker and cook it for approx. 4-5 minutes. When the first one is completely done cooking, cook the second one.
Set aside for 1-2 minutes.
Serve and enjoy!

Chocolate Chips Chaffle Nr. 2

Prep Time: 5 minutes
Cook Time: 8 minutes
Servings: 2 chaffles

Ingredients:
1 egg
½ cup shredded mozzarella cheese
1 tbsp whipping cream
½ tsp coconut flour
¼ tsp baking powder
A pinch of salt
1 tbsp chocolate chips, unsweetened

Instructions:
Heat up the waffle maker.
Mix all ingredients except the chocolate chips in a small mixing bowl.
Grease waffle maker, then pour half of the batter onto the bottom plate of the waffle maker. Sprinkle a few chocolate chips on top and then close.

Cook for approx. 4 minutes or until the chaffle is golden brown.
Repeat with the rest of the batter.
Let chaffle sit for a few minutes so that it begins to crisp.
Serve with sugar-free whipped topping and enjoy!

Chocolate Chips Chaffle Nr. 3

Prep Time: 5 minutes
Cook Time: 8 minutes
Servings: 2 chaffles

Ingredients:
2 tsp coconut flour
2 tbsp sweetener
1 tbsp cocoa powder
¼ tsp baking powder
1 egg
½ cup shredded mozzarella cheese
1 tbsp cream cheese
½ tsp vanilla extract
1 tbsp unsweetened chocolate chips

Instructions:
Heat up the waffle maker.
In a small mixing bowl, beat egg.
Add all the other ingredients, except for chocolate chips, and combine well.
Pour half of the batter onto the bottom plate of the waffle maker. Sprinkle a few chocolate chips on top and then close.
Cook for approx. 4 minutes or until the chaffle is golden brown.
Repeat with the rest of the batter.
Serve with your favorite berries and enjoy!

Crunchy Choco Chaffle

Prep Time: 5 minutes
Cook Time: 16 minutes
Servings: 4 chaffles

Ingredients:
2 eggs, beaten
2 tbsp heavy whipping cream
1 cup mozzarella cheese, shredded

1 tbsp dark cocoa, unsweetened
2 tsp coconut flour
½ tsp baking powder
½ tsp vanilla extract
½ tsp sweetener
1 ½ tbsp almond, minced

Instructions:
Heat up the waffle maker.
Add all the ingredients to a small mixing bowl and stir until well combined.
Pour ¼ of the batter onto the bottom plate of the waffle maker.
Cook for approx. 4 minutes or until the chaffle is golden brown.
Repeat with the rest of the batter.
Serve with ice cream and enjoy!

Brownie Chaffles

Prep Time: 5 minutes
Cook Time: 16 minutes
Servings: 4 chaffles

Ingredients for chaffles:
2 eggs, beaten
1 tbsp dark cocoa, unsweetened
1 tbsp sweetener
1 cup mozzarella cheese, shredded
Ingredients for topping:
3 tbsp keto chocolate, minced
3 tbsp butter, unsalted
½ cup swerve sugar

Instructions for topping:
In a small pan over low heat, pour chocolate, butter and sugar and stir for a few minutes.
Instructions for chaffles:
Heat up the waffle maker.
Add all the ingredients to a small mixing bowl and stir until well combined.
Pour ¼ of the batter onto the bottom plate of the waffle maker.
Cook for approx. 4 minutes or until the chaffle is golden brown.
Repeat with the rest of the batter.
Top the chaffles with chocolate sauce.
Serve with keto ice-cream and enjoy!

Keto Chocolate Chaffle

Prep Time: 5 minutes
Cook Time: 8 minutes
Servings: 2 chaffles

Ingredients:
1 large egg
½ cup Gruyere cheese, shredded
1 tsp almond flour
¼ tsp vanilla extract
1 tsp heavy whipping cream
2 tbsp cocoa powder, unsweetened
¼ tsp baking powder
2 tbsp sweetener
Salt to taste

Instructions:
Heat up the waffle maker.
Add all the ingredients to a small mixing bowl and stir until well combined.
Pour half of the batter onto the bottom plate of the waffle maker.
Cook for approx. 4 minutes or until the chaffle is golden brown.
Repeat with the rest of the batter.
Serve with your favorite berries and enjoy!

Pumpkin Chaffle with Maple Syrup

Prep Time: 5 minutes
Cook Time: 16 minutes
Servings: 4 chaffles

Ingredients:
2 eggs
1 tsp coconut flour
1 cup shredded mozzarella cheese
½ tsp vanilla
½ tsp baking powder
2 tsp pumpkin puree
3/4 tsp pumpkin pie spice
4 tsp heavy whipping cream
2 tsp sugar-free maple syrup

Instructions:
Heat up the waffle maker.
Mix all the ingredients in a small mixing bowl.

Pour ¼ of the batter into the waffle maker and cook for 4 minutes. Repeat with the rest of the batter to make other 3 chaffles.

Let cool for 3 minutes.

Serve with sugar-free maple syrup or keto ice cream and enjoy!

Coffee Chaffle

Prep Time: 5 minutes
Cook Time: 12 minutes
Servings: 3 chaffles

Ingredients for chaffles:
1 egg
½ cup mozzarella cheese, shredded
1 tbs black cocoa
1 tbs sweetener
¼ tsp baking powder
2 tbsp softened cream cheese
¼ tsp instant coffee powder
1 tsp vanilla
Ingredients for frosting:
2 tbs sweetener
2 tbs cream cheese softened
¼ tsp vanilla

Instructions:
Heat up the waffle maker.
Mix the egg and the other ingredients in a small mixing bowl. Mix well until the batter is creamy.
Pour 1/3 of the batter into the waffle maker and cook for 4 minutes. Repeat with the rest of the batter to make the other chaffles.
In a separate bowl, add the sweetener, cream cheese, and vanilla. Mix the frosting until well incorporated. Spread the frosting on the chaffles after it has completely cooled.
Serve and enjoy!

Pumpkin & Pecan Chaffle

Prep Time: 3 minutes
Cook Time: 8 minutes
Servings: 2 chaffles

Ingredients:
1 egg
½ cup grated mozzarella cheese
1 tbsp pumpkin puree
½ tsp pumpkin spice
1 tsp sweetener
2 tbsp almond flour
2 tbsp toasted chopped pecans

Instructions:
Heat up the waffle maker.
Mix the egg, mozzarella, pumpkin, almond flour, pumpkin spice, and sweetener in a large mixing bowl. Combine the pecan pieces.
Pour half of the batter into the waffle maker and cook for 4 minutes. Repeat with the rest of the batter to make another chaffle.
Serve with whipped cream and enjoy!

Mascarpone Cream & Raspberry Chaffle

Prep Time: 5 minutes
Cook Time: 8 minutes
Servings: 2 chaffles

Ingredients for chaffles:
1 large egg, beaten
½ cup mozzarella cheese, shredded
½ tsp sweetener
Ingredients for Mascarpone cream:
2 tbsp Mascarpone cheese, softened
2 tsp sweetener
1 tsp vanilla extract
½ tbsp unsalted butter, melted
Ingredients for topping:
2 tsp unsweetened cocoa powder
2 tbsp raspberries

Instructions for mascarpone cream:
Add all the cream ingredients to a mixing bowl and mix until smoothy.
Instructions:
Heat up the waffle maker.
Add all the chaffles ingredients to a small mixing bowl and stir until well combined.
Pour half of the batter into the waffle maker and cook for 4 minutes until golden brown. Repeat with the rest of the batter to make another chaffle.

Let cool for 3 minutes to let chaffles get crispy. Spread the chaffle with mascarpone cream. Top with raspberries and sprinkle with cocoa powder.
Serve and enjoy!

Red Chaffle

Prep Time: 5 minutes
Cook Time: 8 minutes
Servings: 2 chaffles

Ingredients:
2 tsp processed cocoa
2 tsp sweetener
1 egg
½ cup mozzarella cheese, shredded
2 drops red food coloring
¼ tsp baking powder
1 tbsp heavy whipping cream
Ingredients for the frosting:
2 tsp sweetener
2 tbsp softened cream cheese
¼ tsp vanilla

Instructions:
Heat up the waffle maker.
Mix the egg and the other ingredients in a small mixing bowl. Mix well until the batter is creamy.
Pour half of the batter into the waffle maker and cook for 4 minutes. Repeat with the rest of the batter to make another chaffle.
In a separate bowl, add the sweetener, cream cheese, and vanilla. Mix the frosting until well incorporated. Spread the frosting on the chaffles after it has completely cooled.
Serve and enjoy!

Peanut Butter Chaffle

Prep Time: 4 minutes
Cook Time: 8 minutes
Servings: 2 chaffles

Ingredients:
1 egg
½ cup mozzarella cheese
1 tsp sweetener
2 tbsp peanut butter
1 tsp vanilla extract

Instructions:
Heat up the waffle maker.
Mix all the ingredients in a small mixing bowl.
Pour half of the batter into the waffle maker and cook for 4 minutes until golden brown. Repeat with the rest of the batter to make another chaffle.
Serve and enjoy!

Cinnamon Chaffle
Prep Time: 5 minutes
Cook Time: 8 minutes
Servings: 2 chaffles

Ingredients:
1 egg
½ cup mozzarella cheese, shredded
2 tbsp almond flour
1 tbsp sweetener
½ tsp vanilla extract
¼ tsp cinnamon
½ tsp baking powder

Ingredients for the coating:
1 tbsp butter
2 tbsp sweetener
½ tsp cinnamon

Instructions:
Heat up the waffle maker.
Add all the chaffles ingredients to a small mixing bowl and mix well until creamy.
Pour half of the batter into the waffle maker and cook for 4 minutes. Repeat with the rest of the batter to make another chaffle.
Let cool for 3 minutes to let chaffles get crispy.
In a bowl, combine sweetener and cinnamon for coating.
Melt butter in a microwave safe bowl and brush the chaffles with the butter.
Sprinkle sweetener and cinnamon mixture on both sides of the chaffles once they're brushed with butter.
Serve and enjoy!

Chocolate Peanut Butter Chaffle

Prep Time: 4 minutes

Cook Time: 8 minutes
Servings: 2 chaffles

Ingredients:

1 egg, beaten
½ cup mozzarella cheese, shredded
2 tbsp almond flour
¼ tsp sweetener
1 tbsp unsweetened powdered cocoa
¼ tsp baking powder
2 tbsp unsweetened keto approved peanut butter

Instructions:
Heat up the waffle maker.
Add all the ingredients to a small mixing bowl. Stir well.
Pour half of the batter into the waffle maker and cook for 4 minutes until golden brown. Repeat with the rest of the batter to make another chaffle.
Serve and enjoy!

Cinnamon and Pumpkin Chaffle

Prep Time: 5 minutes
Cook Time: 8 minutes
Servings: 2 chaffles

Ingredients:

1 egg
½ cup mozzarella cheese, shredded
3 tbsp coconut flour
1 tsp baking powder
¼ cup pumpkin puree
½ tsp pumpkin spice seasoning
2 tbsp maple syrup, unsweetened
1 tsp vanilla extract
A pinch of salt
1 tbsp cinnamon powder

Instructions:
Heat up the waffle maker.
Add all the chaffles ingredients to a small mixing bowl and stir until well combined.
Pour half of the batter into the waffle maker and cook for 4 minutes until golden brown. Repeat with the rest of the batter to make another chaffle.
Let cool for 3 minutes to let chaffles get crispy.
Top with maple syrup.

Serve and enjoy!

Chaffle with Crumble

Prep Time: 5 minutes
Cook Time: 8 minutes
Servings: 2 chaffles

Ingredients for the chaffles:
1 tbsp butter
1 egg
½ cup mozzarella cheese, shredded
½ tsp vanilla
1 tbsp almond flour
1 tbsp coconut flour
⅛ tsp baking powder
1 tbsp sweetener
Ingredients for the crumble:
1 tbsp butter, melted
1 tsp sweetener
1 tbsp Pecans, chopped

Instructions:
Heat up the mini waffle maker.
Add all the ingredients for the chaffles to a small mixing bowl and combine well.
In a separate bowl add the melted butter for the crumble, sweetener, and pecans.
Pour half of the batter into the waffle maker, top with half of crumble mixture and cook for 4 minutes. Repeat with the rest of the batter/crumble to make another chaffle.
Let cool for 3 minutes to let chaffles get crispy.
Serve with whipped cream and enjoy!

Orange Cinnamon Chaffle

Prep Time: 5 minutes
Cook Time: 8 minutes
Servings: 2 chaffles

Ingredients:

1 egg, beaten
½ cup mozzarella cheese
2 tbsp almond flour
1 tbsp sweetener
¼ tsp cinnamon

½ tsp baking powder
¼ tsp orange zest
1 tsp orange extract

Instructions:
Heat up the waffle maker.
Add all the chaffles ingredients to a small mixing bowl and mix well until creamy.
Pour half of the batter into the waffle maker and cook for 4 minutes until brown. Repeat with the rest of the batter to make another chaffle.
Let cool for 3 minutes to let chaffles get crispy.
Serve with keto maple syrup and enjoy!

Banana Chaffle

Prep Time: 5 minutes
Cook Time: 4 minutes
Servings: 1 chaffle

Ingredients:
1 tbsp heavy whipping cream
1 tbsp sweetener
1 tbsp coconut flour
1 egg
½ cup mozzarella cheese, shredded
½ tsp vanilla extract
1 tsp banana extract
1 tbsp nuts, chopped

Instructions:
Heat up the waffle maker.
Add all the ingredients to a small mixing bowl and mix well.
Pour the batter into the waffle maker and cook for 4 minutes until golden brown.
Let cool for 3 minutes to let chaffle get crispy.
Serve with sugar free maple syrup and enjoy!

Creamy Chaffle

Prep Time: 5 minutes
Cook Time: 16 minutes
Servings: 4 chaffles

Ingredients for chaffles:
2 tbsp cream cheese
2 eggs

1 cup mozzarella cheese, shredded
1 tbsp butter, melted
1 tsp vanilla extract
½ tsp cinnamon
1 tbsp sweetener
1 tbsp coconut flour
1 tbsp almond flour
1 tsp baking powder
1 tbs chopped walnuts
Ingredients for cream:
4 tbsp cream cheese
2 tbsp butter
2 tsp sweetener
½ tsp vanilla

Instructions:
Heat up the waffle maker.
Add in a blender all the ingredients for the chaffles and blend until creamy.
Pour ¼ of the batter into the waffle maker and cook for 4 minutes. Repeat with the rest of the batter to make the other chaffles.
Let cool for 3 minutes to let chaffles get crispy.
In a small mixing bowl add all the ingredients for the cream and stir them till smoothy.
Frost the cooled chaffles with the cream.
Serve and enjoy!

Cream Chaffles

Prep Time: 5 minutes
Cook Time: 8 minutes
Servings: 2 chaffles

Ingredients for chaffles:
1 tbsp coconut flour
2 tsp confectioner sugar substitute
¼ tsp baking powder
1 egg
½ cup mozzarella cheese, shredded
1 tbsp cream cheese, softened
½ tsp vanilla extract

Instructions:
Heat up the waffle maker.
Add to a blender all the ingredients for the chaffles and blend until creamy.

Pour half of the batter into the waffle maker and cook for 4 minutes until golden brown. Repeat with the rest of the batter to make the other chaffle. Serve with your favorite topping and enjoy!

Chocolate Creamy Chaffle

Prep Time: 5 minutes
Cook Time: 16 minutes
Servings: 4 chaffles

Ingredients for chaffles:
2 tbsp cream cheese
2 eggs
1 cup mozzarella cheese, shredded
1 tbsp butter, melted
1 tsp vanilla extract
1 tbsp sweetener
1 tbsp coconut flour
1 tbsp almond flour
1 tsp baking powder
2 tbsp chocolate chips, unsweetened
Ingredients for cream:
4 tbsp cream cheese
2 tbsp butter
2 tsp sweetener
½ tsp vanilla

Instructions:
Heat up the waffle maker.
Add to a blender all the ingredients for the chaffles and blend until creamy.
Pour ¼ of the batter into the waffle maker and cook for 4 minutes. Repeat with the rest of the batter to make the other chaffles.
Let cool for 3 minutes to let chaffles get crispy.
In a small mixing bowl add all the ingredients for the cream and stir them till smoothy.
Frost the chaffles with the cream.
Serve and enjoy!

Sugar Free Sprinkles Chaffle

Prep Time: 5 minutes
Cook Time: 8 minutes
Servings: 2 chaffles

Ingredients:
1 egg
½ cup shredded mozzarella cheese
1 tbsp almond flour
1 tbsp heavy whipping cream
½ tsp vanilla extract
1 tbsp sugar free sprinkles
2 tsp sweetener

Instructions:
Heat up the mini waffle maker.
Add all the ingredients to a small mixing bowl and combine well.
Pour half of the batter into the waffle maker and cook for 4 minutes. Repeat with the rest of the batter to make another chaffle.
Let cool for 3 minutes to let chaffles get crispy.
Top the chaffle with some sugar free whipped cream and a few sugar free sprinkles.
Serve and enjoy!

Chaffle with Jicama

Prep Time: 5 minutes
Cook Time: 45 minutes
Servings: 5 chaffles

Ingredients for the filling:
2 cups jicama, diced
¼ cup sweetener
4 tbsp butter
1 tsp cinnamon
1/8 tsp nutmeg
¼ tsp cloves, ground
½ tsp vanilla extract
20 drops apple flavoring
Ingredients for the chaffles:
2 eggs
1 cup mozzarella cheese, grated
1 tbsp almond flour
1 tsp coconut flour
½ tsp baking powder
Ingredients for the icing:
1 tbsp butter
2 tsp heavy cream
3 tbsp powdered sweetener
¼ tsp vanilla extract

Instructions for the filling:

In a saucepan over medium heat, add melted butter, sweetener, and jicama.

Simmer approx. 20 minutes until the jicama is soft.

Remove from heat and stir in the spices and flavorings.

Instructions for the chaffles:

Heat up the waffle maker.

Add all the ingredients to a small mixing bowl and combine well. Stir the jicama mix into the egg batter.

Pour 1/5 of the batter into the waffle maker and cook for 4 minutes. Repeat with the rest of the batter to make 4 more chaffles.

Let cool for 3 minutes to let chaffles get crispy.

Instructions for the icing:

In a small pan add melted butter, sweetener, and heavy cream.

Simmer for 4-5 minutes, until thickened. Add vanilla.

Top the chaffles with jicama filling and put the hot glaze over the chaffles.

Serve and enjoy!

Chaffle with Chocolate Icing

Prep Time: 5 minutes
Cook Time: 8 minutes
Servings: 2 chaffles

Ingredients for the chaffles:

2 eggs, beaten
½ cup mozzarella cheese, shredded
½ tsp baking powder
1 tsp vanilla extract
2 tbsp erythritol
3 tbsp almond milk

Ingredients for the chocolate icing:

¼ cup powdered erythritol
1 tbsp cocoa powder
1 tbsp almond milk
½ tsp vanilla extract

Instructions:

Heat up the waffle maker.

Add all the ingredients for chaffles to a small mixing bowl. Stir until well combined.

Pour half of the batter into the waffle maker and cook for 4 minutes. Repeat with the rest of the batter to make another chaffle.

Let cool for 3 minutes to let chaffles get crispy.

Add all the ingredients for the chocolate glaze to a small bowl and combine well.

Top each chaffle with glaze.

Serve and enjoy!

Delicious Chocolate Chaffle

Prep Time: 5 minutes
Cook Time: 16 minutes
Servings: 4 chaffles

Ingredients for the chaffles:

2 eggs
1 cup Gruyere cheese, shredded
2 tbsp heavy cream
1 tbsp coconut flour
2 tbsp cream cheese
3 tbsp cocoa powder, unsweetened
2 tsp vanilla extract
Salt to taste

Ingredients for the chocolate icing:

½ cup heavy cream
2 tbsp unsweetened chocolate, chopped
1 tbsp maple syrup, sugar-free
1 tbsp vanilla extract

Instructions for the chocolate icing:

In a small pan over medium heat simmer the heavy cream for 2-3 minutes.

Remove the pan from heat and add the chocolate: stir until completely melted.

Add maple syrup and vanilla extract.

Instructions for the chaffles:

Heat up the waffle maker.

Add all the ingredients for chaffles to a small mixing bowl. Stir until well combined.

Pour ¼ of the batter into the waffle maker and cook for 4 minutes until golden brown. Repeat with the rest of the batter to prepare the other chaffles.

Let cool for 3 minutes to let chaffles get crispy.

Top each chaffle with chocolate sauce.

Serve and enjoy!

White Chocolate Macadamia Syrup Chaffle

Prep Time: 5 minutes
Cook Time: 8 minutes
Servings: 2 chaffles

Ingredients for chaffles:
1 egg
½ cup mozzarella cheese, grated
1 tsp coconut flour
1 tsp water
¼ tsp baking powder
Ingredients for glaze:
2 tbsp white chocolate chips, unsweetened
1 cup of coconut milk
2 tsp macadamia nut syrup

Instructions for glaze:
In a saucepan, warm up the coconut milk. Remove from heat and add white chocolate chips and macadamia nut syrup.
Wait 5 minutes before stirring. Set aside to allow mixture to cool.
Instructions for chaffles:
Heat up the mini waffle maker.
Add all the ingredients to a small mixing bowl and combine well.
Pour half of the batter into the waffle maker and cook for 4 minutes until brown. Repeat with the rest of the batter to make another chaffle.
Let cool for 3 minutes to let chaffles get crispy.
Serve each chaffle with chocolate glaze and enjoy!

Sweet Eggnog Chaffle

Prep Time: 5 minutes
Cook Time: 8 minutes
Servings: 2 chaffles

Ingredients for chaffles:
1 egg, beaten
2 tbsp cream cheese, softened
2 tsp sweetener
2 tbsp coconut flour
½ tsp baking powder
¼ cup keto eggnog

A pinch of nutmeg
Ingredients for topping:
2 tbsp keto whipped cream
2 tbsp fresh blackberries
2 tsp lemon juice

Instructions:
Heat up the waffle maker.
Add all the chaffles ingredients to a small mixing bowl and stir until well combined.
Pour half of the batter into the waffle maker and cook for 4 minutes until golden brown. Repeat with the rest of the batter to make another chaffle.
Let cool for 3 minutes to let chaffles get crispy.
In a small bowl, combine the lemon juice and blackberries.
Spread the chaffle with whipped cream and top with blackberries.
Serve and enjoy!

Chaffle with Ricotta Cheese

Prep Time: 5 minutes
Cook Time: 16 minutes
Servings: 4 chaffles

Ingredients for the chaffles:
1 egg
1 egg yolk
3 tbsp melted butter
1 tbsp swerve confectioner's sugar substitute
1 cup parmesan cheese, grated
2 tbsp mozzarella cheese, shredded
Ingredients for the topping:
½ cup ricotta cheese
2 tbsp swerve confectioner's sugar substitute
1 tsp vanilla extract

Instructions for the topping:
In a small mixing bowl stir ricotta cheese, vanilla extract and swerve confectioner's sugar substitute until creamy.
Instructions for chaffles:
Heat up the waffle maker.
Add all the chaffles ingredients in a small mixing bowl and stir until well combined.

Pour 1/4 of the batter into the waffle maker and cook for 4 minutes until brown. Repeat with the rest of the batter to make the other chaffles.

Let cool for 3 minutes to let chaffles get crispy.

Top each chaffle with ricotta filling.

Serve and enjoy!

Ricotta and Chocolate Chaffle

Prep Time: 5 minutes
Cook Time: 16 minutes
Servings: 4 chaffles

Ingredients for the chaffles:
1 egg
1 egg yolk
3 tbsp melted butter
1 tbsp swerve confectioner's sugar substitute
1 cup parmesan cheese, grated
2 tbsp mozzarella cheese, shredded

Ingredients for the topping:
½ cup ricotta cheese
2 tbsp swerve confectioner's sugar substitute
1 tsp vanilla extract
2 tbsp milk chocolate chips, unsweetened

Instructions for the topping:
In a small mixing bowl stir ricotta cheese, vanilla extract and swerve confectioner's sugar substitute until creamy.

Add the chocolate chips and mix well.

Instructions for chaffles:
Heat up the waffle maker.

Add all the chaffles ingredients in a small mixing bowl and stir until well combined.

Pour ¼ of the batter into the waffle maker and cook for 4 minutes until brown. Repeat with the rest of the batter to make the other chaffles.

Let cool for 3 minutes to let chaffles get crispy.

Top each chaffle with ricotta and chocolate filling.

Serve and enjoy!

Nuts and Ricotta Chaffles

Prep Time: 5 minutes
Cook Time: 16 minutes
Servings: 4 chaffles

Ingredients for the chaffles:
1 egg
1 egg yolk
3 tbsp melted butter
1 tbsp swerve confectioner's sugar substitute
1 cup parmesan cheese, grated
2 tbsp mozzarella cheese, shredded

Ingredients for the topping:
½ cup ricotta cheese
2 tbsp swerve confectioner's sugar substitute
1 tsp vanilla extract
2 tbsp nuts, minced

Instructions for the topping:
In a small mixing bowl stir ricotta cheese, vanilla extract and swerve confectioner's sugar substitute until creamy.

Add the minced nuts and mix well.

Instructions for chaffles:
Heat up the waffle maker.

Add all the chaffles ingredients to a small mixing bowl and stir until well combined.

Pour ¼ of the batter into the waffle maker and cook for 4 minutes until brown. Repeat with the rest of the batter to make the other chaffles.

Let cool for 3 minutes to let chaffles get crispy.

Top each chaffle with ricotta filling.

Serve and enjoy!

Macadamia Nuts and Cinnamon Chaffle

Prep Time: 5 minutes
Cook Time: 8 minutes
Servings: 2 chaffles

Ingredients for chaffles:
1 tbsp almond flour
½ cup mozzarella cheese, shredded
1 egg, beaten
1 tbsp sweetener
½ tsp vanilla extract
A pinch of salt
1 tbsp Macadamia nuts, minced
½ tsp cinnamon powder

Instructions:
Heat up the waffle maker.

Add all the ingredients to a small mixing bowl and combine well.

Pour ½ of the batter into your waffle maker and cook for 4 minutes until golden brown. Then cook the remaining batter to make another chaffle.

Top the chaffles with unsweetened maple syrup.

Serve and enjoy!

Peppermint Chaffle

Prep Time: 5 minutes
Cook Time: 8 minutes
Servings: 2 chaffles

Ingredients for chaffles:
1 tbsp almond flour
½ cup mozzarella cheese, shredded
1 egg, beaten
1 tbsp sweetener
½ tsp vanilla extract
3-4 chopped mint leaves
A pinch of salt

Instructions:
Heat up the waffle maker.

Add all the ingredients to a small mixing bowl and combine well.

Pour ½ of the batter into your waffle maker and cook for 4 minutes until golden brown. Then cook the remaining batter to make another chaffle.

Top the chaffles with keto ice cream.

Serve and enjoy!

Berries Chaffle

Prep Time: 5 minutes
Cook Time: 16 minutes
Servings: 4 chaffles

Ingredients:
1 cup of mozzarella cheese, shredded
2 tbsp almond flour
2 tsp of sweetener
½ tbsp blackberries
½ tbsp cranberries
1 tsp baking powder
2 eggs, beaten

1 tsp cinnamon
2 tbsp heavy cream for the topping

Instructions:
Heat up the Waffle maker.

Add the mozzarella cheese, baking powder, almond flour, eggs, cinnamon, sweetener, and berries to a medium mixing bowl. Mix well.

Spray the waffle maker with a cooking spray.

Add in about ¼ a cup of batter. Cook the chaffle for 4-5 minutes until it is crispy and brown. Repeat with the remaining batter to prepare the other chaffles.

Serve with heavy cream and enjoy!

Almonds Chaffle

Prep Time: 4 minutes
Cook Time: 8 minutes
Servings: 2 chaffles

Ingredients:
1 large egg, beaten
½ cup of mozzarella cheese, shredded
2 tbsp almond flour
¼ tsp baking powder
2 tbsp almonds, chopped

Instructions:
Heat up the waffle maker.

Add all the ingredients to a small mixing bowl and combine well.

Pour half of the batter into the waffle maker and cook for 4 minutes until brown. Repeat with the rest of the batter to make another chaffle.

Let cool for 3 minutes to let chaffles get crispy.

Serve with keto whipped cream and enjoy!

Almond Chocolate Chaffle

Prep Time: 5 minutes
Cook Time: 8 minutes
Servings: 2 chaffles

Ingredients:
1 egg, beaten
½ cup of mozzarella cheese, shredded
2 tbsp almond chocolate chips, unsweetened
2 tbsp sweetener

1 tbsp whipping cream
1 tbsp almond flour
½ tsp vanilla extract
¼ tsp baking powder

Instructions:
Heat up the waffle maker.
Add all the chaffles ingredients to a small mixing bowl and mix well.
Pour half of the batter into the waffle maker and cook for 4 minutes until golden brown. Repeat with the rest of the batter to make another chaffle.
Let cool for 3 minutes to let chaffles get crispy.
Serve with blackberries, sweetener and enjoy!

Blueberries Syrup Chaffle

Prep Time: 5 minutes
Cook Time: 8 minutes
Servings: 2 chaffles

Ingredients for chaffles:
1 egg, beaten
½ cup cheddar cheese, shredded
1 tsp almond flour
1 tsp sour cream
A pinch of salt
Ingredients for blueberries syrup:
1 cup fresh blueberries
1 tsp vanilla extract
¼ cup sweetener
¼ cup water

Instructions for blueberries syrup:
In a saucepan over low heat add the blueberries, water, sweetener and vanilla extract.
Stir from time to time until you get a syrup.
Remove from heat, set aside and let cool.
Instructions for chaffles:
Heat up the waffle maker.
Add all the chaffles ingredients to a small mixing bowl and stir until well combined.
Pour half of the batter into the waffle maker and cook for 4 minutes until golden brown. Repeat with the rest of the batter to make another chaffle.
Let cool for 3 minutes to let chaffles get crispy.
Top the chaffle with blueberries syrup.
Serve and enjoy!

Raspberry Mousse Chaffle

Prep Time: 5 minutes
Cook Time: 8 minutes
Servings: 2 chaffles

Ingredients for chaffles:
1 large egg, beaten
½ cup mozzarella cheese, grated
1 tsp coconut flour
1 tsp water
¼ tsp baking powder
Ingredients for mousse:
2 tbsp heavy whipping cream
2-3 tbsp fresh raspberries
½ tsp lemon zest
½ tsp vanilla extract
1-2 fresh mint leaves, for garnish

Instructions for mousse:
In a bowl, whip all the mousse ingredients until fluffy. Set aside.
Instructions for chaffles:
Heat up the mini waffle maker.
Add all the chaffles ingredients to a small mixing bowl and combine well.
Pour half of the batter into the waffle maker and cook for 4 minutes until brown. Repeat with the rest of the batter to make another chaffle.
Let cool for 3 minutes to let chaffles get crispy.
Top the chaffle with raspberry mousse and garnish with a fresh mint leaf.
Serve and enjoy!

Crunchy Vanilla Chaffle

Prep Time: 5 minutes
Cook Time: 8 minutes
Servings: 2 chaffles

Ingredients for chaffles:
1 tbsp almond flour
½ cup mozzarella cheese
1 egg, beaten
1 tbsp sweetener
½ tsp vanilla extract
½ tbsp almond, minced

Instructions:

Heat up the waffle maker.

Add all the ingredients to a small mixing bowl and combine well.

Pour ½ of the batter into your waffle maker and cook for 4 minutes until golden brown. Then cook the remaining batter to make another chaffle.

Top the chaffles with unsweetened maple syrup.

Serve and enjoy!

Blackberries Syrup Chaffle

Prep Time: 5 minutes
Cook Time: 8 minutes
Servings: 2 chaffles

Ingredients for chaffles:

1 egg, beaten
½ cup cheddar cheese, shredded
1 tsp almond flour
1 tsp sour cream
A pinch of salt

Ingredients for blackberries syrup:

1 cup fresh blackberries
1 tsp vanilla extract
¼ cup sweetener
¼ cup water

Instructions for blackberries syrup:

In a saucepan over low heat add the blackberries, water, sweetener and vanilla extract.

Stir from time to time until you get a syrup.

Remove from heat, set aside and let cool.

Instructions for chaffles:

Heat up the waffle maker.

Add all the chaffles ingredients to a small mixing bowl and stir until well combined.

Pour half of the batter into the waffle maker and cook for 4 minutes until golden brown. Repeat with the rest of the batter to make another chaffle.

Let cool for 3 minutes to let chaffles get crispy.

Top the chaffles with blackberries syrup.

Serve and enjoy!

Blackberry Cheesy Chaffle

Prep Time: 5 minutes

Cook Time: 20 minutes
Servings: 4 chaffles

Ingredients for chaffles:

2 eggs, beaten
1 cup mozzarella cheese, shredded
A pinch of salt

Ingredients for topping:

1 ½ cup blackberries, minced
1 tsp lemon zest
2 tbsp lemon juice
1 tbsp sweetener
4 slices Brie cheese

Instructions for topping:

In a small saucepan over low heat, add blackberries, lemon zest, lemon juice and sweetener.

Cook for approx. 5 minutes until the sauce thickens. Remove from heat and set aside.

Instructions:

Heat up the waffle maker and preheat oven at 400°.

Add all the chaffles ingredients to a small mixing bowl and stir until well combined.

Pour ¼ of the batter into the waffle maker and cook for 4 minutes until golden brown. Repeat with the rest of the batter to prepare the other chaffles.

Top the chaffle with brie and sauce.

Place the chaffles in a baking sheet lined with parchment paper and cook for 4-5 minutes until cheese bubbles.

Serve and enjoy!

Swiss Chocolate Chaffle

Prep Time: 5 minutes
Cook Time: 8 minutes
Servings: 2 chaffles

Ingredients:

1 egg, beaten
½ cup mozzarella cheese, shredded
1 tbsp cream cheese
1 tbsp sweetener
2 tsp coconut flour
¼ tsp baking powder
1 tbsp unsweetened cocoa powder
1 tbsp unsweetened chocolate chips

Instructions:
Heat up the waffle maker.
Add all the ingredients to a small mixing bowl and stir until well combined.
Pour half of the batter into the waffle maker and cook for 4 minutes until golden brown. Repeat with the rest of the batter to make another chaffle.
Serve and enjoy!

Chaffle Cereals

Prep Time: 5 minutes
Cook Time: 8 minutes
Servings: 2 chaffles

Ingredients:
1 large egg, beaten
½ cup mozzarella cheese, shredded
2 tbsp almond flour
½ tsp coconut flour
1 tbsp cereals, minced
¼ tsp baking powder
1 tbsp butter, melted
1 tbsp cream cheese
¼ tsp vanilla powder
1 tbsp sweetener

Instructions:
Heat up the waffle maker.
Add all the ingredients to a small mixing bowl and stir until well combined.
Pour half of the batter into the waffle maker and cook for 4 minutes. Repeat with the rest of the batter to make another chaffle.
Serve and enjoy!

Whipped Cream Cereals Chaffle

Prep Time: 5 minutes
Cook Time: 8 minutes
Servings: 2 chaffles

Ingredients:
1 large egg, beaten
½ cup mozzarella cheese, shredded
2 tbsp almond flour
½ tsp coconut flour

1 tbsp cereals, minced
¼ tsp baking powder
1 tbsp butter, melted
1 tbsp cream cheese
¼ tsp vanilla powder
1 tbsp sweetener

Ingredients for topping:
2 tbsp whipped cream, unsweetened
2 tsp maple syrup, unsweetened

Instructions:
Heat up the waffle maker.
Add all the chaffles ingredients to a small mixing bowl and stir until well combined.
Pour half of the batter into the waffle maker and cook for 4 minutes. Repeat with the rest of the batter to make another chaffle.
Top the chaffles with whipped cream and maple syrup.
Serve and enjoy!

Sweet Chaffle

Prep Time: 5 minutes
Cook Time: 8 minutes
Servings: 2 chaffles

Ingredients:
1 egg, beaten
½ cup mozzarella cheese, shredded
1 tbsp cocoa powder, unsweetened
2 tbsp almond flour

Instructions:
Heat up the waffle maker.
Add all the ingredients to a small mixing bowl and stir until well combined.
Pour half of the batter into the waffle maker and cook for 4 minutes until golden brown. Repeat with the rest of the batter to make another chaffle.
Serve with strawberries and keto whipped cream and enjoy!

Almond Butter Chaffle

Prep Time: 5 minutes
Cook Time: 8 minutes

Servings: 2 chaffles

Ingredients:
1 large egg, beaten
½ cup of mozzarella cheese, shredded
2 tbsp almond flour
¼ tsp baking powder
2 tbsp almond butter for topping

Instructions:
Heat up the waffle maker.
Add all the ingredients to a small mixing bowl and stir until well combined.
Pour half of the batter into the waffle maker and cook for 4 minutes. Repeat with the rest of the batter to make another chaffle.
Let cool for 3 minutes to let chaffles get crispy.
Spread the chaffles with almond butter.
Serve and enjoy!

Mouth-Watering Chaffle

Prep Time: 5 minutes
Cook Time: 8 minutes
Servings: 2 chaffles

Ingredients for chaffles:
1 large egg, beaten
½ cup of mozzarella cheese, shredded
2 tbsp almond flour
¼ tsp baking powder
Ingredients for topping:
2 tbsp almond butter
2 tbsp unsweetened chocolate chips

Instructions:
Heat up the waffle maker.
Add all the chaffles ingredients to a small mixing bowl and stir until well combined.
Pour half of the batter into the waffle maker and cook for 4 minutes. Repeat with the rest of the batter to make another chaffle.
Let cool for 3 minutes to let chaffles get crispy.
Spread the chaffles with almond butter and garnish with chocolate chips.
Serve and enjoy!

Yogurt Green Chaffle

Prep Time: 5 minutes
Cook Time: 8 minutes
Servings: 2 chaffles

Ingredients:
½ tsp psyllium husk
½ cup mozzarella cheese, shredded
1 egg, beaten
1 tbsp yogurt
¼ tsp baking powder
1 small avocado, sliced for topping

Instructions:
Heat up the mini waffle maker.
Add all the ingredients to a small mixing bowl and stir until well combined.
Pour half of the batter into the waffle maker and cook for 4 minutes until brown. Repeat with the rest of the batter to prepare another chaffle.
Top the chaffles with sliced avocado.
Serve and enjoy!

Almonds & Nutmeg Chaffle

Prep Time: 5 minutes
Cook Time: 8 minutes
Servings: 2 chaffles

Ingredients:
1 large egg, beaten
½ cup of mozzarella cheese, shredded
2 tbsp almond flour
¼ tsp baking powder
2 tbsp almonds, chopped
¼ tsp nutmeg powder

Instructions:
Heat up the waffle maker.
Add all the ingredients to a small mixing bowl and combine well.
Pour half of the batter into the waffle maker and cook for 4 minutes until brown. Repeat with the rest of the batter to make another chaffle.
Let cool for 3 minutes to let chaffles get crispy.
Serve with keto whipped cream and enjoy!

Cashews Chaffle

Prep Time: 5 minutes
Cook Time: 8 minutes
Servings: 2 chaffles

Ingredients:
1 egg, beaten
½ cup mozzarella cheese, grated
1 tsp coconut flour
1 tsp water
¼ tsp baking powder
2 tbsp cashews, chopped for topping
Instructions:
Heat up the mini waffle maker.
Add all the ingredients to a small mixing bowl and combine well.
Pour half of the batter into the waffle maker and cook for 4 minutes until brown. Repeat with the rest of the batter to make another chaffle.
Let cool for 3 minutes to let chaffles get crispy.
Garnish with chopped cashews and unsweetened maple syrup.
Serve and enjoy!

Choco Cashews Chaffle

Prep Time: 4 minutes
Cook Time: 8 minutes
Servings: 2 chaffles

Ingredients for chaffles:
1 egg, beaten
½ cup mozzarella cheese, grated
1 tsp coconut flour
1 tsp water
¼ tsp baking powder
Ingredients for topping:
2 tbsp chocolate chips, unsweetened
2 tsp cashews, chopped
2 tsp sweetener

Instructions:
Heat up the mini waffle maker.
Add all the chaffles ingredients to a small mixing bowl and combine well.

Pour half of the batter into the waffle maker and cook for 4 minutes until brown. Repeat with the rest of the batter to make another chaffle.
Let cool for 3 minutes to let chaffles get crispy.
Garnish with chopped cashews, chocolate chips and sprinkle with sweetener.
Serve and enjoy!

Coconut Flakes Chaffle

Prep Time: 5 minutes
Cook Time: 8 minutes
Servings: 2 chaffles
Ingredients for chaffles:
1 egg, beaten
½ cup mozzarella cheese, grated
1 tsp coconut flour
1 tsp water
¼ tsp baking powder
Ingredients for topping:
2 tbsp caramel sauce, unsweetened
2 tbsp coconut flakes

Instructions:
Heat up the mini waffle maker.
Add all the chaffles ingredients to a small mixing bowl and combine well.
Pour half of the batter into the waffle maker and cook for 4 minutes until brown. Repeat with the rest of the batter to make another chaffle.
Let cool for 3 minutes to let chaffles get crispy.
Top the chaffles with caramel sauce and coconut flakes.
Serve and enjoy!

Caramel Chaffle

Prep Time: 5 minutes
Cook Time: 8 minutes
Servings: 2 chaffles

Ingredients for chaffles:
1 egg, beaten
½ cup mozzarella cheese, grated
1 tsp coconut flour
1 tsp water
¼ tsp baking powder

Ingredients for topping:
2 tbsp keto caramel sauce

Instructions:
Heat up the waffle maker.
Add all the chaffles ingredients to a small mixing bowl and combine well.
Pour half of the batter into the waffle maker and cook for 4 minutes until brown. Repeat with the rest of the batter to make another chaffle.
Let cool for 3 minutes to let chaffles get crispy.
Top the chaffles with caramel sauce.
Serve and enjoy!

Caramel & Chocolate Chips Chaffle

Prep Time: 5 minutes
Cook Time: 8 minutes
Servings: 2 chaffles

Ingredients for chaffles:
1 egg, beaten
½ cup mozzarella cheese, grated
1 tsp coconut flour
1 tsp water
¼ tsp baking powder
Ingredients for topping:
2 tbsp keto caramel sauce
2 tbsp chocolate chips, unsweetened
2 tsp sweetener

Instructions:
Heat up the waffle maker.
Add all the chaffles ingredients to a small mixing bowl and combine well.
Pour half of the batter into the waffle maker and cook for 4 minutes until brown. Repeat with the rest of the batter to make another chaffle.
Let cool for 3 minutes to let chaffles get crispy.
Top the chaffles with caramel sauce and chocolate chips. Sprinkle with sweetener.
Serve and enjoy!

Vanilla & Coconut Whipped Cream Chaffle

Prep Time: 5 minutes

Cook Time: 8 minutes
Servings: 2 chaffles

Ingredients for chaffles:
1 tbsp almond flour
½ cup mozzarella cheese, shredded
1 egg, beaten
1 tbsp sweetener
½ teaspoon vanilla extract
2 tbsp keto coconut whipped cream for topping

Instructions:
Heat up the waffle maker.
Add all the ingredients to a small mixing bowl and combine well.
Pour ½ of the batter into your waffle maker and cook for 4 minutes until golden brown. Cook the remaining batter to make another chaffle.
Top the chaffles with keto coconut whipped cream.
Serve and enjoy!

Choco Coco Chaffle

Prep Time: 5 minutes
Cook Time: 8 minutes
Servings: 2 chaffles

Ingredients:
1 egg, beaten
½ cup mozzarella cheese, grated
1 tsp coconut flour
1 tsp water
¼ tsp baking powder
2 tbsp chocolate chips, unsweetened

Instructions:
Heat up the waffle maker.
Add all the ingredients to a small mixing bowl and stir until well combined.
Pour half of the batter into the waffle maker and cook for 4 minutes until brown. Repeat with the rest of the batter to make another chaffle.
Let cool for 3 minutes to let chaffles get crispy.
Serve with cocoa powder and enjoy!

Coconut Chaffle with Berries

Prep Time: 5 minutes

Cook Time: 16 minutes
Servings: 4 chaffles

Ingredients for chaffles:
2 tbsp softened cream cheese
2 eggs, beaten
1 cup mozzarella cheese, shredded
4 tbsp coconut flour
1 tsp baking powder
1 tbsp butter, melted
2 tsp vanilla extract
1 tbsp sweetener

Ingredients for topping:
4 tsp sweetener
4 tbsp fresh blackberries
4 tbsp fresh raspberries
4 tbsp fresh blueberries

Instructions:
Heat up the waffle maker.
Add all the chaffles ingredients to a small mixing bowl and stir until well combined.
Pour ¼ of the batter into your waffle maker and cook for 4 minutes. Then cook the remaining batter to make the other chaffles.
Top the chaffles with berries and sprinkle with sweetener.
Serve and enjoy!

Cereals & Walnuts Chaffle

Prep Time: 5 minutes
Cook Time: 8 minutes
Servings: 2 chaffles

Ingredients:
1 large egg, beaten
2 tbsp almond flour
1 tbsp cereals, minced
¼ tsp baking powder
1 tbsp butter, melted
1 tbsp cream cheese, softened
¼ tsp vanilla powder
1 tbsp sweetener
½ tbsp walnuts, chopped

Instructions:
Heat up the waffle maker.

Add all the ingredients to a small mixing bowl and stir until well combined.
Pour half of the batter into the waffle maker and cook for 4 minutes. Repeat with the rest of the batter to make another chaffle.
Serve with keto caramel sauce and enjoy!

Eggnog Chaffle

Prep Time: 5 minutes
Cook Time: 8 minutes
Servings: 2 chaffles

Ingredients:
1 egg, beaten
2 tbsp cream cheese, softened
2 tsp sweetener
2 tbsp coconut flour
½ tsp baking powder
¼ cup keto eggnog
A pinch of nutmeg

Instructions:
Heat up the waffle maker.
Add all the ingredients to a small mixing bowl and stir until well combined.
Pour half of the batter into the waffle maker and cook for 4 minutes. Repeat with the rest of the batter to make another chaffle.
Let cool for 3 minutes to let chaffles get crispy.
Serve and enjoy!

Chocolate Chaffle with Eggnog Topping

Prep Time: 5 minutes
Cook Time: 8 minutes
Servings: 2 chaffles

Ingredients for chaffles:
½ cup shredded mozzarella cheese
1 tbsp almond flour
1 egg, beaten
¼ tsp cinnamon
½ tbsp sweetener
2 tbsp low carb chocolate chips

Ingredients for topping:
2 tbsp Keto eggnog

2 tsp cinnamon powder

Instructions:
Heat up the waffle maker.
Add all the chaffles ingredients to a small mixing bowl and stir until well combined.
Add half of the batter into the waffle maker and cook it for approx. 4-5 minutes until golden brown. When the first one is completely done cooking, cook the second one.
Set aside for 1-2 minutes.
Top the chaffle with keto eggnog and sprinkle with cinnamon powder.
Serve and enjoy!

Maple Syrup Crispy Chaffle

Prep Time: 5 minutes
Cook Time: 8 minutes
Servings: 2 chaffles

Ingredients for chaffles:
1 large egg, beaten
¼ cup parmesan cheese, shredded
½ cup mozzarella cheese, shredded
2 tbsp unsweetened maple syrup for topping

Instructions:
Heat up the waffle maker.
Add all the chaffles ingredients except for parmesan cheese to a small mixing bowl and combine well.
Pour half of the batter into the waffle maker, sprinkle with 1-2 tbsp of shredded parmesan cheese and cook for 4 minutes until golden brown. Repeat with the rest of the batter to make another chaffle.
Let cool for 3 minutes to let chaffles get crispy.
Top the chaffles with keto maple syrup.
Serve with coconut flour and enjoy!

White Choco Lemon Chaffle

Prep Time: 5 minutes
Cook Time: 8 minutes
Servings: 2 chaffles

Ingredients for chaffles:
1 large egg, beaten
½ tbsp butter, melted

½ tbsp softened cream cheese
1 tbsp unsweetened white chocolate chips
1 tbsp almond flour
1 tsp coconut flour
1 tbsp sweetener
¼ tsp baking powder
¼ tsp vanilla extract
Ingredients for lemon icing:
2 tbsp sweetener
4 tsp heavy cream
1 tsp lemon juice
Fresh lemon zest

Instructions:
Heat up the waffle maker.
Add all the chaffles ingredients to a small mixing bowl and stir until well combined.
Pour half of the batter into the waffle maker and cook for 4 minutes. Repeat with the rest of the batter to prepare the other chaffle.
Let cool for 3 minutes to let chaffles get crispy.
Combine in a mixing bowl the sweetener, heavy cream, lemon juice and lemon zest. Pour over the chaffles.
Serve and enjoy!

Cherry Chocolate Chaffle

Prep Time: 4 minutes
Cook Time: 8 minutes
Servings: 2 chaffles

Ingredients:
½ cup shredded mozzarella cheese
1 tbsp almond flour
1 egg, beaten
¼ tsp cinnamon
½ tbsp sweetener
1 tbsp low carb chocolate chips
1 tbsp dark sweet cherries, halved

Instructions:
Heat up the waffle maker.
Add all the ingredients to a small mixing bowl and stir until well combined.
Add half of the batter into the waffle maker and cook it for approx. 4-5 minutes. When the first one is completely done cooking, cook the second one.

Set aside for 1-2 minutes.
Serve and enjoy!

Cherries Chaffle

Prep Time: 5 minutes
Cook Time: 8 minutes
Servings: 2 chaffles

Ingredients for chaffles:
1 large egg, beaten
½ cup mozzarella cheese, shredded
¼ tsp sweetener
Ingredients for topping:
2 tbsp dark sweet cherries, halved
2 tbsp keto whipped heavy cream
2 tsp sweetener

Instructions:
Heat up the waffle maker.
Add all the chaffles ingredients to a small mixing bowl and stir until well combined.
Pour half of the batter into the waffle maker and cook for 4 minutes, until brown. Repeat with the rest of the batter to make another chaffle.
Let cool for 3 minutes to let chaffles get crispy.
Spread the chaffles with whipped heavy cream, add cherries and sprinkle with sweetener.
Serve and enjoy!

Ricotta Lemon Chaffle

Prep Time: 5 minutes
Cook Time: 8 minutes
Servings: 2 chaffles

Ingredients:
1 large egg, beaten
½ cup skim ricotta cheese
1 tbsp almond flour
½ tsp baking powder
½ tsp fresh lemon zest
½ tsp fresh lemon juice

Instructions:
Heat up the waffle maker.
Add all the ingredients to a small mixing bowl and stir until well combined.

Pour half of the batter into the waffle maker and cook for 4 minutes until golden brown. Repeat with the rest of the batter to make another chaffle.
Let cool for 3 minutes to let chaffles get crispy.
Serve and enjoy!

Mascarpone Cream Chaffle

Prep Time: 5 minutes
Cook Time: 8 minutes
Servings: 2 chaffles

Ingredients for chaffles:
1 large egg, beaten
½ cup mozzarella cheese, shredded
½ tsp sweetener
Ingredients for Mascarpone cream:
2 tbsp Mascarpone cheese, softened
2 tsp sweetener
1 tsp vanilla extract
½ tbsp unsalted butter, melted
2 tsp unsweetened cocoa powder for topping
Instructions for mascarpone cream:
Add all the cream ingredients to a mixing bowl and mix until smoothy.

Instructions:
Heat up the waffle maker.
Add all the chaffles ingredients to a small mixing bowl and stir until well combined.
Pour half of the batter into the waffle maker and cook for 4 minutes until golden brown. Repeat with the rest of the batter to make another chaffle.
Let cool for 3 minutes to let chaffles get crispy.
Spread the chaffles with mascarpone cream and sprinkle with cocoa powder.
Serve and enjoy!

Coffee Chaffle & Mascarpone Cream

Prep Time: 5 minutes
Cook Time: 8 minutes
Servings: 2 chaffles

Ingredients for chaffles:
1 large egg, beaten
1 tsp sweetener

¼ tsp baking powder
½ cup softened cream cheese
¼ tsp instant coffee powder
Ingredients for Mascarpone cream:
2 tbsp Mascarpone cheese, softened
2 tsp sweetener
1 tsp vanilla extract
½ tbsp unsalted butter, melted

Instructions for mascarpone cream:
Add all the cream ingredients to a mixing bowl and mix until smoothy.
Instructions for chaffles:
Heat up the waffle maker.
Add all the chaffles ingredients to a small mixing bowl and stir until well combined.
Pour half of the batter into the waffle maker and cook for 4 minutes until golden brown. Repeat with the rest of the batter to make another chaffle.
Let cool for 3 minutes to let chaffles get crispy.
Spread the chaffle with mascarpone cream.
Serve and enjoy!

Mouth-Watering Strawberry Chaffle

Prep Time: 5 minutes
Cook Time: 8 minutes
Servings: 2 chaffles

Ingredients for chaffles:
1 large egg, beaten
½ cup of mozzarella cheese, shredded
2 tbsp almond flour
¼ tsp baking powder
Ingredients for topping:
2 tbsp almond butter
2 tbsp fresh strawberries, sliced
Instructions:
Heat up the waffle maker.
Add all the chaffles ingredients to a small mixing bowl and stir until well combined.
Pour half of the batter into the waffle maker and cook for 4 minutes. Repeat with the rest of the batter to make another chaffle.
Let cool for 3 minutes to let chaffles get crispy.
Spread the chaffle with almond butter and garnish with fresh strawberries.

Serve and enjoy!

Crunchy Peach Chaffle

Prep Time: 5 minutes
Cook Time: 8 minutes
Servings: 2 chaffles

Ingredients for chaffles:
1 tbsp almond flour
½ cup mozzarella cheese
1 egg, beaten
½ teaspoon vanilla extract
Ingredients for topping:
1 ripe peach, sliced
1 tbsp unsweetened peach syrup
½ tbsp almond, minced

Instructions for chaffles:
Heat up the waffle maker.
Add all the chaffles ingredients to a small mixing bowl and combine well.
Pour ½ of the batter into your waffle maker and cook for 4 minutes until brown. Then cook the remaining batter to make another chaffle.
Top the chaffle with peach slices, a tbsp of unsweetened peach syrup and sprinkle with minced almonds.
Serve and enjoy!

Orange Glaze Chaffle

Prep Time: 5 minutes
Cook Time: 8 minutes
Servings: 2 chaffles

Ingredients for chaffles:
1 tbsp almond flour
½ cup mozzarella cheese
1 egg, beaten
½ tsp vanilla extract
Ingredients for glaze:
1tbsp unsalted butter, softened
1 tbsp sweetener
2 tbsp cream cheese, softened
¼ tsp orange extract

Instructions for glaze:
Add all the ingredients in a blender and whisk until creamy.

Instructions for chaffles:
Heat up the waffle maker.
Add all the chaffles ingredients to a small mixing bowl and combine well.
Pour ½ of the batter into your waffle maker and cook for 4 minutes until brown. Then cook the remaining batter to make another chaffle.
Top the chaffle with orange frosting.
Serve and enjoy!

Chocolate Chaffle with Orange Glaze

Prep Time: 5 minutes
Cook Time: 8 minutes
Servings: 2 chaffles

Ingredients for chaffles:
1 egg, beaten
½ cup of mozzarella cheese, shredded
2 tbsp chocolate chips, unsweetened
1 tbsp sweetener
1 tbsp whipping cream
1 tbsp almond flour
½ tsp vanilla extract
¼ tsp baking powder

Ingredients for glaze:
1tbsp unsalted butter, softened
1 tbsp sweetener
2 tbsp cream cheese, softened
¼ tsp orange extract

Instructions for glaze:
Add all the ingredients to a blender and whisk until creamy.

Instructions:
Heat up the waffle maker.
Add all the chaffles ingredients to a small mixing bowl and mix well.
Pour half of the batter into the waffle maker and cook for 4 minutes until golden brown. Repeat with the rest of the batter to make another chaffle.
Let cool for 3 minutes to let chaffles get crispy.
Spread the chaffles with orange frosting.
Serve and enjoy!

Sweet Orange Chaffle

Prep Time: 5 minutes
Cook Time: 8 minutes
Servings: 2 chaffles

Ingredients for chaffles:
1 egg, beaten
½ cup mozzarella cheese
1 tsp sweetener
¼ tsp orange zest
1 tsp orange extract

Ingredients for topping:
2 tbsp heavy whipping cream
1 tsp coconut flour

Instructions:
Heat up the waffle maker.
Add all the chaffles ingredients to a small mixing bowl and mix well until creamy.
Pour half of the batter into the waffle maker and cook for 4 minutes until brown. Repeat with the rest of the batter to make another chaffle.
Let cool for 3 minutes to let chaffles get crispy.
Top the chaffles with a spoonful of whipped cream and sprinkle with coconut flour.
Serve and enjoy!

Buttercream Frosting Chaffle

Prep Time: 5 minutes
Cook Time: 8 minutes
Servings: 2 chaffles

Ingredients for chaffles:
1 tbsp almond flour
½ cup mozzarella cheese
1 egg, beaten
1 tbsp sweetener
½ tsp vanilla extract

Ingredients for frosting:
2 tbsp butter, softened
2 tbsp sweetener
¼ tsp vanilla extract

Instruction for frosting:
Mix all the frosting ingredients until the mixture is creamy. Set aside.

Instructions for chaffles:

Heat up the waffle maker.

Add all the chaffles ingredients to a small mixing bowl and combine well.

Pour ½ of the batter into your waffle maker and cook for 4 minutes. Then cook the remaining batter to make another chaffle.

Top the chaffles with buttercream frosting.

Serve and enjoy!

Nutmeg & Cinnamon Chaffle

Prep Time: 5 minutes
Cook Time: 8 minutes
Servings: 2 chaffles

Ingredients for chaffles:

1 tbsp almond flour
½ cup mozzarella cheese, shredded
1 large egg, beaten
¼ tsp baking powder
¼ tsp nutmeg powder
½ tsp cinnamon powder

Instructions:

Heat up the waffle maker.

Add all the chaffles ingredients to a small mixing bowl and combine well.

Pour ½ of the batter into your waffle maker and cook for 4 minutes until golden brown. Then cook the remaining batter to make another chaffle.

Serve with maple syrup and enjoy!

Strawberry Mousse Chaffle

Prep Time: 5 minutes
Cook Time: 8 minutes
Servings: 2 chaffles

Ingredients for chaffles:

1 large egg, beaten
½ cup mozzarella cheese, grated
1 tsp coconut flour
1 tsp water
¼ tsp baking powder
Ingredients for mousse:

2 tbsp heavy whipping cream

2-3 tbsp fresh strawberries
½ tsp lemon zest
½ tsp vanilla extract
1-2 fresh mint leaves, for garnish

Instructions for mousse:

In a bowl, whip all the mousse ingredients until fluffy. Set aside.

Instructions for chaffles:

Heat up the mini waffle maker.

Add all the chaffles ingredients to a small mixing bowl and combine well.

Pour half of the batter into the waffle maker and cook for 4 minutes until brown. Repeat with the rest of the batter to make another chaffle.

Let cool for 3 minutes to let chaffles get crispy.

Top the chaffles with strawberry mousse and garnish with a fresh mint leaf.

Serve and enjoy!

Raspberry Butter Chaffle

Prep Time: 5 minutes
Cook Time: 8 minutes
Servings: 2 chaffles

Ingredients for chaffles:

1 large egg, beaten
½ cup mozzarella cheese, shredded
1 tsp coconut flour
1 tsp water
¼ tsp baking powder
Ingredients for raspberry butter:

3 tbsp butter, softened
1 tbsp fresh raspberries

Instructions for raspberry butter:

In a small mixing bowl, combine all the ingredients. Mix with an electric mixer and set aside.

Instructions for chaffles:

Heat up the waffle maker.

Add all the chaffles ingredients to a small mixing bowl and combine well.

Pour half of the batter into the waffle maker and cook for 4 minutes until brown. Repeat with the rest of the batter to make another chaffle.

Let cool for 3 minutes to let chaffles get crispy.

Spread the chaffles with raspberry butter.

Serve and enjoy!

Peanut Butter Creamy Chaffle

Prep Time: 5 minutes
Cook Time: 8 minutes
Servings: 2 chaffles

Ingredients for chaffles:
1 large egg, beaten
½ cup shredded mozzarella cheese
1 tbsp almond flour
½ tsp baking powder
Ingredients for peanut butter cream:
2 tbsp keto peanut butter
1 tsp sweetener
1 tbsp heavy cream

Instructions for peanut butter cream:
Blend all ingredients in a small bowl. Set aside.
Instructions for chaffles:
Heat up the waffle maker.
Add all the chaffles ingredients to a small mixing bowl and stir until well combined.
Pour half of the batter into the waffle maker and cook for 4 minutes until golden brown. Repeat with the rest of the batter to make another chaffle.
Spread the chaffles with peanut butter cream.
Serve and enjoy!

Chaffle & Custard

Prep Time: 5 minutes
Cook Time: 55 minutes
Servings: 2 chaffles

Ingredients for chaffles:
1 tbsp almond flour
½ cup mozzarella cheese
1 egg, beaten
1 tbsp sweetener
½ tsp vanilla extract
Ingredients for custard:
2 eggs
2 tbsp heavy cream
1 tbsp brown sugar substitute
½ tsp cinnamon powder

½ tsp vanilla extract

Instructions for custard:
Preheat the oven at 350 °.
Place all ingredients in a small bowl and stir until well combined.
Pour the mixture in a baking tin and bake it for about 40-45 minutes.
Remove from heat and set aside to cool.
Instructions for chaffles:
Heat up the waffle maker.
Add all the chaffles ingredients to a small mixing bowl and combine well.
Pour ½ of the batter into your waffle maker and cook for 4 minutes until golden brown. Then cook the remaining batter to make another chaffle.
Top the chaffles with custard.
Serve and enjoy!

Raspberry & Custard Chaffle

Prep Time: 5 minutes
Cook Time: 55 minutes
Servings: 2 chaffles

Ingredients for chaffles:
1 tbsp almond flour
½ cup mozzarella cheese
1 egg, beaten
1 tbsp sweetener
½ tsp vanilla extract
Ingredients for custard:
2 eggs
2 tbsp heavy cream
1 tbsp brown sugar substitute
½ tsp cinnamon powder
½ tsp vanilla extract
Ingredients for topping:
2 tbsp of fresh raspberries

Instructions for custard:
Preheat the oven at 350 °.
Place all ingredients in a small bowl and stir until well combined.
Pour the mixture in a baking tin and bake it for about 40-45 minutes.
Remove from heat and set aside to cool.
Instructions for chaffles:

Heat up the waffle maker.

Add all the chaffles ingredients to a small mixing bowl and combine well.

Pour ½ of the batter into your waffle maker and cook for 4 minutes until golden brown. Then cook the remaining batter to make another chaffle.

Top the chaffles with custard and sprinkle with raspberries.

Serve and enjoy!

Delicious Chaffle

Prep Time: 5 minutes
Cook Time: 55 minutes
Servings: 2 chaffles

Ingredients for chaffles:
½ cup shredded mozzarella cheese
1 tbsp almond flour
1 egg, beaten
¼ tsp cinnamon
½ tbsp sweetener
2 tbsp low carb chocolate chips

Ingredients for custard:
2 eggs
2 tbsp heavy cream
1 tbsp brown sugar substitute
½ tsp cinnamon powder
½ tsp vanilla extract

Instructions for custard:
Preheat the oven at 350°.

Place all ingredients in a small bowl and stir until well combined.

Pour the mixture in a baking tin and bake it for about 40-45 minutes.

Remove from heat and set aside to cool.

Instructions for chaffles:
Heat up the waffle maker.

Add all the chaffles ingredients to a small mixing bowl and combine well.

Pour ½ of the batter into your waffle maker and cook for 4 minutes until golden brown. Then cook the remaining batter to make another chaffle.

Top the chaffles with custard.

Serve and enjoy!

Yogurt Chaffle & Blueberries

Prep Time: 5 minutes
Cook Time: 8 minutes
Servings: 2 chaffles

Ingredients:
½ cup mozzarella cheese, shredded
1 egg, beaten
1 tbsp yogurt
1 tbsp fresh blueberries, chopped
¼ tsp baking powder

Instructions:
Heat up the mini waffle maker.

Add all the ingredients to a small mixing bowl and stir until well combined.

Pour half of the batter into the waffle maker and cook for 4 minutes until brown. Repeat with the rest of the batter to prepare another chaffle.

Serve and enjoy!

Strawberry Yogurt Chaffle

Prep Time: 5 minutes
Cook Time: 8 minutes
Servings: 2 chaffles

Ingredients:
½ cup mozzarella cheese, shredded
1 egg, beaten
1 tbsp yogurt
1 tbsp fresh strawberries, chopped
¼ tsp baking powder

Instructions:
Heat up the waffle maker.

Add all the ingredients to a small mixing bowl and stir until well combined.

Pour half of the batter into the waffle maker and cook for 4 minutes until brown. Repeat with the rest of the batter to prepare another chaffle.

Serve and enjoy!

Vanilla Chaffle with Lemon Icing

Prep Time: 5 minutes

Cook Time: 8 minutes
Servings: 2 chaffles

Ingredients for chaffles:
1 tbsp almond flour
½ cup mozzarella cheese
1 egg, beaten
1 tbsp sweetener
½ tsp vanilla extract

Ingredients for lemon icing:
2 tbsp powdered erythritol
4 tsp heavy cream
1 tsp lemon juice
 Lemon zest

Instructions:
Heat up the waffle maker.
Add all the ingredients for the chaffles to a small mixing bowl and combine well.
Pour ½ of the batter into your waffle maker and cook for 4 minutes. Then cook the remaining batter to make another chaffle.
Combine in a mixing bowl the powdered erythritol, heavy cream, lemon juice and lemon zest.
Pour over vanilla chaffle. Serve and enjoy!

White Chocolate Chaffle with Glaze and Raspberries

Prep Time: 5 minutes
Cook Time: 16 minutes
Servings: 4 chaffles

Ingredients for chaffles:
2 eggs, beaten
1 tbsp butter, melted
1 tbsp softened cream cheese
2 tbsp unsweetened white chocolate chips
1 cup mozzarella cheese, shredded
2 tbsp sweetener
½ tsp baking powder
½ tsp instant coffee granules dissolved in 1 tablespoon hot water
½ tsp vanilla extract
A pinch of salt

Ingredients for glaze:

1 egg yolk
¼ cup heavy cream
2 tbsp sweetener
1 tbsp butter
½ tsp caramel
¼ cup pecans, chopped
¼ cup unsweetened flaked coconut
1 tsp coconut flour
2 tbsp of fresh raspberries for topping

Instructions for chaffles:
Heat up the mini waffle maker.
Add all the chaffles ingredients to a small mixing bowl and mix well.
Pour ¼ of the batter into the waffle maker and cook for 4 minutes. Repeat with the rest of the batter to make 3 more chaffles.
Let cool for 3 minutes to let chaffles get crispy.

Instructions for glaze:
Combine the egg yolk, heavy cream, butter, and sweetener in a pan over medium heat.
Simmer slowly for approx. 4 minutes.
Remove from heat and stir in extract, pecans, flaked coconut, and coconut flour.
Top the chaffle with the glaze and the raspberries. Serve and enjoy!

Glazed Lemon Chaffle

Prep Time: 9 minutes
Cook Time: 4 minutes
Servings: 1 chaffle

Ingredients for chaffles:
1 tbsp heavy whipping cream
1 tbsp sweetener
1 tbsp coconut flour
1 egg
½ cup mozzarella cheese, shredded
½ tsp lemon extract
¼ tsp lemon zest

Ingredients for the glaze:
2 tsp lemon Juice
2 tbsp sweetener

Instructions:
Heat up the waffle maker.

Mix all the ingredients in a small mixing bowl and blend until creamy.

Pour the batter into the waffle maker and cook for about 4 minutes.

Whisk the lemon juice and the sweetener for the glaze in a mixing bowl, adding lemon juice until your desired consistency has been reached.

Pour the glaze over the chaffle.

Serve and enjoy!

Banana & Pecans Chaffle

Prep Time: 5 minutes
Cook Time: 8 minutes
Servings: 2 chaffles

Ingredients:
1 tbsp cream cheese
1 tbsp sweetener
1 egg
½ cup of mozzarella cheese, shredded
½ tsp vanilla extract
1 tsp banana extract, sugar-free
1 tbsp pecans, chopped for topping

Instructions:
Heat up the mini waffle maker.

Add all the ingredients to a small mixing bowl and stir until well combined.

Pour half of the batter into the waffle maker and cook for 4 minutes until brown.

Repeat with the remaining batter to prepare another chaffle.

Let cool for 3 minutes to let chaffles get crispy.

Serve and enjoy!

Macadamia Nuts Chaffle

Prep Time: 5 minutes
Cook Time: 8 minutes
Servings: 2 chaffles

Ingredients for chaffles:
1 tbsp almond flour
½ cup mozzarella cheese, shredded
1 egg, beaten
1 tbsp sweetener

½ tsp vanilla extract
A pinch of salt
1 tbsp Macadamia nuts, minced

Instructions:
Heat up the waffle maker.

Add all the ingredients to a small mixing bowl and combine well.

Pour ½ of the batter into your waffle maker and cook for 4 minutes until golden brown. Then cook the remaining batter to make another chaffle.

Top the chaffles with keto whipped cream.

Serve and enjoy!

Peppermint and Choco Chips Chaffle

Prep Time: 5 minutes
Cook Time: 8 minutes
Servings: 2 chaffles

Ingredients for chaffles:
1 tbsp almond flour
½ cup mozzarella cheese, shredded
1 egg, beaten
1 tbsp sweetener
½ tsp vanilla extract
3-4 chopped mint leaves
2 tsp chocolate chips, unsweetened
A pinch of salt

Instructions:
Heat up the waffle maker.

Add all the ingredients to a small mixing bowl and combine well.

Pour ½ of the batter into your waffle maker and cook for 4 minutes until golden brown. Then cook the remaining batter to make another chaffle.

Serve and enjoy!

Soft Berries Chaffles

Prep Time: 5 minutes
Cook Time: 16 minutes
Servings: 4 chaffles

Ingredients for chaffles:
1 cup of mozzarella cheese, shredded
2 tbsp almond flour

2 tsp of sweetener
½ tbsp blackberries
½ tbsp cranberries
1 tsp baking powder
2 eggs, beaten
1 tsp cinnamon

Ingredients for topping:
4 tbsp unsweetened whipped cream
4 tsp unsweetened maple syrup

Instructions:
Heat up the Waffle Maker.
Add the mozzarella cheese, baking powder, almond flour, eggs, cinnamon, sweetener, and berries to a medium mixing bowl. Mix well.
Spray the waffle maker with a cooking spray.
Add in about ¼ a cup of batter. Cook the chaffle for 4-5 minutes until it is crispy and brown. Repeat with the remaining batter to prepare the other chaffles.
Top the chaffle with a tbsp of keto whipped cream and keto maple syrup.
Serve and enjoy!

Almond Chocolate Chaffle and Jam

Prep Time: 5 minutes
Cook Time: 8 minutes
Servings: 2 chaffles

Ingredients:
1 egg, beaten
½ cup of mozzarella cheese, shredded
2 tbsp almond chocolate chips, unsweetened
2 tbsp sweetener
1 tbsp almond flour
¼ tsp baking powder
2 tbsp whipped cream for topping
2 tbsp raspberries jam, unsweetened for topping

Instructions:
Heat up the waffle maker.
Add all the chaffles ingredients to a small mixing bowl and mix well.
Pour half of the batter into the waffle maker and cook for 4 minutes until golden brown. Repeat with the rest of the batter to make another chaffle.
Let cool for 3 minutes to let chaffles get crispy.

Spread each chaffle with raspberries jam and a tablespoon of whipped cream.
Serve and enjoy!

Caramel & Raspberries Chaffle

Prep Time: 5 minutes
Cook Time: 8 minutes
Servings: 2 chaffles

Ingredients for chaffles:
1 egg, beaten
½ cup mozzarella cheese, grated
1 tsp coconut flour
1 tsp water
¼ tsp baking powder

Ingredients for topping:
2 tbsp keto caramel sauce
2 tbsp fresh raspberries
2 tsp sweetener

Instructions:
Heat up the waffle maker.
Add all the chaffles ingredients to a small mixing bowl and combine well.
Pour half of the batter into the waffle maker and cook for 4 minutes until brown. Repeat with the rest of the batter to make another chaffle.
Let cool for 3 minutes to let chaffles get crispy.
Top the chaffles with caramel sauce and raspberries. Sprinkle with sweetener.
Serve and enjoy!

Choco & Coconut Whipped Cream Chaffle

Prep Time: 5 minutes
Cook Time: 8 minutes
Servings: 2 chaffles

Ingredients for chaffles:
1 tbsp almond flour
½ cup mozzarella cheese, shredded
1 egg, beaten
1 tbsp sweetener
½ tsp vanilla extract
Ingredients for topping:

2 tbsp keto coconut whipped cream
2 tbsp chocolate chips, unsweetened

Instructions:
Heat up the waffle maker.
Add all the ingredients to a small mixing bowl and combine well.
Pour ½ of the batter into your waffle maker and cook for 4 minutes until golden brown. Cook the remaining batter to make another chaffle.
Top the chaffles with keto coconut whipped cream and chocolate chips.
Serve with coconut flakes and enjoy!

Cereals & Raspberries Chaffle

Prep Time: 5 minutes
Cook Time: 8 minutes
Servings: 2 chaffles

Ingredients:
1 large egg, beaten
2 tbsp almond flour
½ tsp coconut flour
1 tbsp cereals, minced
¼ tsp baking powder
1 tbsp butter, melted
1 tbsp cream cheese, softened
¼ tsp vanilla powder
1 tbsp sweetener
1 tbsp fresh raspberries, chopped

Instructions:
Heat up the waffle maker.
Add all the ingredients to a small mixing bowl and stir until well combined.
Pour half of the batter into the waffle maker and cook for 4 minutes. Repeat with the rest of the batter to make another chaffle.
Serve with coconut flour and enjoy!

Gourmet Eggnog Chaffle

Prep Time: 5 minutes
Cook Time: 8 minutes
Servings: 2 chaffles

Ingredients for chaffles:
1 egg, beaten
2 tbsp cream cheese, softened
2 tsp sweetener
2 tbsp coconut flour
½ tsp baking powder
¼ cup keto eggnog
A pinch of nutmeg

Ingredients for topping:
2 tbsp keto whipped cream
2 tbsp dark chocolate chips, unsweetened

Instructions:
Heat up the waffle maker.
Add all the chaffles ingredients to a small mixing bowl and stir until well combined.
Pour half of the batter into the waffle maker and cook for 4 minutes. Repeat with the rest of the batter to make another chaffle.
Let cool for 3 minutes to let chaffles get crispy.
Spread the chaffle with whipped cream and sprinkle with chocolate chips.
Serve and enjoy!

Chaffle Mascarpone and Cocoa

Prep Time: 5 minutes
Cook Time: 8 minutes
Servings: 2 chaffles

Ingredients for chaffles:
1 large egg, beaten
½ cup mozzarella cheese, shredded
½ tsp sweetener

Ingredients for Mascarpone cream:
2 tbsp Mascarpone cheese, softened
2 tsp sweetener
1 tsp vanilla extract
½ tbsp unsalted butter, melted
½ tbsp unsweetened cocoa powder

Instructions for mascarpone cream:
Add all the cream ingredients to a mixing bowl and mix until smoothy.

Instructions:
Heat up the waffle maker.
Add all the chaffles ingredients to a small mixing bowl and stir until well combined.

Pour half of the batter into the waffle maker and cook for 4 minutes until golden brown. Repeat with the rest of the batter to make another chaffle.
Let cool for 3 minutes to let chaffles get crispy.
Serve with coconut flour and enjoy!

Blueberry Mousse Chaffle

Prep Time: 5 minutes
Cook Time: 8 minutes
Servings: 2 chaffles

Ingredients for chaffles:
1 large egg, beaten
½ cup mozzarella cheese, grated
1 tsp coconut flour
1 tsp water
¼ tsp baking powder
Ingredients for mousse:
2 tbsp heavy whipping cream
2-3 tbsp fresh blueberries
½ tsp lemon zest
½ tsp vanilla extract
1-2 fresh mint leaves, for garnish

Instructions for mousse:
In a bowl, whip all the mousse ingredients until fluffy. Set aside.
Instructions for chaffles:
Heat up the mini waffle maker.
Add all the chaffles ingredients to a small mixing bowl and combine well.
Pour half of the batter into the waffle maker and cook for 4 minutes until brown. Repeat with the rest of the batter to make another chaffle.
Let cool for 3 minutes to let chaffles get crispy.
Top the chaffle with blueberry mousse and garnish with a fresh mint leaf.
Serve and enjoy!

Blueberry Butter Chaffle

Prep Time: 5 minutes
Cook Time: 8 minutes
Servings: 2 chaffles
Ingredients for chaffles:
1 large egg, beaten
½ cup mozzarella cheese, shredded
1 tsp coconut flour
1 tsp water
¼ tsp baking powder
Ingredients for blueberry butter:
3 tbsp butter, softened
1 tbsp fresh blueberries

Instructions for blueberry butter:
In a small mixing bowl, combine all the ingredients. Mix with an electric mixer and set aside.
Instructions for chaffles:
Heat up the waffle maker.
Add all the chaffles ingredients to a small mixing bowl and combine well.
Pour half of the batter into the waffle maker and cook for 4 minutes until brown. Repeat with the rest of the batter to make another chaffle.
Let cool for 3 minutes to let chaffles get crispy.
Spread the chaffles with blueberry butter.
Serve and enjoy!

Coffee Chaffle & Custard

Prep Time: 5 minutes
Cook Time: 55 minutes
Servings: 2 chaffles

Ingredients for chaffles:
1 egg, beaten
1 tbs black cocoa, unsweetened
1 tbs sweetener
¼ tsp baking powder
2 tbsp softened cream cheese
¼ tsp instant coffee powder
1 tsp vanilla extract
Ingredients for custard:
2 eggs
2 tbsp heavy cream
1 tbsp brown sugar substitute
½ tsp cinnamon powder
½ tsp vanilla extract

Instructions for custard:
Preheat the oven at 350 °.
Place all ingredients in a small bowl and stir until well combined.

Pour the mixture in a baking tin and bake it for about 40-45 minutes.

Remove from heat and set aside to cool.

Instructions for chaffles:

Heat up the waffle maker.

Add all the chaffles ingredients to a small mixing bowl and combine well.

Pour ½ of the batter into your waffle maker and cook for 4 minutes until golden brown. Then cook the remaining batter to make another chaffle.

Top the chaffles with custard.

Serve and enjoy!

Lemon Chaffle with Icing

Prep Time: 9 minutes
Cook Time: 4 minutes
Servings: 1 chaffle

Ingredients:
1 egg
½ cup mozzarella cheese, shredded
1 tbsp cream cheese
2 tbsp almond flour
1 tbsp lemon juice
2 tsp sweetener
½ tsp lemon zest
¼ tsp baking powder
A pinch of salt

Ingredients for lemon icing:
2 tbsp powdered erythritol
4 tsp heavy cream
1 tsp lemon juice
Lemon zest

Instructions:

Heat up the waffle maker.

Mix egg, cream cheese, mozzarella cheese, almond flour, lemon juice, sweetener, lemon zest, baking powder and salt in a small mixing bowl and blend until creamy.

Pour the batter into the waffle maker and cook for about 4 minutes.

Combine in a mixing bowl the powdered erythritol, heavy cream, lemon juice and lemon zest. Pour over lemon chaffle.

Serve and enjoy!

Chocolate Chaffle

Prep Time: 5 minutes
Cook Time: 16 minutes
Servings: 4 chaffles

Ingredients:
2 eggs
1 cup butter
½ cup sugar-free chocolate chips
¼ cup sweetener
1 tsp vanilla extract

Instructions:

Heat up the waffle maker.

Place butter and chocolate chips on a plate and melt them in microwave for approx. 1 minute. Combine well.

In a small mixing bowl, beat egg.

Add beaten egg, vanilla, sweetener and chocolate mixture in a small mixing bowl and combine well.

Pour ¼ of the batter onto the bottom plate of the waffle maker.

Cook for approx. 4 minutes or until the chaffle is golden brown.

Repeat with the rest of the batter.

Serve with your favorite berries and enjoy!

CHAPTER 4:   SAVORY CHAFFLES RECIPES

Cheddar Chaffle and Egg White

Prep Time: 5 minutes
Cook Time: 16 minutes
Servings: 4 chaffles

Ingredients:
2 eggs white
1 cup shredded cheddar cheese

Instructions:
Heat up the waffle maker.
Add white egg and shredded cheese to a small mixing bowl and combine well.

Pour ¼ of the batter into the waffle maker and cook for 4 minutes until brown. Repeat with the rest of the batter to make the other chaffles.
Let cool for 3 minutes to let chaffles get crispy.
Serve and enjoy!

Savory Garlic Bread Chaffle

Prep Time: 5 minutes
Cook Time: 8 minutes
Servings: 2 chaffles

Ingredients:
1 large egg, beaten
½ cup shredded mozzarella cheese

½ tsp garlic powder
1 tbsp almond flour
1 tbsp butter

Instructions:
Heat up the waffle maker.
Add all the ingredients to a small mixing bowl and combine well.
Pour half of the batter into the waffle maker and cook for 4 minutes until brown. Repeat with the rest of the batter to make another chaffle.
Let cool for 3 minutes to let chaffles get crispy.
Serve and enjoy!

Bacon Chaffle Sticks

Prep Time: 5 minutes
Cook Time: 8 minutes
Servings: 2 chaffles

Ingredients:
1 egg, beaten
½ cup shredded cheddar cheese
2 tbsp bacon bits, browned
A pinch of black pepper

Instructions:
Heat up the waffle maker.
Add all the ingredients to a small mixing bowl and combine well.
Pour half of the batter into the waffle maker and cook for 4 minutes until golden brown. Repeat with the rest of the batter to make another chaffle.
Let cool for 3 minutes to let chaffles get crispy.
Cut the chaffles in sticks and dip into your favorite keto sauce.
Serve and enjoy!

Ham Chaffle with Grilled Eggplant

Prep Time: 4 minutes
Cook Time: 8 minutes
Servings: 2 chaffles

Ingredients for chaffles:
1 egg, beaten
½ cup shredded mozzarella cheese
2 tbsp ham, minced

A pinch of salt
Ingredients for topping:
2-4 slices of grilled eggplants, very thin
2 tbsp sour cream
Fresh parsley to taste

Instructions:
Heat up the waffle maker.
Add all the ingredients except ham to a small mixing bowl and combine well.
Pour half of the batter into the waffle maker, sprinkle with the ham and cook for 4 minutes until brown. Repeat with the rest of the batter/ham to make another chaffle.
Top the chaffle with a slice of grilled eggplant, a teaspoon of sour cream and season with fresh minced parsley.
Serve and enjoy!

Black Olives Chaffle

Prep Time: 5 minutes
Cook Time: 8 minutes
Servings: 2 chaffles

Ingredients:
1 egg, beaten
½ cup of Parmesan cheese, finely grated
1 tbsp almond flour
1 tbsp pitted black olives, finely chopped

Instructions:
Heat up the mini waffle maker.
Add all the ingredients to a small mixing bowl and combine well.
Pour half of the batter into the waffle maker and cook for 4 minutes until brown. Repeat with the rest of the batter to make another chaffle.
Let cool for 3 minutes to let chaffles get crispy.
Serve with Feta cheese and enjoy!

Butter & Poppy Seeds Chaffle

Prep Time: 5 minutes
Cook Time: 8 minutes
Servings: 2 chaffles

Ingredients:
1 large egg, beaten
½ cup shredded mozzarella cheese
2 tbsp almond flour
½ tsp baking powder
½ tsp poppy seeds
2 tbsp unsalted butter for topping

Instructions:
Heat up the waffle maker.
Add all the ingredients to a small mixing bowl and stir until well combined.
Pour half of the batter into the waffle maker and cook for 4 minutes until golden brown. Repeat with the rest of the batter to make another chaffle.
Spread the chaffles with butter and sprinkle with poppy seeds.
Serve and enjoy!

Broccoli Chaffle & Ham Bits

Prep Time: 5 minutes
Cook Time: 8 minutes
Servings: 2 chaffles

Ingredients:
1 large egg, beaten
½ cup boiled, chopped broccoli
½ cup parmesan cheese, shredded
2 tbsp ham bits, browned
A pinch of salt and black pepper

Instructions:
Heat up the waffle maker.
Add all the ingredients to a small mixing bowl and stir until well combined.
Pour half of the batter into the waffle maker and cook for 4 minutes until golden brown. Repeat with the rest of the batter to make another chaffle.
Let cool for 3 minutes to let chaffles get crispy.
Serve warm and enjoy!

Turnip Chaffle with Avocado

Prep Time: 5 minutes
Cook Time: 8 minutes
Servings: 2 chaffles

Ingredients:
1 egg, beaten
½ cup Monterey Jack cheese, shredded
1 turnip, cooked and mashed
2 tbsp bacon bits, cooked
1 small avocado, sliced for topping

Instructions:
Heat up the waffle maker.
Add all the ingredients to a small mixing bowl and stir until well combined.
Pour half of the batter into the waffle maker and cook for 4 minutes until golden brown. Repeat with the rest of the batter to make another chaffle.
Top the chaffle with a few avocado slices.
Serve and enjoy!

Broccoli and Tomatoes Chaffle

Prep Time: 4 minutes
Cook Time: 8 minutes
Servings: 2 chaffles

Ingredients:
½ cup cheddar cheese
¼ cup boiled, chopped broccoli
1 egg
¼ tsp garlic powder
1 tbsp almond flour
1 tbsp tomatoes, diced

Instructions:
Heat up the waffle maker.
Mix almond flour, broccoli, cheddar cheese, egg, tomatoes and garlic powder in a small mixing bowl.
Pour half of the batter into the waffle maker and cook for 4 minutes. Repeat with the rest of the batter to make another chaffle.
Serve and enjoy!

Bagel Chaffle

Prep Time: 5 minutes
Cook Time: 8 minutes
Servings: 2 chaffles

Ingredients for chaffles:
1 egg, beaten

½ cup shredded mozzarella cheese
2 tsp cheddar cheese, shredded
1 tbsp bacon cooked and diced
Ingredients for the topping:
2 tbsp cream cheese
2 tsp everything bagel seasoning

Instructions:
Heat up the waffle maker.
Sprinkle the cheddar cheese to crispy.
Add egg and shredded mozzarella cheese to a small mixing bowl and combine well.
Pour half of the batter into the waffle maker, sprinkle with bacon and cook for 4 minutes until brown. Repeat with the rest of the batter to make another chaffle.
Let cool for 3 minutes to let chaffles get crispy.
Spread the cream cheese over the chaffle and top with everything bagel seasoning.
Serve and enjoy!

Ham and Jalapenos Chaffle

Prep Time: 4 minutes
Cook Time: 8 minutes
Servings: 2 chaffles

Ingredients:
2 tbsp cream cheese
1 egg, beaten
½ cup cheddar cheese
2 tbsp ham, diced
½ tbsp jalapenos
¼ tsp baking powder

Instructions:
Heat up the waffle maker.
In a pan cook ham until brown and crispy.
Mix egg and vanilla extract in a small mixing bowl.
Add baking powder, jalapenos and ham and mix well.
Add the cheese and stir until well combined.
Pour half of the batter into the waffle maker and cook for 4 minutes until golden brown. Repeat with the rest of the batter to make another chaffle.
Serve and enjoy!

Bagels Chaffle

Prep Time: 5 minutes
Cook Time: 8 minutes
Servings: 2 chaffles

Ingredients for chaffles:
1 egg, beaten
1 tsp coconut flour
½ cup shredded mozzarella cheese
Ingredients for topping:
2 tsp cream cheese
1 tsp everything bagel seasoning

Instructions:
Heat up the waffle maker.
Add all the chaffles ingredients to a small mixing bowl and combine well.
Pour half of the batter into the waffle maker and cook for 4 minutes until brown. Repeat with the rest of the batter to make another chaffle.
Let cool for 3 minutes to let chaffles get crispy.
Spread the cream cheese over the chaffle and top with everything bagel seasoning.
Serve and enjoy!

Blueberry and Bacon Chaffle

Prep Time: 5 minutes
Cook Time: 20 minutes
Servings: 4 chaffles

Ingredients:
1 cup of mozzarella cheese
2 tbsp almond flour
2 tsp of sweetener
3 tbsp blueberries
1 tsp baking powder
2 eggs
1 tsp cinnamon
Ingredients for topping:
4 slices of bacon, cooked
4 tbsp Keto Ketchup

Instructions:
Heat up the Mini Waffle Maker.

Add the mozzarella cheese, baking powder, almond flour, eggs, cinnamon, sweetener, and blueberries to a medium mixing bowl. Mix well.

Spray the waffle maker with a cooking spray.

Add in about ¼ a cup of blueberry keto batter and cook the chaffle for 4-5 minutes until it is crispy and brown. Repeat with the remaining batter to prepare the other chaffles.

Top each chaffle with a slice of bacon and a tbsp of keto ketchup.

Serve and enjoy!

Bacon Chaffle

Prep Time: 4 minutes
Cook Time: 8 minutes
Servings: 2 chaffles

Ingredients:
1 egg
½ cup shredded cheddar cheese
1tbsp bacon, cooked and diced

Instructions:
Heat up the waffle maker.

Add egg and shredded cheese to a small mixing bowl and combine well.

Pour half of the batter into the waffle maker, sprinkle with ½ tbsp of diced bacon and cook for 4 minutes. Repeat with the rest of the batter/bacon to make another chaffle.

Let cool for 3 minutes to let chaffles get crispy.

Serve and enjoy!

Topped Grilled Radishes Chaffle

Prep Time: 5 minutes
Cook Time: 8 minutes
Servings: 2 chaffles

Ingredients for chaffles:
1 large egg, beaten
½ cup mozzarella cheese, shredded
½ tsp baking powder
2 tbsp radishes, grilled and thin sliced
A pinch of salt and black pepper
Ingredients for topping:

2 tbsp butter
2 slices of deli ham
2 tsp fresh parsley, minced

Instructions:
Heat up the waffle maker.

Add all the ingredients to a small mixing bowl and stir until well combined.

Pour half of the batter into the waffle maker and cook for 4 minutes until golden brown. Repeat with the rest of the batter to make another chaffle.

Spread the chaffle with butter, top with a slice of deli ham and sprinkle the fresh parsley.

Serve and enjoy!

Onion Chaffle with Dip

Prep Time: 4 minutes
Cook Time: 16 minutes
Servings: 4 chaffles

Ingredients:
2 eggs
1 cup shredded mozzarella cheese
1 large sweet onion, rings
Ingredients for the dip:
2 tbsp mayonnaise
2 tsp keto ketchup
1 tsp grated horseradish
¼ tsp paprika
1/7 tsp garlic powder
1/8 tsp onion powder
1/8 tsp dried oregano
4-5 drops hot sauce

Instructions:
Heat up the waffle maker.

In a small bowl, whisk the egg until beaten and then combine mozzarella cheese and onion. Mix well.

Pour ¼ of the batter into the waffle maker and cook for about 4 minutes. Repeat with the rest of the batter to make other 3 chaffles.

Let cool for 3 minutes to let chaffles get crispy.

Combine all dip ingredients into a mixing bowl and whisk until smoothy.

Top every chaffles with a tablespoon of dip.

Serve and enjoy!

Zucchini & Onion Chaffle

Prep Time: 5 minutes
Cook Time: 8 minutes
Servings: 2 chaffles

Ingredients:
1 egg
½ cup grated zucchini
½ cup mozzarella cheese, shredded
1 tbsp onion, minced
1 garlic clove, minced
Fresh dill, chopped

Instructions:
Heat up the mini waffle maker.
Whisk eggs in bowl and stir in zucchini, onions, garlic, herbs, and most of the cheese. You can reserve some of the cheese to make the crispy coating.
Pour half of the batter into the waffle maker and cook for 4 minutes until brown. Repeat with the rest of the batter to make another chaffle.
Let cool for 3 minutes to let chaffles get crispy.
Serve with sour cream and enjoy!

Asparagus & Egg Chaffle

Prep Time: 10 minutes
Cook Time: 8 minutes
Servings: 2 chaffles

Ingredients:
1 egg, beaten
2 asparagus, boiled and finely cut
½ cup parmesan cheese, shredded
¼ cup Provolone cheese, shredded
A pinch of salt and pepper
Ingredients for topping:
1 small hard-boiled egg, sliced
1 tsp of keto mayonnaise

Instructions:
Heat up the waffle maker.
Add all the ingredients except for parmesan cheese to a small mixing bowl and combine well.
Pour half of the batter into the waffle maker, sprinkle with 1-2 tbsp of shredded parmesan cheese and cook

for 4 minutes. Repeat with the rest of the batter to make another chaffle.
Spread the chaffle with keto mayonnaise and a few slices of boiled egg.
Serve immediately and enjoy!

Ham Chaffle

Prep Time: 5 minutes
Cook Time: 8 minutes
Servings: 2 chaffles

Ingredients:
1 egg
½ cup shredded mozzarella cheese
2 tbsp ham, minced
Fresh basil to taste
Instructions:
Heat up the waffle maker.
Add all the ingredients except ham to a small mixing bowl and combine well.
Pour half of the batter into the waffle maker, sprinkle with the ham and cook for 4 minutes until brown. Repeat with the rest of the batter/ham to make another chaffle.
Serve and enjoy!

Onion & Ham Chaffle

Prep Time: 4 minutes
Cook Time: 16 minutes
Servings: 4 chaffles

Ingredients:
2 eggs
1 cup cheese, shredded
2 tbsp ham, minced
½ cup red onion, sliced
2 tbsp almond flour

Instructions:
Heat up the waffle maker.
Add all the ingredients to a small mixing bowl and combine well.
Pour ¼ of the batter into the waffle maker and cook for 4 minutes until brown. Repeat with the rest of the batter to prepare the other chaffles.

Serve immediately and enjoy!

Chaffle Taco Shells

Prep Time: 4 minutes
Cook Time: 20 minutes
Servings: 4 chaffles

Ingredients:
1 tbsp almond flour
1 cup taco blend cheese
2 eggs
¼ tsp taco seasoning

Instructions:
Heat up the waffle maker.
Mix almond flour, taco blend cheese, eggs, and taco seasoning in a small mixing bowl.
Add ¼ of batter to the waffle maker at a time. Cook chaffle batter for approx. 4 minutes.
Remove the chaffle from the waffle maker and drape over the side of a bowl.
Continue making chaffles until you are out of batter. Then fill your taco shells with taco meat and your favorite toppings.
Serve and enjoy!

Broccoli Chaffle

Prep Time: 4 minutes
Cook Time: 8 minutes
Servings: 2 chaffles

Ingredients:
½ cup cheddar cheese
¼ cup boiled and chopped broccoli
1 egg
¼ tsp garlic powder
1 tbsp almond flour

Instructions:
Heat up the waffle maker.
Mix almond flour, broccoli, cheddar cheese, egg, and garlic powder in a small mixing bowl.
Pour half of the batter into the waffle maker and cook for 4 minutes. Repeat with the rest of the batter to make another chaffle.
Serve and enjoy alone or dipping in sour cream!

Bacon & Chicken Chaffle

Prep Time: 4 minutes
Cook Time: 8 minutes
Servings: 2 chaffles

Ingredients:
1 egg
1/3 cup diced cooked chicken
1 slice bacon cooked and crumbled
½ cup shredded cheddar cheese
1 tsp powdered ranch dressing

Instructions:
Heat up the waffle maker.
Mix the egg, ranch dressing and cheese in a small mixing bowl.
Add the bacon and chicken and combine.
Pour half of the batter into the waffle maker and cook for 4 minutes. Repeat with the rest of the batter to make another chaffle.
Let cool for 3 minutes to let chaffles get crispy.
Serve with ranch dressing and enjoy!

Jalapeno Peppers Chaffle

Prep Time: 5 minutes
Cook Time: 16 minutes
Servings: 4 chaffles

Ingredients:
2 tbsp coconut flour
½ tsp baking powder
4 slices bacon, cooked and chopped
2 large eggs
2 jalapeno peppers, de-seeded and sliced
1 tbsp cream cheese
1 cup shredded cheddar cheese
A pinch of salt

Instructions:
Heat up the waffle maker.
Mix flour, baking powder, and salt in a small mixing bowl.
In a separate bowl, beat cream cheese until fluffy and in another bowl add egg and beat until fluffy.
Add ½ cup cream cheese and the shredded cheese, then beat until well mixed.

Add dry ingredients to egg mixture until well combined.

Fold in 1/3 jalapeno peppers.

Pour ¼ of the batter into the waffle maker and cook for 4 minutes. Repeat with the rest of the batter to make the other chaffles.

Let cool for 3 minutes then top with the rest of the cream cheese, jalapeno slices, and crumbled bacon pieces.

Serve and enjoy!

Easy Chaffle with Dip

Prep Time: 4 minutes
Cook Time: 16 minutes
Servings: 4 chaffles

Ingredients:
2 eggs
1 cup shredded mozzarella cheese
A pinch of salt
Ingredients for the dip:
2 tbsp mayonnaise
2 tsp keto ketchup
1 tsp grated horseradish
¼ tsp paprika
1/7 tsp garlic powder
1/8 tsp onion powder
1/8 tsp dried oregano
4-5 drops hot sauce

Instructions:
Heat up the waffle maker.

In a small bowl, whisk the egg until beaten and then combine mozzarella cheese. Mix well and season with salt.

Pour ¼ of the batter into the waffle maker and cook for about 4 minutes until golden brown. Repeat with the rest of the batter to make other 3 chaffles.

Let cool for 3 minutes to let chaffles get crispy.

Combine all dip ingredients into a mixing bowl and whisk until smoothy.

Top every chaffles with a tablespoon of dip.

Serve and enjoy!

Onion Chaffle

Prep Time: 4 minutes
Cook Time: 16 minutes
Servings: 4 chaffles

Ingredients:
2 eggs
1 cup shredded mozzarella cheese
1 large sweet onion, rings
A pinch of salt

Instructions:
Heat up the mini waffle maker.

In a small bowl, whisk the egg until beaten and then combine mozzarella cheese and onion. Mix well and add a pinch of salt.

Pour ¼ of the batter into the waffle maker and cook for about 4 minutes until golden brown. Repeat with the rest of the batter to make other 3 chaffles.

Let cool for 3 minutes to let chaffles get crispy.

Serve and enjoy!

Artichoke and Spinach Chaffle

Prep Time: 5 minutes
Cook Time: 8 minutes
Servings: 2 chaffles

Ingredients:
1 large egg, beaten
½ cup mozzarella cheese, shredded
1 tbsp cream cheese, softened
¼ tsp garlic powder
1/3 cup artichoke hearts marinated, minced
1/3 cup spinach, cooked and minced
A pinch of salt and pepper

Instructions:
Heat up the waffle maker.

Add all the ingredients to a small mixing bowl and stir until well combined.

Pour half of the batter into the waffle maker and cook for 4 minutes until golden brown. Repeat with the rest of the batter to make another chaffle.

Let cool for 3 minutes to let chaffles get crispy.

Serve with sour cream and enjoy!

Scrambled Eggs on an Onion Chaffle

Prep Time: 5 minutes
Cook Time: 16 minutes
Servings: 4 chaffles

Ingredients for chaffles:
2 large eggs
1 cup shredded mozzarella cheese
1 large sweet onion, rings
½ tsp garlic powder
2 tbsp almond flour
2 tbsp coconut flour
A pinch of salt

Ingredients for topping:
3 eggs
1 tsp dried herbs
1 tbsp olive oil
A pinch of salt

Instructions for chaffles:
Heat up the waffle maker.
In a small bowl, whisk the egg until beaten and then combine mozzarella cheese, onion, almond and coconut flour. Mix well, add a pinch of salt and the garlic powder.
Pour ¼ of the batter into the waffle maker and cook for about 4 minutes until golden brown. Repeat with the rest of the batter to make other 3 chaffles.
Let cool for 3 minutes to let chaffles get crispy.

Instructions for topping:
Whisk the eggs for 1-2 minutes. Add the dried herbs and a pinch of salt.
In a small saucepan heat the oil over medium heat.
Cook the eggs.
Top each chaffles with the scrambled eggs.
Serve with Keto Ketchup and enjoy!

Chicken Chaffle

Prep Time: 4 minutes
Cook Time: 8 minutes
Servings: 2 chaffles

Ingredients:
1/3 cup cooked chicken, chopped
1 egg

½ cup cheddar cheese, shredded
¼ tsp taco seasoning

Instructions:
Heat up the mini waffle maker.
Mix all the ingredients to a small mixing bowl and combine well.
Pour half of the batter into the waffle maker and cook for 4 minutes. Repeat with the rest of the batter to make another chaffle.
Let cool for 3 minutes to let chaffles get crispy.
Serve and enjoy!

Chicken and Jalapeno Chaffle

Prep Time: 4 minutes
Cook Time: 8 minutes
Servings: 2 chaffles

Ingredients:
½ cup cooked chicken breasts, chopped
1 large egg, beaten
½ cup cheddar cheese, shredded
1 jalapeno, deseeded and chopped
1/8 tsp garlic powder
1/8 tsp onion powder
1 tsp cream cheese

Instructions:
Heat up the waffle maker.
Mix all the ingredients to a small mixing bowl and combine well.
Pour half of the batter into the waffle maker and cook for 4 minutes until golden brown. Repeat with the rest of the batter to make another chaffle.
Serve and enjoy!

Coriander Butter Chaffle

Prep Time: 5 minutes
Cook Time: 8 minutes
Servings: 2 chaffles

Ingredients for chaffles:
1 large egg, beaten
½ cup of mozzarella cheese, shredded
2 tbsp almond flour
¼ tsp baking powder

Ingredients for Coriander butter:
1 tsp olive oil
2 tbsp butter, softened
1 tbsp fresh coriander, chopped
1 tsp lime juice
A pinch of salt and black pepper

Instructions for Coriander butter:
In a small mixing bowl, combine all the ingredients and stir well. Set aside.

Instructions for chaffles:
Heat up the waffle maker.
Add all the chaffles ingredients to a small mixing bowl and combine well.
Pour half of the batter into the waffle maker and cook for 4 minutes until brown. Repeat with the rest of the batter to make another chaffle.
Let cool for 3 minutes to let chaffles get crispy.
Spread the chaffle with coriander butter.
Serve and enjoy!

Chicken Creamy Chaffle

Prep Time: 4 minutes
Cook Time: 8 minutes
Servings: 2 chaffles

Ingredients for topping:
1 cup chicken breast, shredded
¼ all-purpose cream
A pinch of salt and pepper
Ingredients for chaffles:
1 egg
½ cup shredded mozzarella cheese

Instructions for chicken:
In a small saucepan over medium heat, add the shredded chicken fillet and the cream.
Taste with a pinch of salt and pepper. Set aside.

Instructions for chaffles:
Heat up the mini waffle maker.
Mix all the ingredients to a small mixing bowl and combine well.
Pour half of the batter into the waffle maker and cook for 4 minutes. Repeat with the rest of the batter to make another chaffle.
Let cool for 3 minutes to let chaffles get crispy.
Top each chaffle with the chicken mixture.

Serve and enjoy!

Chicken Garlic Chaffle

Prep Time: 4 minutes
Cook Time: 8 minutes
Servings: 2 chaffles

Ingredients for topping:
1 cup chicken breast fillet, shredded
¼ all-purpose cream
A pinch of salt and pepper
Ingredients for chaffles:
1 egg
½ cup shredded mozzarella cheese
¼ tsp garlic powder

Instructions for chicken:
In a small saucepan over medium heat, add the shredded chicken fillet and the cream.
Taste with a pinch of salt and pepper. Set aside.

Instructions for chaffles:
Heat up the mini waffle maker.
Mix all the ingredients in a small mixing bowl and combine well.
Pour half of the batter into the waffle maker and cook for 4 minutes. Repeat with the rest of the batter to make another chaffle.
Let cool for 3 minutes to let chaffles get crispy.
Top each chaffle with the chicken mixture.
Serve and enjoy!

Tuna & Pork Chaffle

Prep Time: 5 minutes
Cook Time: 16 minutes
Servings: 4 chaffles

Ingredients:
2 cans tuna, drained
2 eggs
1 cup shredded mozzarella cheese
1 tsp garlic, minced
3 tbsp mayonnaise
1 tbsp lemon juice
¼ cup pork rinds, crushed
½ tsp onion powder

2 tbsp butter, melted
Instructions:
Heat up the waffle maker.
Mix all the ingredients in a small mixing bowl and combine well.
Pour ¼ of the batter into the waffle maker and cook for 4 minutes. Repeat with the rest of the batter to make other chaffles.
Let cool for 3 minutes to let chaffles get crispy.
Serve and enjoy!

Zucchini Chaffle

Prep Time: 5 minutes
Cook Time: 8 minutes
Servings: 2 chaffles

Ingredients:
1 egg, beaten
1 cup grated zucchini
¼ cup parmesan cheese, shredded
½ cup mozzarella cheese, shredded
1 tsp dried basil
A pinch of salt and pepper

Instructions:
Heat up the waffle maker.
Add all the ingredients except for parmesan cheese in a small mixing bowl and combine well.
Pour half of the batter into the waffle maker, sprinkle with 1-2 tbsp of shredded parmesan cheese and cook for 4 minutes. Repeat with the rest of the batter to make another chaffle.
Let cool for 3 minutes to let chaffles get crispy.
Serve and enjoy!

Zucchini & Bacon Chaffle

Prep Time: 10 minutes
Cook Time: 8 minutes
Servings: 2 chaffles

Ingredients:
1 egg, beaten
½ cup grated zucchini
½ cup parmesan cheese, shredded
¼ cup cheddar cheese, shredded

1 tbsp bacon, diced
A pinch of salt and pepper
Instructions:
Heat up the waffle maker.
Add all the ingredients except for parmesan cheese to a small mixing bowl and combine well.
Pour half of the batter into the waffle maker, sprinkle with 1-2 tbsp of shredded parmesan cheese and cook for 4 minutes. Repeat with the rest of the batter to make another chaffle.
Let cool for 3 minutes to let chaffles get crispy.
Serve and enjoy!

Spinach Chaffle

Prep Time: 10 minutes
Cook Time: 8 minutes
Servings: 2 chaffles

Ingredients:
1 egg, beaten
1 cup spinach, boiled and chopped
½ cup parmesan cheese, shredded
½ cup mozzarella cheese, shredded
1 tsp dried basil
A pinch of salt and pepper

Instructions:
Heat up the waffle maker.
Add all the ingredients except for parmesan cheese to a small mixing bowl and combine well.
Pour half of the batter into the waffle maker, sprinkle with 1-2 tbsp of shredded parmesan cheese and cook for 4 minutes. Repeat with the rest of the batter to make another chaffle.
Let cool for 3 minutes to let chaffles get crispy.
Serve and enjoy!

Spinach and Ham Chaffle

Prep Time: 10 minutes   **Cook Time:** 8 minutes   **Servings:** 2 chaffles
Ingredients:
1 egg, beaten
1 cup spinach, boiled and chopped

¼ cup parmesan cheese, shredded
½ cup mozzarella cheese, shredded
1 tbsp ham, diced
1 tsp dried basil
A pinch of salt and pepper

Instructions:
Heat up the waffle maker.
Add all the ingredients except for parmesan cheese to a small mixing bowl and combine well.
Pour half of the batter into the waffle maker, sprinkle with 1-2 tbsp of shredded parmesan cheese and cook for 4 minutes. Repeat with the rest of the batter to make another chaffle.
Let cool for 3 minutes to let chaffles get crispy.
Serve and enjoy!

Popeye Chaffle

Prep Time: 10 minutes
Cook Time: 8 minutes
Servings: 2 chaffles

Ingredients:
1 egg, beaten
1 cup spinach, boiled and chopped
¼ cup parmesan cheese, shredded
½ cup mozzarella cheese, shredded
1 tbsp bacon, diced
1 tsp dried basil
A pinch of salt and pepper

Instructions:
Heat up the waffle maker.
Add all the ingredients except for parmesan cheese to a small mixing bowl and combine well.
Pour half of the batter into the waffle maker, sprinkle with 1-2 tbsp of shredded parmesan cheese and cook for 4 minutes. Repeat with the rest of the batter to make another chaffle.
Let cool for 3 minutes to let chaffles get crispy.
Serve and enjoy!

Tomatoes and Basil Chaffle

Prep Time: 10 minutes
Cook Time: 8 minutes

Servings: 2 chaffles
Ingredients:
1 egg, beaten
1 cup tomatoes, chopped
¼ cup parmesan cheese, shredded
½ cup swiss cheese, shredded
1 tsp fresh basil
A pinch of salt and pepper

Instructions:
Heat up the waffle maker.
Add all the ingredients except for parmesan cheese to a small mixing bowl and combine well.
Pour half of the batter into the waffle maker, sprinkle with 1-2 tbsp of shredded parmesan cheese and cook for 4 minutes. Repeat with the rest of the batter to make another chaffle.
Let cool for 3 minutes to let chaffles get crispy.
Serve with sour cream and enjoy!

Asparagus Chaffle

Prep Time: 10 minutes
Cook Time: 8 minutes
Servings: 2 chaffles

Ingredients:
1 egg, beaten
2 asparagus, boiled and finely cut
¼ cup parmesan cheese, shredded
½ cup Provolone cheese, shredded
A pinch of salt and pepper

Instructions:
Heat up the waffle maker.
Add all the ingredients except for parmesan cheese to a small mixing bowl and combine well.
Pour half of the batter into the waffle maker, sprinkle with 1-2 tbsp of shredded parmesan cheese and cook for 4 minutes. Repeat with the rest of the batter to make another chaffle.
Serve immediately and enjoy!

Cauliflower & Smoked Salmon Chaffle

Prep Time: 10 minutes
Cook Time: 8 minutes

Servings: 2 chaffles

Ingredients for chaffles:
1 egg, beaten
½ cup cauliflower, boiled and chopped
¼ cup parmesan cheese, shredded
½ cup mozzarella cheese, shredded
A pinch of salt and pepper

Ingredients for topping:
2 slices of smoked salmon
1 tbsp sour cream

Instructions:
Heat up the waffle maker.
Add all the ingredients except for parmesan cheese to a small mixing bowl and combine well.
Pour half of the batter into the waffle maker, sprinkle with 1-2 tbsp of shredded parmesan cheese and cook for 4 minutes. Repeat with the rest of the batter to make another chaffle.
Let cool for 3 minutes to let chaffles get crispy.
Top the chaffle with a slice of smoked salmon.
Serve with sour cream and enjoy!

Cauliflower and Tomato Chaffle

Prep Time: 10 minutes
Cook Time: 8 minutes
Servings: 2 chaffles

Ingredients for chaffles:
1 egg, beaten
½ cup cauliflower, boiled and chopped
¼ cup parmesan cheese, shredded
½ cup mozzarella cheese, shredded
1 tbsp tomato, diced
A pinch of salt and pepper

Instructions:
Heat up the waffle maker.
Add all the ingredients except for parmesan cheese to a small mixing bowl and combine well.
Pour half of the batter into the waffle maker, sprinkle with 1-2 tbsp of shredded parmesan cheese and cook for 4 minutes until golden brown. Repeat with the rest of the batter to make another chaffle.
Let cool for 3 minutes to let chaffles get crispy.
Serve with sour cream and enjoy!

Jicama Chaffle

Prep Time: 5 minutes
Cook Time: 24 minutes
Servings: 4 chaffles

Ingredients:
2 garlic cloves, pressed
1 cup cheese
2 eggs, whisked
1 jicama root, peeled, drained, and chopped
½ onion, minced
Salt and Pepper to taste

Instructions:
Heat up the mini waffle maker.
Microwave the jicama for about 8-9 minutes.
Add all the ingredients to a small mixing bowl and combine well.
Pour ¼ of the batter into the waffle maker, sprinkle a little cheese on top and cook for 4 minutes. Repeat with the rest of the batter to make the other chaffles.
Let cool for 3 minutes to let chaffles get crispy.
Serve and enjoy!

Basil and Hard-Boiled Egg Chaffle

Prep Time: 4 minutes
Cook Time: 8 minutes
Servings: 2 chaffles

Ingredients for chaffles:
1 large egg, beaten
½ cup of mozzarella cheese, shredded
2 tbsp almond flour
¼ tsp baking powder

Ingredients for topping:
1 tbsp chopped fresh basil
2 tbsp keto mayonnaise
1 hard-boiled egg, thin sliced

Instructions:
Heat up the waffle maker.
Add all the chaffles ingredients to a small mixing bowl and combine well.
Pour half of the batter into the waffle maker and cook for 4 minutes until brown. Repeat with the rest of the batter to make another chaffle.

Let cool for 3 minutes to let chaffles get crispy. Spread the chaffle with mayonnaise, garnish with a few slices of hard-boiled egg and sprinkle with basil. Serve and enjoy!

Rose Pepper Butter and Roast Beef Chaffle

Prep Time: 5 minutes
Cook Time: 8 minutes
Servings: 2 chaffles

Ingredients for chaffles:
1 large egg, beaten
½ cup of mozzarella cheese, shredded
2 tbsp almond flour
¼ tsp baking powder
Ingredients for Rose pepper butter:
2 tbsp butter, softened
2 tbsp Parmesan cheese, shredded
1 tsp rose pepper, chopped
¼ tsp lemon juice
A pinch of salt and black pepper
Ingredients for topping:
2 thin slices of Roast beef
Lettuce leaves

Instructions for Rose Pepper butter:
In a small mixing bowl, combine all the ingredients and stir well. Set aside.
Instructions for chaffles:
Heat up the waffle maker.
Add all the chaffles ingredients to a small mixing bowl and combine well.
Pour half of the batter into the waffle maker and cook for 4 minutes until brown. Repeat with the rest of the batter to make another chaffle.
Let cool for 3 minutes to let chaffles get crispy.
Spread the chaffle with Rose pepper butter. Top with lettuce and roast-beef.
Serve and enjoy!

Sausage Chaffle

Prep Time: 6 minutes
Cook Time: 8 minutes

Servings: 2 chaffles
Ingredients for the chaffles:
1 egg
½ cup mozzarella cheese, grated
1 tsp coconut flour
1 tsp water
¼ tsp baking powder
Ingredients for the sausage sauce:
¼ cup browned sausage
3 tbsp chicken broth
2 tbsp whipping cream
2 tsp softened cream cheese
garlic powder

Instructions for the sausage sauce:
In a large pan over medium heat add the sausage and all the other ingredients for the sauce and bring to a boil.
Continue to cook until the sauce begins to thicken, approx. 8 minutes.
Instructions:
Heat up the mini waffle maker.
Add all the ingredients for the chaffles to a small mixing bowl and combine well.
Pour half of the batter into the waffle maker and cook for 4 minutes. Repeat with the rest of the batter to make another chaffle.
Spoon the gravy over chaffles.
Serve and enjoy!

Herbs & Parmesan Cheese Chaffle

Prep Time: 4 minutes
Cook Time: 8 minutes
Servings: 2 chaffles

Ingredients:
½ cup mozzarella cheese, shredded
1 egg
1 tbsp almond flour
¼ tsp garlic powder
¼ tsp Italian seasoning
1 tbsp heavy whipping cream
¼ cup grated parmesan cheese

Instructions:
Heat up the mini waffle maker.

Add all the ingredients to a small mixing bowl and combine well.

Pour half of the batter into the waffle maker and cook for 4 minutes. Repeat with the rest of the batter to make another chaffle.

Let cool for 3 minutes to let chaffles get crispy.

Serve and enjoy!

Savory Feta Chaffle

Prep Time: 5 minutes
Cook Time: 5 minutes
Servings: 1 chaffle

Ingredients for chaffle:
1 white egg
¼ cup mozzarella cheese, shredded
2 tbsp almond flour
1 tsp Cajun seasoning
Ingredients for topping:
1 egg
1 thin slice Feta cheese
1 tomato, sliced

Instructions:
Heat up the waffle maker.

Add all the ingredients for the chaffle to a small mixing bowl and stir until well combined.

Pour the batter into the waffle maker and cook for 4 minutes until golden brown.

Let cool for 3 minutes to let chaffle get crispy.

In the meantime, in a small pan fry the egg for approx. 2 minutes.

Top the chaffle with the fried egg, a slice of feta cheese and a slice of tomato.

Serve and enjoy!

Spicy Bacon Chaffle

Prep Time: 5 minutes
Cook Time: 8 minutes
Servings: 2 chaffles

Ingredients for chaffles:
1 large egg, beaten
½ cup of mozzarella cheese, shredded
2 tbsp almond flour

¼ tsp baking powder
Ingredients for topping:
2 slices of bacon, browned
2 tsp hot sauce, unsweetened
Lettuce leaves

Instructions:
Heat up the waffle maker.

Add all the chaffles ingredients to a small mixing bowl and combine well.

Pour half of the batter into the waffle maker and cook for 4 minutes until brown. Repeat with the rest of the batter to make another chaffle.

Let cool for 3 minutes to let chaffles get crispy.

Spread the chaffle with hot sauce and top with lettuce and bacon.

Serve and enjoy!

Salmon Chaffle

Prep Time: 5 minutes
Cook Time: 8 minutes
Servings: 2 chaffles

Ingredients for the chaffles:
½ cup mozzarella cheese, grated
1 large egg
A pinch of salt and pepper
Ingredients for the filling:
2 slices of smoked salmon
2 tbsp cream cheese
½ tsp cress
A handful of arugulas
A pinch of salt and pepper
Lemon zest

Instructions:
Heat up the mini waffle maker.

Add all the chaffles ingredients to a small mixing bowl and stir until well combined.

Pour half of the batter into the waffle maker and cook for 4 minutes. Repeat with the rest of the batter to make another chaffle.

Let cool for 3 minutes to let chaffles get crispy.

Brush chaffles with cream cheese and top with salmon and garnish. Season to taste with salt, pepper.

Serve and enjoy!

Chaffle Strips

Prep Time: 10 minutes
Cook Time: 10 minutes
Servings: 2 chaffles

Ingredients:
1 egg
1 tbsp almond flour
½ tsp vanilla extract
1 tsp cinnamon
¼ tsp baking powder
½ cup mozzarella, shredded
1 tbsp sweetener
1 tbsp melted butter

Instructions:
Heat up the mini waffle maker.
Add all the chaffles ingredients to a small mixing bowl and stir until well combined.
Pour half of the batter into the waffle maker and cook for 4 minutes. Repeat with the rest of the batter to make another chaffle.
Let cool for 3 minutes to let chaffles get crispy.
Cut the chaffles into strips and place them into a bowl. Cover in the melted butter.
Pour sweetener and a pinch of cinnamon over the chaffles.
Serve and enjoy!

Cucumber and Bacon Cream Chaffle

Prep Time: 5 minutes
Cook Time: 8 minutes
Servings: 2 chaffles

Ingredients for chaffles:
1 large egg, beaten
½ cup of mozzarella cheese, shredded
2 tbsp almond flour
¼ tsp baking powder
Ingredients for cucumber cream:
2 tbsp cream cheese, softened
2 tbsp fresh cucumber, chopped
Ingredients for topping:
2 slices of bacon, cooked
A pinch of black pepper

2 tsp sesame seeds

Instructions for cream:
In a small bowl, whisk cream cheese and cucumber until smoothy. Set aside.
Instructions for chaffles:
Heat up the mini waffle maker.
Add all the chaffles ingredients to a small mixing bowl and combine well.
Pour half of the batter into the waffle maker and cook for 4 minutes until brown. Repeat with the rest of the batter to make another chaffle.
Let cool for 3 minutes to let chaffles get crispy.
Spread the chaffle with cucumber cream and top with bacon slices. Season with pepper to taste.
Sprinkle with sesame seeds.
Serve and enjoy!

Chaffle Cheeseburger

Prep Time: 10 minutes
Cook Time: 25 minutes
Servings: 2 chaffles

Ingredients for burger:
6 oz. ground beef burger
A pinch of salt and pepper
Ingredients for chaffles:
½ cup mozzarella cheese, grated
1 egg
A pinch of salt and pepper, garlic powder and oregano
Ingredients for 1 burger sauce:
½ egg yolks
1 tsp of linseed oil
1 tsp olive oil
1 tbsp cream cheese
½ tsp sugar-free mustard
½ tsp lemon juice
A pinch of salt and pepper
1 tbsp red onion, finely chopped
Ingredients for filling:
1 tbsp low-carb ketchup
2 slices of tomatoes, diced
2 slices of onion, diced
4 slices of cucumber, diced
1 large sheet of lettuce

1 tbsp grated cheddar cheese

Instructions for burger sauce:
Put the egg yolk and all the other ingredients in a tall container and puree with the blender until a firm emulsion has formed. Season with salt, pepper, and lemon juice.

Instructions for burger:
In a saucepan over medium heat add the ground beef burger and cook it for about 10 minutes.
Once cooked, remove from heat, and add salt and pepper to taste.

Instructions for chaffles:
Heat up the waffle maker.
Add all the chaffles ingredients to a small mixing bowl and stir until well combined.
Pour half of the batter into the waffle maker and cook for 4 minutes. Repeat with the rest of the batter to make another chaffle.
Let cool for 3 minutes to let chaffles get crispy.
Top chaffle with burger, sauce, and all filling ingredients.
Serve immediately and enjoy!

Avocado and Shrimp Chaffle

Prep Time: 10 minutes
Cook Time: 16 minutes
Servings: 4 chaffles

Ingredients for chaffles:
2 eggs
1 cup mozzarella cheese, shredded
1 tsp Cajun seasoning
Ingredients for filling:
1 lb. shrimps, peeled, deveined, and cooked
4 slices cooked bacon
1 sliced avocado
1/3 cup onion, sliced and cooked
2 tbsp cream cheese
1 tsp Cajun seasoning

Instructions:
Heat up the mini waffle maker.
Add all the chaffles ingredients to a small mixing bowl and stir until well combined.

Pour ¼ of the batter into the waffle maker and cook for 4 minutes until brown. Repeat with the rest of the batter to prepare the other chaffles.
Let cool for 3 minutes to let chaffles get crispy.
In a small bowl, toss shrimps with the Cajun seasoning.
Spread the chaffle with cream cheese, top with shrimps, bacon, onion and avocado. Cover with another chaffle.
Serve and enjoy!

Chaffle Bacon Burger

Prep Time: 10 minutes
Cook Time: 25 minutes
Servings: 2 chaffles

Ingredients for burger:
180 g ground beef burger
A pinch of salt and pepper
Ingredients for chaffles:
½ cup mozzarella cheese, grated
1 egg
A pinch of salt and pepper
Garlic powder to taste
Ingredients for filling:
2 tbsp low-carb ketchup
4 slices of bacon, crispy
2 slices of tomatoes, diced
2 slices of onion, diced
4 slices of cucumber, diced
1 large sheet of lettuce

Instructions for burger:
In a saucepan over medium heat add the ground beef burger and cook it for about 10 minutes.
Once cooked, remove from heat, and add salt and pepper to taste.

Instructions for chaffles:
Heat up the waffle maker.
Add all the chaffles ingredients to a small mixing bowl and stir until well combined.
Pour half of the batter into the waffle maker and cook for 4 minutes. Repeat with the rest of the batter to make another chaffle.
Let cool for 3 minutes to let chaffles get crispy.

Top chaffle with burger, and all other filling ingredients.
Serve immediately and enjoy!

Hot dog Chaffle

Prep Time: 5 minutes
Cook Time: 15 minutes
Servings: 2 chaffles

Ingredients for chaffles:
1 egg, beaten
½ cup shredded cheddar cheese
½ tsp baking powder
2 tbsp almond flour
A pinch of salt and pepper
Ingredients for topping:
2 tbsp keto ketchup or keto mayonnaise
½ cup shredded cheese
1 hot dog, sliced and cooked

Instructions:
Heat up the waffle maker.
Mix all the ingredients for chaffles to a small mixing bowl and stir until well combined.
Pour half of the batter into the waffle maker and cook for 4 minutes. Repeat with the rest of the batter to make another chaffle.
Let cool for 3 minutes to let chaffles get crispy.
Top the chaffle with sliced hot dog, a tbsp of keto ketchup/mayonnaise and sprinkle with cheddar cheese.
Serve and enjoy!

Mayo Chaffle

Prep Time: 5 minutes
Cook Time: 8 minutes
Servings: 2 chaffles

Ingredients:
2 large eggs
2 tbsp mayonnaise
2 tbsp almond flour
½ tsp corn syrup substitute
¼ tsp baking powder

Instructions:
Heat up the mini waffle maker.
Mix all the ingredients in a small mixing bowl.
Pour half of the batter into the waffle maker and cook for 4 minutes until brown. Repeat with the rest of the batter to make another chaffle.
Let cool for 3 minutes to let chaffles get crispy.
Serve and enjoy!

Paprika Bacon Chaffle

Prep Time: 5 minutes
Cook Time: 8 minutes
Servings: 2 chaffles

Ingredients for chaffles:
1 large egg, beaten
½ cup cheddar cheese, shredded
½ tbsp paprika powder
1 tbsp bacon bits, browned

Instructions:
Heat up the waffle maker.
Add all the chaffles ingredients to a small mixing bowl and stir until well combined.
Pour half of the batter into the waffle maker and cook for 4 minutes, until brown. Repeat with the rest of the batter to make another chaffle.
Let cool for 3 minutes to let chaffles get crispy.
Serve with sliced avocado and enjoy!

BBQ Pork Chaffle

Prep Time: 10 minutes
Cook Time: 10 minutes
Servings: 2 chaffles

Ingredients for rib patties:
½ pound ground pork
1 tsp liquid smoke hickory flavor
A pinch of salt and pepper
2 tbsp sugar-free BBQ sauce
Ingredients for the chaffles:
2 eggs, beaten
2 tbsp mayonnaise
2 tbsp almond flour
¼ tsp baking powder

Ingredients for the filling:
1 tbsp sugar free barbecue sauce
10 pickle chips
¼ onion, chopped

Instructions for patties:
Mix the ribs ingredients except for BBQ sauce in a mixing bowl.
Divide the pork into two balls, then roll them.
Heat a grill pan over medium heat. Grill the patties for 6 minutes per side, brushing them with 1/2 tablespoon of barbecue sauce after you flip them. Allow them to cook for 1 more minute per side to caramelize the sauce, then remove.

Instructions for the chaffles:
Heat up the mini waffle maker.
Add all the chaffles ingredients to a small mixing bowl and stir until well combined.
Pour half of the batter into the waffle maker and cook for 4 minutes until brown. Repeat with the rest of the batter to make another chaffle.
Let cool for 3 minutes to let chaffles get crispy.

Instructions for filling:
Spread the chaffle with BBQ sauce and stack the patties.
Top with chopped onions and pickle chips before placing the remaining chaffle on top.
Serve and enjoy!

Roast Beef, Brie and Cranberries Chaffle

Prep Time: 5 minutes
Cook Time: 8 minutes
Servings: 2 chaffles

Ingredients for the chaffles:
1 large egg, beaten
½ cup mozzarella cheese, shredded
2 tbsp almond flour

Ingredients for the filling:
1 slice of roast beef, very thin
1 slice of Brie cheese
1 tbsp chia cranberry jam

Instructions for the chaffles:
Heat up the waffle maker.
Add all the chaffles ingredients to a small mixing bowl and combine well.

Pour half of the batter into the waffle maker and cook for 4 minutes until golden brown. Repeat with the rest of the batter to prepare the remaining chaffle.
Let cool for 3 minutes to let chaffles get crispy.
Spread the chaffle with chia cranberry jam and top with a slice of brie and of roast beef.
Serve and enjoy!

Red Hot Chili Chaffle

Prep Time: 5 minutes
Cook Time: 16 minutes
Servings: 4 chaffles

Ingredients:
2 eggs, beaten
½ cup parmesan cheese, grated
1 cup cheddar cheese, shredded
1 red hot chili pepper
½ tsp garlic powder
1 tsp dried basil
2 tbsp almond flour

Instructions:
Heat up the waffle maker.
Add all the ingredients to a small mixing bowl and stir until well combined.
Pour half of the batter into the waffle maker and cook for 4 minutes until golden brown. Repeat with the rest of the batter to make the other chaffles.
Let cool for 3 minutes to let chaffles get crispy.
Serve and enjoy!

Parmesan Butter Chaffle

Prep Time: 5 minutes
Cook Time: 8 minutes
Servings: 2 chaffles

Ingredients for chaffles:
1 large egg, beaten
½ cup of mozzarella cheese, shredded
2 tbsp almond flour
¼ tsp baking powder

Ingredients for Parmesan butter:
2 tbsp butter, softened

2 tbsp Parmesan cheese, shredded
A pinch of salt and black pepper

Instructions for Parmesan butter:
In a small mixing bowl, combine all the ingredients and stir well. Set aside.
Instructions for chaffles:
Heat up the waffle maker.
Add all the chaffles ingredients to a small mixing bowl and combine well.
Pour half of the batter into the waffle maker and cook for 4 minutes until brown. Repeat with the rest of the batter to make another chaffle.
Let cool for 3 minutes to let chaffles get crispy.
Spread the chaffle with Parmesan butter.
Serve and enjoy!

Pesto Chaffle

Prep Time: 5 minutes
Cook Time: 13 minutes
Servings: 2 chaffles

Ingredients for the chaffles:
1 egg
½ cup shredded cheddar cheese
Ingredients for topping:
2 tbsp marinara sauce
2 tbsp mozzarella cheese, shredded
1 tbsp olives, minced
1 tomato, sliced
1 tbsp keto pesto sauce

Instructions for the chaffles:
Heat up the waffle maker and preheat oven at 400°.
Add egg and shredded cheese to a small mixing bowl and combine well.
Pour half of the batter into the waffle maker and cook for 4 minutes until golden brown. Repeat with the rest of the batter to make another chaffle.
Let cool for 3 minutes to let chaffles get crispy.
Spread the marinara sauce and the keto pesto on the chaffle.
Top with olives, mozzarella cheese and olives.
Bake the chaffles for approx. 5 minutes.
Serve and enjoy!

Roasted Pepper & Tuna Chaffle

Prep Time: 5 minutes
Cook Time: 8 minutes
Servings: 2 chaffles

Ingredients for chaffles:
1 large egg, beaten
½ cup mozzarella cheese, shredded
Ingredients for roasted pepper sauce:
2 tbsp roasted green peppers
2 tbsp mayonnaise
¼ tsp garlic powder
1 tbsp olive oil
A pinch of salt and black pepper
Ingredients for topping:
1 can of tuna, drained
2 tsp of fresh coriander, minced

Instructions for sauce:
Mix in a blender all the sauce ingredients and set aside.
Instructions for chaffles:
Heat up the waffle maker.
Add all the chaffles ingredients to a small mixing bowl and stir until well combined.
Pour half of the batter into the waffle maker and cook for 4 minutes until golden brown. Repeat with the rest of the batter to make another chaffle.
Let cool for 3 minutes to let chaffles get crispy.
Spread the chaffle with pepper cream and tuna.
Sprinkle with fresh coriander.
Serve and enjoy!

Shredded Pork Chaffle

Prep Time: 5 minutes
Cook Time: 16 minutes
Servings: 4 chaffles

Ingredients:
2 eggs, beaten
1 cup mozzarella cheese, shredded
¼ tsp baking powder
2 cups cooked pork, shredded
1 tbsp Keto BBQ sauce
2 cups coleslaw mix, shredded

2 tbsp apple cider vinegar
A pinch of salt and pepper
¼ cup ranch dressing

Instructions for topping:
Mix the shredded pork and the keto BBQ sauce in a small bowl.
In a separate mixing bowl, combine coleslaw mix with apple cider vinegar, salt, pepper and ranch dressing.

Instructions for the chaffles:
Heat up the waffle maker.
Add the eggs, mozzarella cheese and baking powder to a small mixing bowl and stir until well combined.
Pour ¼ of the batter into the waffle maker and cook for 4 minutes until golden brown. Repeat with the rest of the batter to make the other chaffles.
Top each chaffle with the pork and the coleslaw mix.
Serve and enjoy!

Shrimps Spicy Chaffle

Prep Time: 5 minutes
Cook Time: 16 minutes
Servings: 4 chaffles

Ingredients for shrimps:
1 tsp olive oil
1 lb. shrimps, peeled and deveined
1 tbsp Creole seasoning
A pinch of salt
2 tbsp hot sauce
3 tbsp butter

Ingredients for the chaffles:
2 eggs
1 cup Monterey Jack cheese, shredded

Instructions for shrimps:
In a small saucepan over medium heat, heat the olive oil and cook the shrimps for approx. 3-4 minutes.
Season the shrimps with Creole seasoning.
Pour in the butter and the hot sauce. Mix well.

Instructions for the chaffles:
Heat up the waffle maker.
Add all the chaffles ingredients to a small mixing bowl and stir until well combined.

Pour ¼ of the batter into the waffle maker and cook for 4 minutes until golden brown. Repeat with the rest of the batter to make the other chaffles.
Let cool for 3 minutes to let chaffles get crispy.
Top the chaffles with shrimps.
Serve and enjoy!

Hot Sauce Cheddar Chaffle

Prep Time: 5 minutes
Cook Time: 8 minutes
Servings: 2 chaffles

Ingredients:
1 egg
½ cup shredded cheddar cheese
1 tbsp keto hot sauce

Instructions:
Heat up the waffle maker.
Add all the ingredients to a small mixing bowl and combine well.
Pour half of the batter into the waffle maker and cook for 4 minutes until golden brown. Repeat with the rest of the batter to make another chaffle.
Let cool for 3 minutes to let chaffles get crispy.
Serve and enjoy!

Asiatic Cauliflower Rice Chaffle

Prep Time: 10 minutes
Cook Time: 16 minutes
Servings: 4 chaffles

Ingredients for chaffles:
1 cup cauliflower rice, steamed
2 eggs, beaten
1 cup parmesan cheese, shredded
A pinch of salt and pepper
Ingredients for the sauce:
3 tbsp coconut aminos
1 tbsp vinegar
1 tsp garlic powder
1 tsp fresh ginger puree
3 tbsp sesame oil
1 tsp fish sauce
1 tsp red chili peppers powder

Ingredients for topping:
1 tsp sesame seeds
¼ cup red onion, sliced

Instructions for the sauce:
In a bowl add all the sauce ingredients and mix well.
Instructions for the chaffles:
Heat up the mini waffle maker.
Add all the ingredients except for parmesan cheese to a small mixing bowl and combine well.
Pour ¼ of the batter into the waffle maker, sprinkle with 1 tbsp of shredded parmesan cheese and cook for 4 minutes until golden brown. Repeat with the rest of the batter to make the other chaffles.
Top the chaffle with the sauce, sesame seeds and red onion slices.
Serve and enjoy!

Bacon, Olives & Cheddar Chaffle

Prep Time: 4 minutes
Cook Time: 8 minutes
Servings: 2 chaffles

Ingredients:
1 egg, beaten
½ cup shredded cheddar cheese
A pinch of salt
1 tbsp bacon bits
½ tbsp black olives, pitted and chopped

Instructions:
Heat up the waffle maker.
Add all the ingredients to a small mixing bowl and stir until well combined.
Pour half of the batter into the waffle maker and cook for 4 minutes until golden brown. Repeat with the rest of the batter to make another chaffle.
Let cool for 3 minutes to let chaffles get crispy.
Serve and enjoy!

Veggie Chaffle

Prep Time: 5 minutes
Cook Time: 8 minutes
Servings: 2 chaffles

Ingredients:
1 egg
½ cup zucchini, grated
½ cup mozzarella cheese, shredded
½ tbsp onion, minced
½ tbsp tomato, diced
1 garlic clove, minced
Fresh dill, chopped
A pinch of salt

Instructions:
Heat up the waffle maker.
Whisk eggs in bowl and stir in zucchini, onions, garlic, herbs, tomatoes and most of the cheese. You can reserve some of the cheese to make the crispy coating.
Pour half of the batter into the waffle maker and cook for 4 minutes until brown. Repeat with the rest of the batter to make another chaffle.
Let cool for 3 minutes to let chaffles get crispy.
Serve and enjoy!

Vegetables Chaffle

Prep Time: 5 minutes
Cook Time: 8 minutes
Servings: 2 chaffles

Ingredients:
1 egg
½ tbsp spinach, boiled and chopped
½ cup mozzarella cheese, shredded
1 tsp onion, minced, browned
½ tbsp broccoli, boiled and chopped
1 garlic clove, minced
A pinch of salt and pepper

Instructions:
Heat up the waffle maker.
Add all the ingredients to a small mixing bowl and stir until well combined.
Pour half of the batter into the waffle maker and cook for 4 minutes until brown. Repeat with the rest of the batter to make another chaffle.
Let cool for 3 minutes to let chaffles get crispy.
Serve with sour cream and enjoy!

Scallion Chaffle

Prep Time: 5 minutes
Cook Time: 8 minutes
Servings: 2 chaffles

Ingredients:
1 large egg, beaten
½ cup of mozzarella cheese, shredded
2 tbsp almond flour
¼ tsp baking powder
1 tbsp scallion browned and chopped
1 tsp fresh basil
A pinch of salt

Instructions:
Heat up the waffle maker.
Add all the ingredients to a small mixing bowl and combine well.
Pour half of the batter into the waffle maker and cook for 4 minutes until brown. Repeat with the rest of the batter to make another chaffle.
Let cool for 3 minutes to let chaffles get crispy.
Serve and enjoy!

Fresh Dill Chaffle

Prep Time: 5 minutes
Cook Time: 8 minutes
Servings: 2 chaffles

Ingredients:
1 egg, beaten
½ cup shredded cheddar cheese
½ tbsp fresh dill, finely chopped

Instructions:
Heat up the waffle maker.
Add egg, shredded cheddar cheese, and dill to a small mixing bowl and combine well.
Pour half of the batter into the waffle maker and cook for 4 minutes until brown. Repeat with the rest of the batter to make another chaffle.
Serve with your favorite keto dressing and enjoy!

Israelian Chaffle

Prep Time: 10 minutes
Cook Time: 20 minutes
Servings: 4 chaffles

Ingredients for chaffles:
2 large eggs, beaten
1 cup cheddar cheese, shredded
2 scallions, minced
A pinch of salt and pepper
Ingredients for topping:
2 chicken breasts, cooked and shredded
¼ cup keto buffalo sauce
3 tbsp keto hummus
2 celery stalks, minced
¼ cup cheddar cheese, shredded

Instructions:
Heat up the waffle maker and preheat oven at 400°.
In a mixing bowl add hummus, chicken, sauce and celery stalks. Combine well and set aside.
Add all the chaffles ingredients in a separate mixing bowl and stir until well combined.
Pour ¼ of the batter into the waffle maker and cook for 4 minutes until golden brown. Repeat with the rest of the batter to prepare the other chaffles.
Arrange the chaffles in the baking sheet lined with parchment paper.
Top each chaffle with the chicken mixture and sprinkle with cheddar cheese.
Bake for approx. 5 minutes or until the cheese bubbles.
Serve and enjoy!

Keto Mayonnaise Chaffle

Prep Time: 5 minutes
Cook Time: 16 minutes
Servings: 4 chaffles

Ingredients:
2 large eggs, beaten
2 tbsp keto mayonnaise
1 tbsp almond flour
1 tbsp cream cheese
¼ tsp baking powder

A pinch of salt and pepper

Instructions:
Heat up the waffle maker.
Add all the ingredients to a small mixing bowl and stir until well combined.
Pour ¼ of the batter into the waffle maker and cook for 4 minutes until brown. Repeat with the rest of the batter to make the other chaffles.
Let cool for 3 minutes to let chaffles get crispy.
Serve and enjoy!

Herbs Chaffle with Grilled Eggplant

Prep Time: 4 minutes
Cook Time: 8 minutes
Servings: 2 chaffles

Ingredients for chaffles:
1 egg, beaten
½ cup shredded parmesan cheese
1 tsp fresh basil
½ tsp dried oregano
½ tsp dried thyme
Ingredients for topping:
2-4 slices of grilled eggplant
2 tbsp keto mustard

Instructions:
Heat up the waffle maker.
Add all the ingredients to a small mixing bowl and combine well.
Pour half of the batter into the waffle maker and cook for 4 minutes. Repeat with the rest of the batter to make another chaffle.
Spread the chaffle with keto mustard and garnish with 1-2 slices of grilled eggplant.
Serve and enjoy!

Tasty Eggplant & Feta Chaffle

Prep Time: 5 minutes
Cook Time: 5 minutes
Servings: 1 chaffle

Ingredients for chaffle:
1 white egg
¼ cup mozzarella cheese, shredded

2 tbsp almond flour
1 tsp Italian seasoning
Ingredients for topping:
1 egg
4 oz Feta cheese
1 tomato, sliced
2-4 thin slices of grilled eggplant

Instructions:
Heat up the waffle maker.
Add all the ingredients for the chaffle to a small mixing bowl and stir until well combined.
Pour the batter into the waffle maker and cook for 4 minutes until golden brown.
Let cool for 3 minutes to let chaffle get crispy.
In the meantime, in a small pan fry the egg for approx. 2 minutes.
Top the chaffle with the fried egg, a slice of feta cheese, a slice of tomato and the grilled eggplant.
Serve and enjoy!

Savory Aubergine Chaffle

Prep Time: 5 minutes
Cook Time: 8 minutes
Servings: 2 chaffles

Ingredients for the chaffles:
1 large egg, beaten
½ cup mozzarella cheese, shredded
2 tbsp almond flour
Ingredients for the filling:
2 slices of roast beef, very thin
2 slices of Brie cheese
2 thin slices of grilled eggplant

Instructions for the chaffles:
Heat up the waffle maker.
Add all the chaffles ingredients to a small mixing bowl and combine well.
Pour half of the batter into the waffle maker and cook for 4 minutes until golden brown. Repeat with the rest of the batter to prepare the remaining chaffle.
Let cool for 3 minutes to let chaffles get crispy.
Garnish the chaffle with a slice of brie, eggplants and roast beef.
Serve warm and enjoy!

Parmigiana Chaffle

Prep Time: 4 minutes
Cook Time: 8 minutes
Servings: 2 chaffles

Ingredients for chaffles:
1 large egg, beaten
½ cup of mozzarella cheese, shredded
2 tbsp almond flour
¼ tsp baking powder
Ingredients for Parmigiana:
2 round eggplant slices, grilled
2 tbsp low carb pasta sauce
2 tbsp Parmesan cheese, finely grated
2 tsp fresh parsley, chopped

Instructions for chaffles:
Heat up the waffle maker and preheat oven.
Add all the ingredients to a small mixing bowl and combine well.
Pour half of the batter into the waffle maker and cook for 4 minutes until brown. Repeat with the rest of the batter to make another chaffle.
Let cool for 3 minutes to let chaffles get crispy.
Instructions for Parmigiana topping:
Top the chaffle with a slice of grilled eggplant; spread the eggplant with a tablespoon of pasta sauce. Sprinkle with Parmesan and parsley.
Place the parmigiana chaffles in the baking sheet with parchment paper.
Bake in the oven for approx. 5 minutes or until cheese is melted.
Serve and enjoy!

Basil Cream & Ham Chaffle

Prep Time: 5 minutes
Cook Time: 8 minutes
Servings: 2 chaffles

Ingredients for chaffles:
1 large egg, beaten
½ cup of mozzarella cheese, shredded
2 tbsp almond flour
¼ tsp baking powder
Ingredients for basil cream:

2 tbsp cream cheese, softened
2 tbsp fresh basil, chopped
Ingredients for topping:
2 slices of ham
A pinch of black pepper
2 tsp sesame seeds
2 tsp pickled cucumbers, sliced

Instructions for cream:
In a small bowl, whisk cream cheese and basil until smoothy. Set aside.
Instructions for chaffles:
Heat up the mini waffle maker.
Add all the chaffles ingredients to a small mixing bowl and combine well.
Pour half of the batter into the waffle maker and cook for 4 minutes until brown. Repeat with the rest of the batter to make another chaffle.
Let cool for 3 minutes to let chaffles get crispy.
Spread the chaffle with basil cream. Top with a slice of ham and pickled cucumbers. Season with pepper to taste and sprinkle with sesame seeds.
Serve and enjoy!

Turnip Chaffle

Prep Time: 5 minutes
Cook Time: 8 minutes
Servings: 2 chaffles

Ingredients:
1 egg, beaten
½ cup Monterey Jack cheese, shredded
1 turnip, cooked and mashed
2 tbsp bacon bits, cooked

Instructions:
Heat up the waffle maker.
Add all the ingredients to a small mixing bowl and stir until well combined.
Pour half of the batter into the waffle maker and cook for 4 minutes until golden brown. Repeat with the rest of the batter to make another chaffle.
Serve and enjoy!

Ground Beef and Bell Peppers Chaffle

Prep Time: 5 minutes
Cook Time: 20 minutes
Servings: 2 chaffles

Ingredients for chaffles:
1 egg, beaten
½ cup shredded cheddar cheese
½ tbsp fresh basil, finely chopped
A pinch of salt
Ingredients for beef:
1 tsp olive oil
2 cups ground beef
½ tsp garlic powder
2 bell peppers, sliced
1 scallion, chopped
2 tsp mayonnaise for topping

Instructions for chaffles:
Heat up the waffle maker.
Add egg, shredded cheddar cheese, a pinch of salt and basil to a small mixing bowl and combine well.
Pour half of the batter into the waffle maker and cook for 4 minutes until brown. Repeat with the rest of the batter to make another chaffle.
Instructions for beef:
In a saucepan over medium heat cook the ground beef in olive oil. Season with salt and pepper if needed and add bell peppers and scallion. Stir occasionally and cook until the meat is browned.
Instruction for topping:
Spread the chaffle with keto mayonnaise and garnish with beef and vegetables.
Serve immediately and enjoy!

Shrimps Chaffle with Sauce

Prep Time: 5 minutes
Cook Time: 26 minutes
Servings: 4 chaffles

Ingredients for shrimps:
1 tsp olive oil
1 lb. shrimps, peeled and deveined
A pinch of salt and pepper
1 tsp lemon juice

Ingredients for the chaffles:
2 eggs, beaten
1 cup cheddar cheese, shredded
Ingredients for the topping:
4 tbsp Keto Thousand Island Sauce
6-8 fresh spinach leaves

Instructions for shrimps:
In a small saucepan over medium heat, heat the olive oil and cook the shrimps for approx. 8-10 minutes. Season with salt and pepper and add the lemon juice.
Instructions for the chaffles:
Heat up the waffle maker.
Add all the chaffles ingredients to a small mixing bowl and stir until well combined.
Pour ¼ of the batter into the waffle maker and cook for 4 minutes until golden brown. Repeat with the rest of the batter to make the other chaffles.
Let cool for 3 minutes to let chaffles get crispy.
Spread the chaffle with keto thousand island sauce. Top the chaffle with spinach leaves and shrimps. Serve and enjoy!

Butter and Spinach Leaves Chaffle

Prep Time: 4 minutes
Cook Time: 8 minutes
Servings: 2 chaffles

Ingredients for chaffles:
1 large egg, beaten
½ cup of mozzarella cheese, shredded
2 tbsp almond flour
¼ tsp baking powder
A pinch of salt
Ingredients for topping:
4 fresh spinach leaves
2 tbsp butter, melted
2 tsp parmesan cheese, flakes

Instructions:
Heat up the waffle maker.
Add all the ingredients to a small mixing bowl and combine well.
Pour half of the batter into the waffle maker and cook for 4 minutes until brown. Repeat with the rest of the batter to make another chaffle.
Let cool for 3 minutes to let chaffles get crispy.

Top the chaffle with spinach leaves. Sprinkle with melted butter and parmesan flakes.
Serve immediately and enjoy!

Chives and Salami Chaffle

Prep Time: 5 minutes
Cook Time: 8 minutes
Servings: 2 chaffles

Ingredients:
1 large egg, beaten
½ cup of mozzarella cheese, shredded
2 tbsp almond flour
¼ tsp baking powder
1 tbsp chopped fresh chives
2-4 slices of salami for topping

Instructions:
Heat up the waffle maker.
Add all the ingredients to a small mixing bowl and combine well.
Pour half of the batter into the waffle maker and cook for 4 minutes until brown. Repeat with the rest of the batter to make another chaffle.
Let cool for 3 minutes to let chaffles get crispy.
Top the chaffle with 1-2 slices of salami.
Serve with your favorite keto sauce and enjoy!

Chicken Chaffle & BBQ Sauce

Prep Time: 5 minutes
Cook Time: 8 minutes
Servings: 2 chaffles

Ingredients for chaffles:
½ cup cooked chicken, chopped
1 egg, beaten
½ cup cheddar cheese, shredded
Ingredients for topping:
2 tbsp of Keto BBQ sauce
2-4 slices bacon cooked and crumbled

Instructions:
Heat up the waffle maker.
Mix all the ingredients to a small mixing bowl and combine well.

Pour half of the batter into the waffle maker and cook for 4 minutes until golden brown. Repeat with the rest of the batter to make another chaffle.
Let cool for 3 minutes to let chaffles get crispy.
Garnish the chaffle with BBQ sauce and bacon.
Serve warm and enjoy!

Colby Jack Chaffle

Prep Time: 5 minutes
Cook Time: 8 minutes
Servings: 2 chaffles

Ingredients:
1 egg, beaten
4 slices of Colby Jack cheese

Instructions:
Heat up the waffle maker and use cooking spray to grease it.
Place 1 slice of cheese on the waffle maker. Add the beaten egg.
Cover with another slice of cheese on top.
Cook for 4 minutes until golden brown. Repeat with the rest of the batter to make another chaffle.
Serve and enjoy!

Chives Creamy Chaffle

Prep Time: 4 minutes
Cook Time: 8 minutes
Servings: 2 chaffles

Ingredients for chaffles:
1 large egg, beaten
½ cup of mozzarella cheese, shredded
2 tbsp almond flour
¼ tsp baking powder
1 tbsp chopped fresh chives
Ingredients for topping:
2 tbsp of softened cream cheese
2 tsp of raspberries jam, unsweetened

Instructions:
Heat up the waffle maker.
Add all the chaffles ingredients to a small mixing bowl and combine well.

Pour half of the batter into the waffle maker and cook for 4 minutes until brown. Repeat with the rest of the batter to make another chaffle.

Let cool for 3 minutes to let chaffles get crispy.

Spread the chaffle with cream cheese and with a spoonful of raspberries jam.

Serve and enjoy!

Pickles and Colby Jack Chaffle

Prep Time: 5 minutes
Cook Time: 8 minutes
Servings: 2 chaffles

Ingredients for chaffles:
1 egg, beaten
4 slices of Colby Jack cheese
Ingredients for topping:
4 pickles, thin sliced
2 tbsp of keto Tzatziki sauce

Instructions:
Heat up the waffle maker and use cooking spray to grease it.

Place 1 slice of cheese on the waffle maker. Add the beaten egg.

Cover with another slice of cheese on top.

Cook for 4 minutes until golden brown. Repeat with the rest of the batter to make another chaffle.

Spread the chaffle with Tzatziki sauce and sprinkle with sliced pickles.

Serve and enjoy!

Zucchini Tasty Chaffle

Prep Time: 5 minutes
Cook Time: 8 minutes
Servings: 2 chaffles

Ingredients:
1 large egg, beaten
½ cup grated zucchini
½ cup parmesan cheese, shredded
A pinch of salt

Instructions:
Heat up the waffle maker.

Add all the ingredients to a small mixing bowl and combine well.

Pour half of the batter into the waffle maker and cook for 4 minutes until golden brown. Repeat with the rest of the batter to make another chaffle.

Let cool for 3 minutes to let chaffles get crispy.

Serve and enjoy!

Chives and Hard-Boiled Egg Chaffle

Prep Time: 5 minutes
Cook Time: 8 minutes
Servings: 2 chaffles

Ingredients for chaffles:
1 large egg, beaten
½ cup of mozzarella cheese, shredded
2 tbsp almond flour
¼ tsp baking powder
Ingredients for topping:
1 tbsp chopped fresh chives
2 tbsp keto mayonnaise
1 hard-boiled egg, thin sliced

Instructions:
Heat up the waffle maker.

Add all the chaffles ingredients to a small mixing bowl and combine well.

Pour half of the batter into the waffle maker and cook for 4 minutes until brown. Repeat with the rest of the batter to make another chaffle.

Let cool for 3 minutes to let chaffles get crispy.

Spread the chaffle with mayonnaise, garnish with a few slices of hard-boiled egg and sprinkle with chives.

Serve and enjoy!

Basil Creamy Chaffle

Prep Time: 5 minutes
Cook Time: 8 minutes
Servings: 2 chaffles

Ingredients for chaffles:
1 large egg, beaten
½ cup of mozzarella cheese, shredded
2 tbsp almond flour

¼ tsp baking powder

1 tbsp chopped fresh basil

Ingredients for topping:

2 tbsp of softened cream cheese

2 tsp of raspberries jam, unsweetened

Instructions:

Heat up the waffle maker.

Add all the chaffles ingredients to a small mixing bowl and combine well.

Pour half of the batter into the waffle maker and cook for 4 minutes until brown. Repeat with the rest of the batter to make another chaffle.

Let cool for 3 minutes to let chaffles get crispy.

Spread the chaffle with cream cheese and with a spoonful of raspberries jam.

Serve and enjoy!

Parsley Creamy Chaffle

Prep Time: 5 minutes

Cook Time: 8 minutes

Servings: 2 chaffles

Ingredients for chaffles:

1 large egg, beaten

½ cup of mozzarella cheese, shredded

2 tbsp almond flour

¼ tsp baking powder

1 tbsp chopped fresh parsley

Ingredients for topping:

2 tbsp of softened cream cheese

2 tsp of blueberries jam, unsweetened

Instructions:

Heat up the waffle maker.

Add all the chaffles ingredients to a small mixing bowl and combine well.

Pour half of the batter into the waffle maker and cook for 4 minutes until brown. Repeat with the rest of the batter to make another chaffle.

Let cool for 3 minutes to let chaffles get crispy.

Spread the chaffle with cream cheese and with a spoonful of blueberries jam.

Serve and enjoy!

Bacon Butter Chaffle

Prep Time: 5 minutes

Cook Time: 8 minutes

Servings: 2 chaffles

Ingredients for chaffles:

1 large egg, beaten

½ cup of mozzarella cheese, shredded

2 tbsp almond flour

¼ tsp baking powder

Ingredients for bacon butter:

2 tbsp butter, softened

1 tbsp scallion, browned and chopped

1 tbsp bacon, browned and chopped

1 tsp basil, minced

½ tsp tomato paste

A pinch of salt and black pepper

Instructions for bacon butter:

In a small mixing bowl, combine all the ingredients and stir well. Set aside.

Instructions for chaffles:

Heat up the waffle maker.

Add all the chaffles ingredients to a small mixing bowl and combine well.

Pour half of the batter into the waffle maker and cook for 4 minutes until brown. Repeat with the rest of the batter to make another chaffle.

Let cool for 3 minutes to let chaffles get crispy.

Spread the chaffle with bacon butter.

Serve and enjoy!

Broccoli Tasty Chaffle

Prep Time: 5 minutes

Cook Time: 8 minutes

Servings: 2 chaffles

Ingredients:

1 large egg, beaten

½ cup boiled, chopped broccoli

½ cup parmesan cheese, shredded

A pinch of salt

Instructions:

Heat up the waffle maker.

Add all the ingredients to a small mixing bowl and combine well.
Pour half of the batter into the waffle maker and cook for 4 minutes until golden brown. Repeat with the rest of the batter to make another chaffle.
Let cool for 3 minutes to let chaffles get crispy.
Serve with sour cream and enjoy!

Tasty Onion Chaffle

Prep Time: 5 minutes
Cook Time: 8 minutes
Servings: 2 chaffles

Ingredients:
1 large egg, beaten
½ cup parmesan cheese, finely grated
A pinch of salt and pepper
2 tbsp red onion, browned and chopped

Instructions:
Heat up the waffle maker.
Add all the ingredients to a small mixing bowl and combine well.
Pour half of the batter into the waffle maker and cook for 4 minutes until golden brown. Repeat with the rest of the batter to make another chaffle.
Let cool for 3 minutes to let chaffles get crispy.
Serve with sliced avocado and enjoy!

Parmesan and Scallion Chaffle

Prep Time: 5 minutes
Cook Time: 8 minutes
Servings: 2 chaffles

Ingredients:
1 large egg, beaten
½ cup parmesan cheese, finely grated
A pinch of salt and pepper
2 tbsp scallion browned and chopped

Instructions:
Heat up the waffle maker.
Add all the ingredients to a small mixing bowl and combine well.

Pour half of the batter into the waffle maker and cook for 4 minutes until golden brown. Repeat with the rest of the batter to make another chaffle.
Let cool for 3 minutes to let chaffles get crispy.
Serve and enjoy!

Chives & Bacon Tasty Chaffle

Prep Time: 4 minutes
Cook Time: 8 minutes
Servings: 2 chaffles

Ingredients:
1 large egg, beaten
½ cup of parmesan cheese, shredded
2 tbsp almond flour
¼ tsp baking powder
1 tbsp chopped fresh chives
1 tbsp bacon bits, cooked
A pinch of black pepper

Instructions:
Heat up the waffle maker.
Add all the ingredients to a small mixing bowl and combine well.
Pour half of the batter into the waffle maker and cook for 4 minutes until brown. Repeat with the rest of the batter to make another chaffle.
Let cool for 3 minutes to let chaffles get crispy.
Serve and enjoy!

Baked Pumpkin Bacon Chaffle

Prep Time: 5 minutes
Cook Time: 28 minutes
Servings: 2 chaffles

Ingredients for chaffles:
1 large egg, beaten
½ cup mozzarella cheese, shredded
Ingredients for topping:
2 tbsp of fresh pumpkin, diced
1 tsp rosemary fresh or dried, minced
1 tbsp olive oil, extra virgin
A pinch of salt and pepper
2-4 slices of bacon, cooked

Instructions for baked pumpkin:

Preheat your oven at 350°.

In the baking dish lined with parchment paper, place the diced pumpkin and drizzle with olive oil.

Cook for about 15-20 minutes until tender.

Remove and set aside.

Instructions for chaffles:

Heat up the waffle maker.

Add all the chaffles ingredients to a small mixing bowl and stir until well combined.

Pour half of the batter into the waffle maker and cook for 4 minutes until golden brown. Repeat with the rest of the batter to make another chaffle.

Let cool for 3 minutes to let chaffles get crispy.

Top the chaffle with diced baked pumpkin and 1 or 2 slices of bacon. Sprinkle with rosemary.

Serve with sour cream and enjoy!

Parmesan and Jalapenos Chaffle

Prep Time: 5 minutes
Cook Time: 8 minutes
Servings: 2 chaffles

Ingredients:

1 large egg, beaten
½ cup parmesan cheese, finely grated
A pinch of salt and pepper
3 jalapeno peppers, de-seeded and sliced

Instructions:

Heat up the waffle maker.

Add all the ingredients to a small mixing bowl and combine well.

Pour half of the batter into the waffle maker and cook for 4 minutes until golden brown. Repeat with the rest of the batter to make another chaffle.

Let cool for 3 minutes to let chaffles get crispy.

Serve with keto hot sauce and enjoy!

Tasty Parsley Chaffle

Prep Time: 5 minutes
Cook Time: 8 minutes
Servings: 2 chaffles

Ingredients:

1 large egg, beaten
½ cup parmesan cheese, finely grated
A pinch of salt and black pepper
1 tbsp fresh parsley, finely chopped

Instructions:

Heat up the waffle maker.

Add all the ingredients to a small mixing bowl and combine well.

Pour half of the batter into the waffle maker and cook for 4 minutes until golden brown. Repeat with the rest of the batter to make another chaffle.

Let cool for 3 minutes to let chaffles get crispy.

Serve with a sliced tomato and enjoy!

Veggie Parmesan Chaffle

Prep Time: 5 minutes
Cook Time: 8 minutes
Servings: 2 chaffles

Ingredients:

1 large egg
½ cup zucchini, grated
½ cup parmesan cheese, finely grated
½ tbsp onion, minced and browned
½ tbsp tomato, diced
1 garlic clove, minced
Fresh dill, chopped
A pinch of salt and black pepper

Instructions:

Heat up the waffle maker.

Whisk eggs in bowl and stir in zucchini, onions, garlic, herbs, tomatoes and most of the cheese. You can reserve some of the cheese to make the crispy coating.

Pour half of the batter into the waffle maker and cook for 4 minutes until brown. Repeat with the rest of the batter to make another chaffle.

Let cool for 3 minutes to let chaffles get crispy.

Serve and enjoy!

Broccoli Chaffle & Bacon Bits

Prep Time: 5 minutes

Cook Time: 8 minutes
Servings: 2 chaffles

Ingredients:
1 large egg, beaten
½ cup boiled, chopped broccoli
½ cup parmesan cheese, shredded
2 tbsp bacon bits, browned
A pinch of salt and black pepper

Instructions:
Heat up the waffle maker.
Add all the ingredients to a small mixing bowl and stir until well combined.
Pour half of the batter into the waffle maker and cook for 4 minutes until golden brown. Repeat with the rest of the batter to make another chaffle.
Let cool for 3 minutes to let chaffles get crispy.
Serve warm and enjoy!

Vegetables Chaffle with Brie and Sausage

Prep Time: 5 minutes
Cook Time: 18 minutes
Servings: 2 chaffles

Ingredients for chaffles:
1 egg, beaten
½ tbsp spinach, boiled and chopped
½ cup mozzarella cheese, shredded
1 tsp onion, minced, browned
½ tbsp broccoli, boiled and chopped
1 garlic clove, minced
A pinch of salt and black pepper
Ingredients for topping:
½ cup chicken sausage, browned and chopped
2 slices of Brie cheese

Instructions:
Heat up the waffle maker.
Add all the chaffles ingredients to a small mixing bowl and stir until well combined.
Pour half of the batter into the waffle maker and cook for 4 minutes until brown. Repeat with the rest of the batter to make another chaffle.
Top the chaffle with warm sausage and a slice of brie cheese. Season with black pepper if desired.
Serve immediately and enjoy!

Grilled Radishes Chaffle

Prep Time: 5 minutes
Cook Time: 8 minutes
Servings: 2 chaffles

Ingredients:
1 large egg, beaten
½ cup mozzarella cheese, shredded
½ tsp baking powder
2 tbsp radishes, grilled and thin sliced
A pinch of salt and black pepper

Instructions:
Heat up the waffle maker.
Add all the ingredients to a small mixing bowl and stir until well combined.
Pour half of the batter into the waffle maker and cook for 4 minutes until golden brown. Repeat with the rest of the batter to make another chaffle.
Let cool for 3 minutes to let chaffles get crispy.
Serve and enjoy!

Chaffle Sticks

Prep Time: 5 minutes
Cook Time: 8 minutes
Servings: 2 chaffles

Ingredients:
1 egg, beaten
½ cup shredded cheddar cheese

Instructions:
Heat up the waffle maker.
Add egg and shredded cheese to a small mixing bowl and combine well.
Pour half of the batter into the waffle maker and cook for 4 minutes until golden brown. Repeat with the rest of the batter to make another chaffle.
Let cool for 3 minutes to let chaffles get crispy.
Cut the chaffles in sticks and dip into your favorite keto sauce.
Serve and enjoy!

Fried Radishes Chaffle

Prep Time: 5 minutes
Cook Time: 8 minutes
Servings: 2 chaffles

Ingredients for chaffles:
1 large egg, beaten
½ cup mozzarella cheese, shredded
½ tsp baking powder
A pinch of salt and black pepper
Ingredients for topping:
2 tbsp fresh radishes, thin sliced
1 tbsp olive oil
2 tbsp keto mayonnaise

Instructions:
Heat up the waffle maker.
Add all the chaffles ingredients to a small mixing bowl and stir until well combined.
Pour half of the batter into the waffle maker and cook for 4 minutes until golden brown. Repeat with the rest of the batter to make another chaffle.
In a small saucepan over medium heat, cook the radishes in olive oil until crispy.
Spread the chaffle with mayonnaise and top with fried radishes.
Serve and enjoy!

Ham Chaffle Sticks

Prep Time: 5 minutes
Cook Time: 8 minutes
Servings: 2 chaffles

Ingredients:
1 egg, beaten
½ cup shredded cheddar cheese
2 tbsp ham bits, browned
A pinch of black pepper

Instructions:
Heat up the waffle maker.
Add all the ingredients to a small mixing bowl and combine well.
Pour half of the batter into the waffle maker and cook for 4 minutes until golden brown. Repeat with the rest of the batter to make another chaffle.

Let cool for 3 minutes to let chaffles get crispy.
Cut the chaffles in sticks and dip into keto ketchup.
Serve and enjoy!

Creamy Salmon Chaffle

Prep Time: 5 minutes
Cook Time: 8 minutes
Servings: 2 chaffles

Ingredients for the chaffles:
½ cup mozzarella cheese, shredded
1 large egg, beaten
2 tbsp smoked salmon, chopped
1 tbsp cream cheese, softened
1 tsp fresh parsley, chopped
A pinch of black pepper

Instructions:
Heat up the waffle maker.
Add all the chaffles ingredients to a small mixing bowl and stir until well combined.
Pour half of the batter into the waffle maker and cook for 4 minutes until golden brown. Repeat with the rest of the batter to make another chaffle.
Let cool for 3 minutes to let chaffles get crispy.
Serve and enjoy!

Garlic Chaffle with Smoked Salmon

Prep Time: 4 minutes
Cook Time: 8 minutes
Servings: 2 chaffles

Ingredients:
1 egg, beaten
½ cup shredded mozzarella cheese
¼ tsp garlic powder
2 tbsp smoked salmon, chopped

Instructions:
Heat up the waffle maker.
Add all the ingredients to a small mixing bowl and combine well.
Pour half of the batter into the waffle maker and cook for 4 minutes until golden brown. Repeat with the rest of the batter to make another chaffle.
Serve with sour cream and enjoy!

Ranch Chaffle

Prep Time: 5 minutes
Cook Time: 8 minutes
Servings: 2 chaffles

Ingredients:
1 egg, beaten
½ cup cheddar cheese, shredded
¼ cup chicken cooked, shredded
1 tbsp bacon bits, browned
1 tsp Ranch seasoning

Instructions:
Heat up the waffle maker.
Add all the chaffles ingredients to a small mixing bowl and stir until well combined.
Pour half of the batter into the waffle maker and cook for 4 minutes until golden brown. Repeat with the rest of the batter to make another chaffle.
Serve warm and enjoy!

Chaffle BBQ

Prep Time: 5 minutes
Cook Time: 8 minutes
Servings: 2 chaffles

Ingredients:
1 egg, beaten
½ cup mozzarella cheese, shredded
¼ tsp BBQ seasoning
½ tsp baking powder

Instructions:
Heat up the waffle maker.
Add all the ingredients to a small mixing bowl and stir until well combined.
Pour half of the batter into the waffle maker and cook for 4 minutes. Repeat with the rest of the batter to make another chaffle.
Let cool for 3 minutes to let chaffles get crispy.
Serve and enjoy!

Softened Cabbage Chaffle

Prep Time: 2 minutes
Cook Time: 15 minutes
Servings: 2 chaffles

Ingredients for chaffles:
1 large egg, beaten
½ cup of mozzarella cheese, shredded
2 tbsp almond flour
¼ tsp baking powder
Ingredients for topping:
2 tbsp bacon strips, browned
2 tsp onion, browned and chopped
½ cup fresh cabbage, shredded
½ tsp paprika powder
1 tbsp olive oil
A pinch of salt and black pepper

Instructions for cabbage:
In a small saucepan over medium heat, cook the cabbage in olive oil until it's softened. Season with paprika powder.
Stir in the bacon and onions. Cook 2 minutes to combine flavors.
Instructions for chaffles:
Heat up the waffle maker.
Add all the chaffles ingredients to a small mixing bowl and stir until well combined.
Pour half of the batter into the waffle maker and cook for 4 minutes until golden brown. Repeat with the rest of the batter to make another chaffle.
Let cool for 3 minutes to let chaffles get crispy.
Top the chaffle with cabbage-bacon mixture.
Serve and enjoy!

Mayonnaise and Berries Chaffle

Prep Time: 5 minutes
Cook Time: 16 minutes
Servings: 4 chaffles

Ingredients for chaffles:
2 large eggs, beaten
2 tbsp mayonnaise
2 tbsp almond flour
½ tsp corn syrup substitute
¼ tsp baking powder
Ingredients for topping:
1 tbsp blackberries
1 tbsp strawberries

Instructions:
Heat up the waffle maker.
Add all the chaffles ingredients to a small mixing bowl and stir until well combined.
Pour ¼ of the batter into the waffle maker and cook for 4 minutes until brown. Repeat with the rest of the batter to prepare the other chaffles.
Let cool for 3 minutes to let chaffles get crispy.
Top the chaffles with berries.
Serve and enjoy!

Ranch Seasoning Chaffle

Prep Time: 5 minutes
Cook Time: 8 minutes
Servings: 2 chaffles

Ingredients:
1 large egg, beaten
½ cup of mozzarella cheese, shredded
2 tbsp almond flour
¼ tsp baking powder
¼ tsp Ranch seasoning

Instructions:
Heat up the mini waffle maker.
Add all the ingredients to a small mixing bowl and combine well.
Pour half of the batter into the waffle maker and cook for 4 minutes until brown. Repeat with the rest of the batter to make another chaffle.
Let cool for 3 minutes to let chaffles get crispy.
Serve and enjoy!

Spicy Chaffle

Prep Time: 5 minutes
Cook Time: 8 minutes
Servings: 2 chaffles

Ingredients:
1 large egg, beaten
½ cup of mozzarella cheese, shredded
2 tbsp almond flour
¼ tsp baking powder
1 tbsp hot sauce, unsweetened

Instructions:
Heat up the waffle maker.
Add all the ingredients to a small mixing bowl and combine well.
Pour half of the batter into the waffle maker and cook for 4 minutes until brown. Repeat with the rest of the batter to make another chaffle.
Let cool for 3 minutes to let chaffles get crispy.
Serve and enjoy!

Chaffle with Melt Cheese

Prep Time: 5 minutes
Cook Time: 10 minutes
Servings: 2 chaffles

Ingredients for chaffles:
1 large egg, beaten
½ cup of cheddar cheese, shredded
¼ tsp dried oregano
Ingredients for filling:
1 tbsp butter
¼ cup shredded cheese

Instructions:
Heat up the waffle maker.
Add all the ingredients to a small mixing bowl and stir until well combined.
Pour half of the batter into the waffle maker and cook for 4 minutes until golden brown. Repeat with the rest of the batter to make another chaffle.
Top the chaffle with shredded cheese and cover with another chaffle.
In a small saucepan over low heat melt the butter and cook the chaffle part by part for about 2 minutes or until the filling is melt.
Serve and enjoy!

Asiatic Gourmet Chaffle

Prep Time: 5 minutes
Cook Time: 8 minutes
Servings: 2 chaffles

Ingredients:
1 egg, beaten
½ cup mozzarella cheese, shredded

2 tsp sweetener
1/8 tsp pandan extract
½ tsp psyllium hush powder
2 tsp coconut flour

Instructions:
Heat up the waffle maker.
Add all the ingredients to a small mixing bowl and stir until well combined.
Pour half of the batter into the waffle maker and cook for 4 minutes until golden brown. Repeat with the rest of the batter to make another chaffle.
Let cool for 3 minutes to let chaffles get crispy.
Serve with whipped cream and enjoy!

Lemon Sauce Chicken Chaffle

Prep Time: 5 minutes
Cook Time: 18 minutes
Servings: 2 chaffles

Ingredients for chaffles:
1 large egg, beaten
½ cup cheddar cheese, shredded
Ingredients for chicken:
½ cup of chicken breast, shredded
¼ tsp garlic powder
¼ tsp paprika powder
1 tsp lemon juice
A pinch of salt and black pepper
2 tbsp heavy cream
1 tbsp finely grated Parmesan cheese
½ tsp fresh thyme, minced
½ tsp fresh parsley, minced
1 tbsp unsalted butter
½ cup chicken broth

Instructions for chicken:
In a saucepan over medium heat, cook the chicken breast in the unsalted butter part by part, for approx. 10 minutes. Season with a pinch of salt, black pepper and paprika.
Set aside the meat.
In the same saucepan, add garlic powder, chicken broth, heavy cream, parmesan cheese, lemon juice and thyme. Bring to a boil and simmer until the sauce thickens. Add the chicken and mix well.
Instructions for chaffles:

Heat up the waffle maker.
Add all the chaffles ingredients to a small mixing bowl and stir until well combined.
Pour half of the batter into the waffle maker and cook for 4 minutes until golden brown. Repeat with the rest of the batter to make another chaffle.
Top the chaffle with lemon sauce chicken.
Serve warm and enjoy!

Sliced Beef Chaffle

Prep Time: 5 minutes
Cook Time: 8 minutes
Servings: 2 chaffles

Ingredients for chaffles:
1 large egg, beaten
½ cup mozzarella cheese, shredded
Ingredients for topping:
2-4 slices of sliced beef (seared in butter)
2 tbsp of keto mayonnaise
A pinch of black pepper
Instructions for chaffles:
Heat up the waffle maker.
Add all the chaffles ingredients to a small mixing bowl and stir until well combined.
Pour half of the batter into the waffle maker and cook for 4 minutes until golden brown. Repeat with the rest of the batter to make another chaffle.
Spread the chaffle with keto mayonnaise and top with 1-2 slices of sliced beef.
Season with black pepper according to your taste.
Serve immediately and enjoy!

Lemon Sauce Salmon Chaffle

Prep Time: 5 minutes
Cook Time: 18 minutes
Servings: 2 chaffles

Ingredients for chaffles:
1 large egg, beaten
½ cup cheddar cheese, shredded
Ingredients for lemon sauce:
¼ tsp garlic powder
¼ tsp paprika powder
1 tsp lemon juice

A pinch of salt and black pepper
2 tbsp heavy cream
1 tbsp finely grated Parmesan cheese
½ tsp fresh thyme, minced
½ tsp fresh parsley, minced
½ cup chicken broth

Ingredients for topping:
2 slices of smoked salmon
Lettuce leaves

Instructions for lemon sauce:
In a saucepan over medium heat, add all the sauce ingredients and bring to a boil. Simmer until the sauce thickens.

Instructions for chaffles:
Heat up the waffle maker.
Add all the chaffles ingredients to a small mixing bowl and stir until well combined.
Pour half of the batter into the waffle maker and cook for 4 minutes until golden brown. Repeat with the rest of the batter to make another chaffle.
Top the chaffle with lettuce, lemon sauce and a slice of smoked salmon.
Serve and enjoy!

Bell Peppers Chaffle

Prep Time: 5 minutes
Cook Time: 8 minutes
Servings: 2 chaffles

Ingredients:
1 large egg, beaten
½ cup of mozzarella cheese, shredded
2 tbsp almond flour
¼ tsp baking powder
1 tbsp red bell pepper, minced
1 tbsp yellow bell pepper, minced
1 tsp fresh parsley, minced

Instructions:
Heat up the waffle maker.
Add all the chaffles ingredients to a small mixing bowl and combine well.
Pour half of the batter into the waffle maker and cook for 4 minutes until brown. Repeat with the rest of the batter to make another chaffle.
Let cool for 3 minutes to let chaffles get crispy.

Serve and enjoy!

Fried Fish Chaffle

Prep Time: 5 minutes
Cook Time: 8 minutes
Servings: 2 chaffles

Ingredients for chaffles:
1 large egg, beaten
½ cup of mozzarella cheese, shredded
2 tbsp almond flour
¼ tsp baking powder

Ingredients for topping:
2 tbsp keto mayonnaise
2 fried white fish cutlets
A pinch of salt and black pepper

Instructions:
Heat up the waffle maker.
Add all the chaffles ingredients to a small mixing bowl and combine well.
Pour half of the batter into the waffle maker and cook for 4 minutes until brown. Repeat with the rest of the batter to make another chaffle.
Spread the chaffle with mayonnaise and top it with fried fish cutlet. Season with salt and pepper to taste.
Serve warm and enjoy!

Peppers & Camembert Chaffle

Prep Time: 5 minutes
Cook Time: 8 minutes
Servings: 2 chaffles

Ingredients for chaffles:
1 large egg, beaten
½ cup of cheddar cheese, shredded

Ingredients for topping:
1 tbsp green bell pepper, thinly sliced
1 tbsp yellow bell pepper, thinly sliced
1 tsp fresh parsley, minced
2 slices of Camembert cheese, very thin

Instructions:
Heat up the waffle maker.
Add all the chaffles ingredients in a small mixing bowl and combine well.

Pour half of the batter into the waffle maker and cook for 4 minutes until brown. Repeat with the rest of the batter to make another chaffle.
Spread the chaffle with mayonnaise. Top in with bell peppers and a slice of Camembert. Sprinkle with fresh parsley.
Serve immediately and enjoy!

Gourmet Fried Fish Chaffle

Prep Time: 5 minutes
Cook Time: 8 minutes
Servings: 2 chaffles

Ingredients for chaffles:
1 large egg, beaten
½ cup of mozzarella cheese, shredded
2 tbsp almond flour
¼ tsp baking powder
Ingredients for topping:
2 tbsp keto mayonnaise
2 fried white fish cutlets
1 small avocado, sliced
1 tomato, sliced
A pinch of salt and black pepper

Instructions:
Heat up the waffle maker.
Add all the chaffles ingredients to a small mixing bowl and combine well.
Pour half of the batter into the waffle maker and cook for 4 minutes until brown. Repeat with the rest of the batter to make another chaffle.
Spread the chaffle with mayonnaise. Top it with fried fish cutlet and season with salt and pepper to taste.
Add avocado and tomato slices.
Serve warm and enjoy!

Grilled Prawns Chaffle

Prep Time: 5 minutes
Cook Time: 8 minutes
Servings: 2 chaffles

Ingredients for chaffles:
1 large egg, beaten
½ cup mozzarella cheese, shredded

A pinch of salt
Ingredients for topping:
6-8 grilled prawns
2 tsp fresh parsley, minced
2 tbsp butter, unsalted

Instructions:
Heat up the waffle maker.
Add all the chaffles ingredients to a small mixing bowl and stir until well combined.
Pour half of the batter into the waffle maker and cook for 4 minutes until golden brown. Repeat with the rest of the batter to make another chaffle.
Spread the chaffles with butter and top with grilled prawns. Sprinkle with fresh parsley.
Serve immediately and enjoy!

Cauliflower Chaffle

Prep Time: 5 minutes
Cook Time: 8 minutes
Servings: 2 chaffles

Ingredients for chaffles:
1 egg, beaten
½ cup steamed cauliflower mash
¼ cup parmesan cheese, shredded
½ cup mozzarella cheese, shredded
A pinch of salt and black pepper

Instructions:
Heat up the waffle maker.
Add all the chaffles ingredients except for parmesan cheese to a small mixing bowl and combine well.
Pour half of the batter into the waffle maker, sprinkle with 1-2 tbsp of shredded parmesan cheese and cook for 4 minutes until golden brown. Repeat with the rest of the batter to make another chaffle.
Let cool for 3 minutes to let chaffles get crispy.
Serve and enjoy!

Crispy Chaffle

Prep Time: 5 minutes
Cook Time: 8 minutes
Servings: 2 chaffles

Ingredients for chaffles:
1 large egg, beaten
¼ cup parmesan cheese, shredded
½ cup mozzarella cheese, shredded
A pinch of salt and black pepper

Instructions:
Heat up the waffle maker.
Add all the chaffles ingredients except for parmesan cheese to a small mixing bowl and combine well.
Pour half of the batter into the waffle maker, sprinkle with 1-2 tbsp of shredded parmesan cheese and cook for 4 minutes until golden brown. Repeat with the rest of the batter to make another chaffle.
Let cool for 3 minutes to let chaffles get crispy.
Serve and enjoy!

Paprika Chaffle

Prep Time: 5 minutes
Cook Time: 8 minutes
Servings: 2 chaffles

Ingredients for chaffles:
1 large egg, beaten
½ cup cheddar cheese, shredded
½ tbsp paprika powder

Instructions:
Heat up the waffle maker.
Add all the chaffles ingredients to a small mixing bowl and stir until well combined.
Pour half of the batter into the waffle maker and cook for 4 minutes, until brown. Repeat with the rest of the batter to make another chaffle.
Let cool for 3 minutes to let chaffles get crispy.
Serve with sour cream and enjoy!

Cabbage Chaffle

Prep Time: 5 minutes
Cook Time: 8 minutes
Servings: 2 chaffles

Ingredients for chaffles:
1 large egg, beaten
½ cup of mozzarella cheese, shredded
2 tbsp almond flour

¼ tsp baking powder
1 tbsp cabbage, boiled and thinly chopped
A pinch of salt and black pepper

Instructions for chaffles:
Heat up the waffle maker.
Add all the chaffles ingredients to a small mixing bowl and stir until well combined.
Pour half of the batter into the waffle maker and cook for 4 minutes until golden brown. Repeat with the rest of the batter to make another chaffle.
Let cool for 3 minutes to let chaffles get crispy.
Serve and enjoy!

Artichoke Chaffle

Prep Time: 5 minutes
Cook Time: 8 minutes
Servings: 2 chaffles

Ingredients:
1 large egg, beaten
½ cup cheddar cheese, shredded
½ tsp garlic powder
1/3 cup artichoke hearts marinated, minced
A pinch of salt and pepper

Instructions:
Heat up the waffle maker.
Add all the ingredients to a small mixing bowl and stir until well combined.
Pour half of the batter into the waffle maker and cook for 4 minutes until golden brown. Repeat with the rest of the batter to make another chaffle.
Let cool for 3 minutes to let chaffles get crispy.
Serve and enjoy!

Creamy Boiled Cabbage Chaffle

Prep Time: 5 minutes
Cook Time: 8 minutes
Servings: 2 chaffles

Ingredients for chaffles:
1 large egg, beaten
½ cup of mozzarella cheese, shredded
2 tbsp almond flour
¼ tsp baking powder

1 tbsp cabbage, boiled and thinly chopped
A pinch of salt and black pepper
2 tbsp of cream cheese, softened, for topping

Instructions for chaffles:
Heat up the waffle maker.
Add all the chaffles ingredients to a small mixing bowl and stir until well combined.
Pour half of the batter into the waffle maker and cook for 4 minutes until golden brown. Repeat with the rest of the batter to make another chaffle.
Let cool for 3 minutes to let chaffles get crispy.
Spread the chaffles with cream cheese. Season with salt and black pepper if needed.
Serve and enjoy!

Artichoke and Turkey Chaffle

Prep Time: 5 minutes
Cook Time: 8 minutes
Servings: 2 chaffles

Ingredients:
1 large egg, beaten
½ cup mozzarella cheese, shredded
1 tbsp cream cheese, softened
¼ tsp garlic powder
1/3 cup artichoke hearts marinated, minced
1/3 cup turkey, cooked and shredded
A pinch of salt and pepper

Instructions:
Heat up the waffle maker.
Add all the ingredients to a small mixing bowl and stir until well combined.
Pour half of the batter into the waffle maker and cook for 4 minutes until golden brown. Repeat with the rest of the batter to make another chaffle.
Let cool for 3 minutes to let chaffles get crispy.
Serve with sour cream and enjoy!

Sardine's Pate Chaffle

Prep Time: 5 minutes
Cook Time: 8 minutes
Servings: 2 chaffles

Ingredients for chaffles:
1 large egg, beaten
½ cup shredded mozzarella cheese
Ingredients for Sardine's Pate:
½ tbsp pickled capers
½ can sardines in extra virgin olive oil
1 filet anchovies, canned
1 tbsp butter
½ tbsp keto mayonnaise
A pinch of black pepper

Instructions for pate:
Add all the pate ingredients to a blender and mix until smoothy.
Instructions for chaffles:
Heat up the waffle maker.
Add all the chaffles ingredients to a small mixing bowl and stir until well combined.
Pour half of the batter into the waffle maker and cook for 4 minutes until golden brown. Repeat with the rest of the batter to make another chaffle.
Top the chaffle with sardine's pate. Season with black pepper to taste.
Serve and enjoy!

Artichoke and Chicken Chaffle

Prep Time: 5 minutes
Cook Time: 8 minutes
Servings: 2 chaffles

Ingredients:
1 large egg, beaten
½ cup mozzarella cheese, shredded
1 tbsp cream cheese, softened
¼ tsp garlic powder
1/3 cup artichoke hearts marinated, minced
1/3 cup chicken, cooked and shredded
A pinch of salt and pepper

Instructions:
Heat up the waffle maker.
Add all the ingredients to a small mixing bowl and stir until well combined.
Pour half of the batter into the waffle maker and cook for 4 minutes until golden brown. Repeat with the rest of the batter to make another chaffle.
Let cool for 3 minutes to let chaffles get crispy.

Serve and enjoy!

Sardines Chaffle

Prep Time: 5 minutes
Cook Time: 8 minutes
Servings: 2 chaffles

Ingredients for chaffles:
1 large egg, beaten
½ cup shredded mozzarella cheese
Ingredients for topping:
½ can sardines in extra virgin olive oil
2 tbsp keto mayonnaise
A pinch of black pepper

Instructions for chaffles:
Heat up the waffle maker.
Add all the chaffles ingredients to a small mixing bowl and stir until well combined.
Pour half of the batter into the waffle maker and cook for 4 minutes until golden brown. Repeat with the rest of the batter to make another chaffle.
Spread the chaffle with mayonnaise and top the chaffle with sardines. Season with black pepper to taste.
Serve and enjoy!

Anchovies Filets Chaffle

Prep Time: 5 minutes
Cook Time: 8 minutes
Servings: 2 chaffles

Ingredients for chaffles:
1 large egg, beaten
½ cup shredded mozzarella cheese
Ingredients for topping:
4 filets anchovies, canned
2 tbsp keto mayonnaise
A pinch of black pepper

Instructions for chaffles:
Heat up the waffle maker.
Add all the chaffles ingredients to a small mixing bowl and stir until well combined.

Pour half of the batter into the waffle maker and cook for 4 minutes until golden brown. Repeat with the rest of the batter to make another chaffle.
Spread the chaffle with mayonnaise and top the chaffle with anchovies. Season with black pepper to taste.
Serve and enjoy!

Keto Chaffle Onions and Mushrooms

Prep Time: 5 minutes
Cook Time: 8 minutes
Servings: 2 chaffles

Ingredients:
1 large egg, beaten
½ cup mozzarella cheese, shredded
1 tbsp onion, minced and browned
1 tbsp fresh mushrooms, browned and chopped
1 tsp garlic powder
A pinch of salt and black pepper

Instructions:
Heat up the mini waffle maker.
Add all the ingredients to a small mixing bowl and stir until well combined.
Pour half of the batter into the waffle maker and cook for 4 minutes until brown. Repeat with the rest of the batter to make another chaffle.
Let cool for 3 minutes to let chaffles get crispy.
Serve with sour cream and enjoy!

Chaffle with Basil Cream

Prep Time: 5 minutes
Cook Time: 8 minutes
Servings: 2 chaffles

Ingredients for chaffles:
1 large egg, beaten
½ cup of mozzarella cheese, shredded
2 tbsp almond flour
¼ tsp baking powder
Ingredients for basil cream:
2 tbsp cream cheese, softened
2 tbsp fresh basil, chopped

Instructions for cream:
In a small bowl, whisk cream cheese and basil until smoothy. Set aside.
Instructions for chaffles:
Heat up the mini waffle maker.
Add all the chaffles ingredients to a small mixing bowl and combine well.
Pour half of the batter into the waffle maker and cook for 4 minutes until brown. Repeat with the rest of the batter to make another chaffle.
Let cool for 3 minutes to let chaffles get crispy.
Spread the chaffle with basil cream.
Serve with slices of cucumber and enjoy!

Keto Chaffle with Cucumber Cream

Prep Time: 5 minutes
Cook Time: 8 minutes
Servings: 2 chaffles

Ingredients for chaffles:
1 large egg, beaten
½ cup of mozzarella cheese, shredded
2 tbsp almond flour
¼ tsp baking powder
Ingredients for cucumber cream:
2 tbsp cream cheese, softened
2 tbsp fresh cucumber, chopped

Instructions for cream:
In a small bowl, whisk cream cheese and cucumber until smoothy. Set aside.
Instructions for chaffles:
Heat up the mini waffle maker.
Add all the chaffles ingredients to a small mixing bowl and combine well.
Pour half of the batter into the waffle maker and cook for 4 minutes until brown. Repeat with the rest of the batter to make another chaffle.
Let cool for 3 minutes to let chaffles get crispy.
Spread the chaffle with cucumber cream.
Serve and enjoy!

Scallion Cream Chicken Chaffle

Prep Time: 5 minutes
Cook Time: 8 minutes

Servings: 2 chaffles

Ingredients for chaffles:
1 large egg, beaten
½ cup of mozzarella cheese, shredded
2 tbsp almond flour
¼ tsp baking powder
Ingredients for scallion cream:
2 tbsp cream cheese, softened
2 tbsp scallion, browned and chopped
Ingredients for topping:
½ cup chicken, cooked and shredded
2 tsp sesame seeds
A pinch of black pepper

Instructions for cream:
In a small bowl, whisk cream cheese and scallion until smoothy. Set aside.
Instructions for chaffles:
Heat up the mini waffle maker.
Add all the chaffles ingredients to a small mixing bowl and combine well.
Pour half of the batter into the waffle maker and cook for 4 minutes until brown. Repeat with the rest of the batter to make another chaffle.
Spread the chaffle with scallion cream. Top with chicken and season with pepper to taste. Sprinkle with sesame seeds.
Serve warm and enjoy!

Fontina Cheese & Ham Chaffle

Prep Time: 5 minutes
Cook Time: 8 minutes
Servings: 2 chaffles

Ingredients:
1 large egg, beaten
½ cup of Fontina cheese, shredded
1 tbsp ham, diced
1 tsp fresh basil, minced

Instructions:
Heat up the waffle maker.
Add all the ingredients to a small mixing bowl and combine well.

Pour half of the batter into the waffle maker and cook for 4 minutes until golden brown. Repeat with the rest of the batter to make another chaffle.
Let cool for 3 minutes to let chaffles get crispy.
Serve and enjoy!

Pork Tenderloin Chaffle

Prep Time: 5 minutes
Cook Time: 8 minutes
Servings: 2 chaffles

Ingredients for chaffles:
1 large egg, beaten
½ cup of Fontina cheese, shredded
Ingredients for topping:
2 thin slices of cooked pork tenderloin
2 tsp of poppy seeds
2 tbsp sour cream

Instructions:
Heat up the waffle maker.
Add all the chaffles ingredients to a small mixing bowl and combine well.
Pour half of the batter into the waffle maker and cook for 4 minutes until golden brown. Repeat with the rest of the batter to make another chaffle.
Spread the chaffle with sour cream and top with a slice of pork tenderloin. Sprinkle with poppy seeds.
Serve warm and enjoy!

Ricotta and Spinach Chaffle

Prep Time: 5 minutes
Cook Time: 8 minutes
Servings: 2 chaffles

Ingredients:
1 large egg, beaten
½ cup skim ricotta cheese
1 tbsp almond flour
½ tsp baking powder
2 tbsp spinach, boiled, drained and minced
A pinch of salt
½ tsp unsalted butter

Instructions:
Heat up the waffle maker.

Add all the ingredients to a small mixing bowl and stir until well combined.
Pour half of the batter into the waffle maker and cook for 4 minutes until golden brown. Repeat with the rest of the batter to make another chaffle.
Let cool for 3 minutes to let chaffles get crispy.
Serve and enjoy!

Egg Salad Chaffle

Prep Time: 5 minutes
Cook Time: 8 minutes
Servings: 2 chaffles

Ingredients for chaffles:
1 large egg, beaten
½ cup mozzarella cheese, shredded
Ingredients for egg salad:
1 hard-boiled egg
2 tsp avocado pulp, smashed
2 tsp keto mayonnaise
A pinch of salt and black pepper
Instructions for egg salad:
Combine all the salad ingredients in a bowl and mix well.

Instructions for chaffles:
Heat up the waffle maker.
Add all the chaffles ingredients to a small mixing bowl and stir until well combined.
Pour half of the batter into the waffle maker and cook for 4 minutes until golden brown. Repeat with the rest of the batter to make another chaffle.
Let cool for 3 minutes to let chaffles get crispy.
Spread the chaffle with egg salad.
Serve and enjoy!

Arugula & Pecans Chaffle

Prep Time: 5 minutes
Cook Time: 8 minutes
Servings: 2 chaffles

Ingredients for chaffles:
1 large egg, beaten
½ cup mozzarella cheese, shredded
Ingredients for topping:

2 tsp sour cream
2 tbsp fresh arugula
2 tbsp of chopped pecans

Instructions:
Heat up the waffle maker.
Add all the ingredients to a small mixing bowl and stir until well combined.
Pour half of the batter into the waffle maker and cook for 4 minutes until golden brown. Repeat with the rest of the batter to make another chaffle.
Let cool for 3 minutes to let chaffles get crispy.
Top the chaffle with sour cream and arugula. Sprinkle with chopped pecans.
Serve and enjoy!

Alfalfa Sprouts Chaffle

Prep Time: 5 minutes
Cook Time: 8 minutes
Servings: 2 chaffles

Ingredients for chaffles:
1 large egg, beaten
½ cup mozzarella cheese, shredded
Ingredients for topping:
2 tsp keto mayonnaise
2 slices of turkey breast
2 tbsp alfalfa sprouts

Instructions:
Heat up the waffle maker.
Add all the chaffles ingredients to a small mixing bowl and stir until well combined.
Pour half of the batter into the waffle maker and cook for 4 minutes until golden brown. Repeat with the rest of the batter to make another chaffle.
Let cool for 3 minutes to let chaffles get crispy.
Spread the chaffle with mayonnaise. Top with alfalfa sprouts and turkey breast.
Serve and enjoy!

Italian Chaffle

Prep Time: 5 minutes
Cook Time: 8 minutes
Servings: 2 chaffles

Ingredients for the chaffles:
1 large egg, beaten
½ cup shredded cheddar cheese
Ingredients for the filling:
1 small tomato, sliced
Fresh spinach leaves
1-2 slices of mozzarella cheese
1 tsp keto mayonnaise
1 tsp keto ketchup

Instructions for the chaffles:
Heat up the waffle maker.
Add egg and shredded cheese to a small mixing bowl and combine well.
Pour half of the batter into the waffle maker and cook for 4 minutes until golden brown. Repeat with the rest of the batter to prepare the remaining chaffles.
Let cool for 3 minutes to let chaffles get crispy.
Spread the chaffle with mayonnaise and ketchup.
Top with a slice of tomato, spinach leaves, a slice of mozzarella.
Serve and enjoy!

Arugula Chaffle

Prep Time: 5 minutes
Cook Time: 8 minutes
Servings: 2 chaffles

Ingredients for chaffles:
1 large egg, beaten
½ cup mozzarella cheese, shredded
Ingredients for topping:
2 tsp keto mayonnaise
2 tbsp fresh arugula
2 tsp Parmesan cheese, shredded

Instructions:
Heat up the waffle maker.
Add all the ingredients to a small mixing bowl and stir until well combined.
Pour half of the batter into the waffle maker and cook for 4 minutes until golden brown. Repeat with the rest of the batter to make another chaffle.
Let cool for 3 minutes to let chaffles get crispy.
Spread the chaffle with mayonnaise. Top with arugula. Sprinkle with Parmesan cheese.

Serve and enjoy!

Caprese Chaffle

Prep Time: 5 minutes
Cook Time: 8 minutes
Servings: 2 chaffles

Ingredients for the chaffles:
1 large egg, beaten
½ cup shredded cheddar cheese
Ingredients for the topping:
1-2 slices of tomato
Fresh basil leaves
1-2 slices of mozzarella cheese

Instructions for the chaffles:
Heat up the waffle maker.
Add egg and shredded cheese to a small mixing bowl and combine well.
Pour half of the batter into the waffle maker and cook for 4 minutes until golden brown. Repeat with the rest of the batter to prepare the remaining chaffles.
Let cool for 3 minutes to let chaffles get crispy.
Top the chaffle with a slice of tomato, basil leaves and a slice of mozzarella.
Serve and enjoy!

Chaffle with Roasted Pepper Sauce

Prep Time: 5 minutes
Cook Time: 8 minutes
Servings: 2 chaffles

Ingredients:
1 large egg, beaten
½ cup mozzarella cheese, shredded
Ingredients for roasted pepper sauce:
2 tbsp roasted green peppers
2 tbsp mayonnaise
¼ tsp garlic powder
1 tbsp olive oil
A pinch of salt and black pepper

Instructions for sauce:
Mix in a blender all the sauce ingredients and set aside.

Instructions for chaffles:
Heat up the waffle maker.
Add all the chaffles ingredients to a small mixing bowl and stir until well combined.
Pour half of the batter into the waffle maker and cook for 4 minutes until golden brown. Repeat with the rest of the batter to make another chaffle.
Let cool for 3 minutes to let chaffles get crispy.
Spread the chaffle with the pepper cream.
Serve and enjoy!

Coriander and Capers Chaffle

Prep Time: 5 minutes
Cook Time: 8 minutes
Servings: 2 chaffles

Ingredients:
1 egg, beaten
¼ cup shredded mozzarella cheese
1 tsp coconut flour
¼ tsp baking powder
¼ tsp garlic powder
½ tsp fresh coriander, minced
1 tsp capers, chopped

Instructions:
Heat up the waffle maker.
Add all the ingredients to a small mixing bowl and combine well.
Pour half of the batter into the waffle maker and cook for 4 minutes until golden brown. Repeat with the rest of the batter to make another chaffle.
Let cool for 3 minutes to let chaffles get crispy.
Serve and enjoy!

Quick Coriander Chaffle

Prep Time: 5 minutes
Cook Time: 8 minutes
Servings: 2 chaffles

Ingredients for chaffles:
1 egg, beaten
½ cup mozzarella cheese
1 tsp coconut flour
¼ tsp baking powder

½ tsp fresh coriander, minced
Ingredients for topping:
2 tbsp sour cream
2 tbsp raspberries

Instructions:
Heat up the waffle maker.
Add all the chaffles ingredients to a small mixing bowl and combine well.
Pour half of the batter into the waffle maker and cook for 4 minutes until golden brown. Repeat with the rest of the batter to make another chaffle.
Let cool for 3 minutes to let chaffles get crispy.
Spread the chaffle with sour cream and top with raspberries.
Serve and enjoy!

Chaffle with Chives Cream

Prep Time: 5 minutes
Cook Time: 8 minutes
Servings: 2 chaffles

Ingredients for chaffles:
1 large egg, beaten
½ cup of mozzarella cheese, shredded
2 tbsp almond flour
¼ tsp baking powder
Ingredients for chives cream:
2 tbsp cream cheese, softened
1 tbsp fresh chives, chopped

Instructions for cream:
In a small bowl, whisk cream cheese and chives until smoothy. Set aside.
Instructions for chaffles:
Heat up the mini waffle maker.
Add all the chaffles ingredients to a small mixing bowl and combine well.
Pour half of the batter into the waffle maker and cook for 4 minutes until brown. Repeat with the rest of the batter to make another chaffle.
Let cool for 3 minutes to let chaffles get crispy.
Spread the chaffle with chives cream.
Serve with everything bagel seasoning and enjoy!

Capers Chaffle

Prep Time: 5 minutes
Cook Time: 8 minutes
Servings: 2 chaffles

Ingredients for chaffles:
1 egg, beaten
½ cup mozzarella cheese
1 tsp coconut flour
¼ tsp baking powder
1 tbsp capers, minced

Instructions:
Heat up the waffle maker.
Add all the chaffles ingredients to a small mixing bowl and combine well.
Pour half of the batter into the waffle maker and cook for 4 minutes until golden brown. Repeat with the rest of the batter to make another chaffle.
Let cool for 3 minutes to let chaffles get crispy.
Serve and enjoy!

Provolone and Genoa Salami Chaffle

Prep Time: 5 minutes
Cook Time: 8 minutes
Servings: 2 chaffles

Ingredients for chaffles:
1 large egg, beaten
½ cup of Provolone cheese, shredded
Ingredients for topping:
2 slices of Genoa Salami
1 tsp fresh parsley, minced
2 tsp pickled cucumber, sliced

Instructions:
Heat up the waffle maker.
Add all the ingredients to a small mixing bowl and combine well.
Pour half of the batter into the waffle maker and cook for 4 minutes until golden brown. Repeat with the rest of the batter to make another chaffle.
Let cool for 3 minutes to let chaffles get crispy.
Top the chaffle with a slice of Genoa Salami and pickled cucumbers. Sprinkle with fresh parsley.
Serve and enjoy!

Swiss Cheese & Ham Chaffle

Prep Time: 5 minutes
Cook Time: 8 minutes
Servings: 2 chaffles

Ingredients:
1 large egg, beaten
½ cup of Swiss cheese, shredded
1 tbsp ham, diced
1 tsp fresh basil, minced

Instructions:
Heat up the waffle maker.
Add all the ingredients to a small mixing bowl and combine well.
Pour half of the batter into the waffle maker and cook for 4 minutes until golden brown. Repeat with the rest of the batter to make another chaffle.
Let cool for 3 minutes to let chaffles get crispy.
Serve with your favorite keto dressing and enjoy!

Deli Ham and Mascarpone Chaffle

Prep Time: 5 minutes
Cook Time: 8 minutes
Servings: 2 chaffles

Ingredients for chaffles:
1 large egg, beaten
½ cup of mozzarella cheese, shredded
Ingredients for topping:
2 slices of Deli Ham
2 tbsp Mascarpone cheese, softened

Instructions:
Heat up the waffle maker.
Add all the chaffles ingredients to a small mixing bowl and combine well.
Pour half of the batter into the waffle maker and cook for 4 minutes until golden brown. Repeat with the rest of the batter to make another chaffle.
Let cool for 3 minutes to let chaffles get crispy.
Spread the chaffle with mascarpone and top with a slice of deli ham.
Serve and enjoy!

Baked Pumpkin Chaffle

Prep Time: 5 minutes
Cook Time: 28 minutes
Servings: 2 chaffles

Ingredients for chaffles:
1 large egg, beaten
½ cup mozzarella cheese, shredded
Ingredients for topping:
2 tbsp of fresh pumpkin, diced
1 tsp rosemary fresh or dried, minced
1 tbsp olive oil, extra virgin
A pinch of salt and pepper

Instructions for baked pumpkin:
Preheat your oven at 350°.
In the baking dish lined with parchment paper, place the diced pumpkin and drizzle with olive oil.
Cook for about 15-20 minutes until tender.
Remove and set aside.
Instructions for chaffles:
Heat up the waffle maker.
Add all the chaffles ingredients to a small mixing bowl and stir until well combined.
Pour half of the batter into the waffle maker and cook for 4 minutes until golden brown. Repeat with the rest of the batter to make another chaffle.
Let cool for 3 minutes to let chaffles get crispy.
Top the chaffle with diced baked pumpkin. Sprinkle with rosemary.
Serve with sour cream and enjoy!

Ragù Chaffle

Prep Time: 5 minutes
Cook Time: 20-25 minutes
Servings: 2 chaffles

Ingredients for chaffles:
1 egg, beaten
½ cup cheddar cheese, shredded
A pinch of salt
Ingredients for beef:
1 tsp olive oil, extra virgin
2 cups ground beef
½ tsp basil, minced

1 scallion, chopped
2 tbsp tomato sauce
A pinch of salt and pepper

Instructions for beef:
In a saucepan over medium heat brown the scallion in olive oil. Add the ground beef, season with salt and pepper and cook for 5-6 minutes. Add basil and tomato sauce. Stir occasionally and cook until the meat is browned.

Instructions for chaffles:
Heat up the waffle maker.
Add egg, shredded cheddar cheese, a pinch of salt in a small mixing bowl and combine well.
Pour half of the batter into the waffle maker and cook for 4 minutes until brown. Repeat with the rest of the batter to make another chaffle.
Top the chaffle with beef.
Serve immediately and enjoy!

Ground Pork Chaffle

Prep Time: 5 minutes
Cook Time: 20 minutes
Servings: 2 chaffles

Ingredients for chaffles:
1 egg, beaten
½ cup shredded mozzarella cheese
½ tbsp fresh basil, finely chopped
A pinch of salt

Ingredients for pork:
1 tsp olive oil, extra virgin
2 cups ground pork
1 small red onion, chopped
1 tsp fresh parsley, minced
A pinch of salt and black pepper

Instructions for pork:
In a saucepan over low heat brown the onion in olive oil. Season with salt and pepper if needed. Add the ground pork and the fresh parsley. Stir occasionally and cook until the meat is browned.

Instructions for chaffles:
Heat up the waffle maker.
Add egg, shredded cheddar cheese, a pinch of salt and basil in a small mixing bowl and combine well.

Pour half of the batter into the waffle maker and cook for 4 minutes until brown. Repeat with the rest of the batter to make another chaffle.
Garnish the chaffle with ground pork.
Serve immediately and enjoy!

Turkey Creamy Chaffle

Prep Time: 5 minutes
Cook Time: 8 minutes
Servings: 2 chaffles

Ingredients for topping:
1 cup turkey breast, shredded
¼ all-purpose cream
A pinch of salt and black pepper

Ingredients for chaffles:
1 egg, beaten
½ cup shredded cheddar cheese

Instructions for chicken:
In a small saucepan over medium heat, add the shredded turkey fillet and the cream.
Taste with a pinch of salt and pepper. Set aside.

Instructions for chaffles:
Heat up the mini waffle maker.
Mix all the ingredients to a small mixing bowl and combine well.
Pour half of the batter into the waffle maker and cook for 4 minutes. Repeat with the rest of the batter to make another chaffle.
Let cool for 3 minutes to let chaffles get crispy.
Top each chaffle with the turkey mixture.
Serve and enjoy!

Grated Cauliflower Chaffle

Prep Time: 5 minutes
Cook Time: 8 minutes
Servings: 2 chaffles

Ingredients for chaffles:
1 egg, beaten
2 tbsp cauliflower, grated
¼ cup parmesan cheese, shredded
½ cup mozzarella cheese, shredded
A pinch of salt and black pepper

Instructions:
Heat up the waffle maker.
Add all the chaffles ingredients except for parmesan cheese to a small mixing bowl and combine well.
Pour half of the batter into the waffle maker, sprinkle with 1-2 tbsp of shredded parmesan cheese and cook for 4 minutes until golden brown. Repeat with the rest of the batter to make another chaffle.
Let cool for 3 minutes to let chaffles get crispy.
Serve and enjoy!

Tuna Salad Chaffle

Prep Time: 5 minutes
Cook Time: 8 minutes
Servings: 2 chaffles

Ingredients for chaffles:
1 large egg, beaten
½ cup mozzarella cheese, shredded
Ingredients for tuna salad:
1 can tuna, drained
1 tbsp keto mayonnaise
2 tbsp cream cheese, softened
1 tsp capers
½ tsp paprika powder
A pinch of salt and black pepper

Instructions for tuna salad:
Combine all the salad ingredients in a bowl and mix well.
Instructions for chaffles:
Heat up the waffle maker.
Add all the chaffles ingredients to a small mixing bowl and stir until well combined.
Pour half of the batter into the waffle maker and cook for 4 minutes until golden brown. Repeat with the rest of the batter to make another chaffle.
Let cool for 3 minutes to let chaffles get crispy.
Spread the chaffle with tuna salad.
Serve and enjoy!

Garlic Turkey Chaffle

Prep Time: 5 minutes
Cook Time: 8 minutes
Servings: 2 chaffles

Ingredients for chaffles:
1 egg, beaten
½ cup shredded mozzarella cheese
¼ tsp garlic powder
Ingredients for topping:
½ cup turkey breast fillet, shredded
¼ all-purpose cream
A pinch of salt and pepper

Instructions for turkey:
In a small saucepan over medium heat, add the shredded turkey fillet and the cream.
Taste with a pinch of salt and pepper. Set aside.
Instructions for chaffles:
Heat up the mini waffle maker.
Mix all the ingredients to a small mixing bowl and combine well.
Pour half of the batter into the waffle maker and cook for 4 minutes. Repeat with the rest of the batter to make another chaffle.
Let cool for 3 minutes to let chaffles get crispy.
Top each chaffle with the turkey mixture.
Serve and enjoy!

Dill Creamy Butter Chaffle

Prep Time: 5 minutes
Cook Time: 8 minutes
Servings: 2 chaffles

Ingredients for chaffles:
1 large egg, beaten
½ cup mozzarella cheese, shredded
Ingredients for dill creamy butter:
½ tbsp cream cheese, softened
1 tbsp butter, softened
1 tbsp fresh dill, minced
1 tsp lemon juice
A pinch of salt and pepper

Instructions for dill creamy butter:
Mix all the ingredients in a blender and whisk until creamy.
Instructions:
Heat up the waffle maker.
Add all the chaffles ingredients to a small mixing bowl and stir until well combined.

Pour half of the batter into the waffle maker and cook for 4 minutes until golden brown. Repeat with the rest of the batter to make another chaffle. Let cool for 3 minutes to let chaffles get crispy. Spread the chaffle with dill creamy butter. Serve and enjoy!

Shrimps Chaffle & Dill Creamy Butter

Prep Time: 5 minutes
Cook Time: 15 minutes
Servings: 2 chaffles

Ingredients for shrimps:
1 tsp olive oil
2 tbsp shrimps, peeled and deveined
1 tsp of lemon juice
½ tsp paprika powder
A pinch of salt and black pepper
Ingredients for the chaffles:
1 large egg, beaten
½ cup mozzarella cheese, shredded
Ingredients for dill creamy butter:
½ tbsp cream cheese, softened
1 tbsp butter, softened
1 tbsp fresh dill, minced
1 tsp lemon juice
A pinch of salt and pepper

Instructions for dill creamy butter:
Mix all the ingredients in a blender and whisk until creamy.
Instructions for shrimps:
In a small saucepan over medium heat, heat the olive oil and cook the shrimps for approx. 3-4 minutes. Season the shrimps with paprika, lemon juice, salt and pepper.
Instructions for chaffles:
Heat up the waffle maker.
Add all the chaffles ingredients to a small mixing bowl and stir until well combined.
Pour half of the batter into the waffle maker and cook for 4 minutes until golden brown. Repeat with the rest of the batter to make another chaffle. Let cool for 3 minutes to let chaffles get crispy. Spread the chaffle with dill creamy butter and top with shrimps.

Serve and enjoy!

Rose Pepper Chaffle

Prep Time: 5 minutes
Cook Time: 8 minutes
Servings: 2 chaffles

Ingredients for chaffles:
1 large egg, beaten
½ cup of mozzarella cheese, shredded
2 tbsp almond flour
¼ tsp baking powder
Ingredients for Rose pepper butter:
2 tbsp butter, softened
2 tbsp Parmesan cheese, shredded
1 tsp rose pepper, chopped
¼ tsp lemon juice
A pinch of salt and black pepper

Instructions for Rose Pepper butter:
In a small mixing bowl, combine all the ingredients and stir well. Set aside.
Instructions for chaffles:
Heat up the waffle maker.
Add all the chaffles ingredients to a small mixing bowl and combine well.
Pour half of the batter into the waffle maker and cook for 4 minutes until brown. Repeat with the rest of the batter to make another chaffle. Let cool for 3 minutes to let chaffles get crispy. Spread the chaffle with Rose pepper butter. Serve and enjoy!

Chaffle with Spinach Cream

Prep Time: 5 minutes
Cook Time: 8 minutes
Servings: 2 chaffles

Ingredients for chaffles:
1 large egg, beaten
½ cup of mozzarella cheese, shredded
2 tbsp almond flour
¼ tsp baking powder
Ingredients for Spinach cream:
1 tbsp fresh spinach, boiled, drained and chopped

2 tbsp mayonnaise
1 tsp olive oil, extra virgin
1 tsp fresh parsley, chopped
½ tsp lemon juice
1 tsp sour cream
¼ tsp onion powder
A pinch of salt and black pepper

Instructions for spinach cream:
In a small mixing bowl, combine all the ingredients and stir well. Set aside.

Instructions for chaffles:
Heat up the waffle maker.
Add all the chaffles ingredients to a small mixing bowl and combine well.
Pour half of the batter into the waffle maker and cook for 4 minutes until brown. Repeat with the rest of the batter to make another chaffle.
Let cool for 3 minutes to let chaffles get crispy.
Spread the chaffle with spinach cream.
Serve and enjoy!

Curry Bacon Chaffle

Prep Time: 5 minutes
Cook Time: 8 minutes
Servings: 2 chaffles

Ingredients:
1 egg, beaten
½ cup shredded mozzarella cheese
¼ tsp curry powder
½ tbsp fresh basil, finely chopped
1 tbsp bacon bits, browned
A pinch of salt and pepper

Instructions:
Heat up the waffle maker.
Add egg, shredded mozzarella cheese, curry powder and basil to a small mixing bowl and combine well.
Pour half of the batter into the waffle maker and cook for 4 minutes until brown. Repeat with the rest of the batter to make another chaffle. Season with salt and pepper.
Serve and enjoy!

Chicken Salad Chaffle

Prep Time: 5 minutes
Cook Time: 8 minutes
Servings: 2 chaffles

Ingredients for chaffles:
1 large egg, beaten
½ cup shredded cheddar cheese

Ingredients for chicken salad:
½ cup chicken, cooked and shredded
1 tbsp fresh celery, chopped
1 tsp scallion, browned and minced
2 tbsp avocado pulp, smashed
1 tsp fresh basil, minced
2 tbsp keto mayonnaise
1 tsp keto mustard
1 tsp lemon juice
A pinch of salt and pepper

Instructions for chicken salad:
Combine all the ingredients in a mixing bowl and stir well. Set aside.

Instructions for chaffles:
Heat up the waffle maker.
Add egg and shredded cheese to a small mixing bowl and combine well.
Pour half of the batter into the waffle maker and cook for 4 minutes until golden brown. Repeat with the rest of the batter to make another chaffle.
Let cool for 3 minutes to let chaffles get crispy.
Garnish the chaffle with chicken salad.
Serve and enjoy!

Cabbage and Corned Beef Chaffle

Prep Time: 5 minutes
Cook Time: 8 minutes
Servings: 2 chaffles

Ingredients for chaffles:
1 large egg, beaten
½ cup of cheddar cheese, shredded
1 tbsp almond flour
¼ tsp baking powder

Ingredients for topping:
½ cup fresh cabbage, shredded

2 slices of corned beef
2 tbsp keto mustard
A pinch of salt and black pepper

Instructions:
Heat up the waffle maker.
Add all the chaffles ingredients to a small mixing bowl and stir until well combined.
Pour half of the batter into the waffle maker and cook for 4 minutes until golden brown. Repeat with the rest of the batter to make another chaffle.
Let cool for 3 minutes to let chaffles get crispy.
Spread the chaffle with mustard and top it with cabbage and corned beef. Season with salt and pepper.
Serve and enjoy!

Sauerkraut Chaffle

Prep Time: 5 minutes
Cook Time: 8 minutes
Servings: 2 chaffles

Ingredients for chaffles:
1 large egg, beaten
½ cup of cheddar cheese, shredded
1 tbsp almond flour
¼ tsp baking powder
Ingredients for topping:
2 tbsp sauerkraut
2 tbsp keto mustard
A pinch of salt and black pepper

Instructions:
Heat up the waffle maker.
Add all the chaffles ingredients to a small mixing bowl and stir until well combined.
Pour half of the batter into the waffle maker and cook for 4 minutes until golden brown. Repeat with the rest of the batter to make another chaffle.
Let cool for 3 minutes to let chaffles get crispy.
Spread the chaffle with mustard and top it with sauerkraut. Season with salt and pepper.
Serve and enjoy!

Onion and Corned Beef Chaffle

Prep Time: 5 minutes
Cook Time: 8 minutes
Servings: 2 chaffles

Ingredients for chaffles:
1 large egg, beaten
½ cup of cheddar cheese, shredded
1 tbsp almond flour
¼ tsp baking powder
Ingredients for topping:
2 slices of corned beef
2 tbsp keto ketchup
1 tbsp red onion, browned and chopped
A pinch of salt and black pepper

Instructions:
Heat up the waffle maker.
Add all the chaffles ingredients to a small mixing bowl and stir until well combined.
Pour half of the batter into the waffle maker and cook for 4 minutes until golden brown. Repeat with the rest of the batter to make another chaffle.
Let cool for 3 minutes to let chaffles get crispy.
Spread the chaffle with ketchup. Top it with corned beef and onions. Season with salt and pepper.
Serve and enjoy!

Bacon and Sauerkraut Chaffle

Prep Time: 5 minutes
Cook Time: 8 minutes
Servings: 2 chaffles

Ingredients for chaffles:
1 large egg, beaten
½ cup of swiss cheese, shredded
1 tbsp almond flour
¼ tsp baking powder
Ingredients for topping:
2 tbsp sauerkraut
2 tbsp keto mayonnaise
2 slices of bacon, browned
A pinch of salt and black pepper

Instructions:
Heat up the waffle maker.

Add all the chaffles ingredients to a small mixing bowl and stir until well combined.

Pour half of the batter into the waffle maker and cook for 4 minutes until golden brown. Repeat with the rest of the batter to make another chaffle.

Let cool for 3 minutes to let chaffles get crispy.

Spread the chaffle with mayonnaise and top it with sauerkraut and bacon. Season with salt and pepper.

Serve and enjoy!

Savory Asparagus Chaffle

Prep Time: 4 minutes
Cook Time: 8 minutes
Servings: 2 chaffles

Ingredients for chaffles:
1 large egg, beaten
½ cup of mozzarella cheese, shredded
2 tbsp almond flour
¼ tsp baking powder

Ingredients for topping:
4 asparagus, boiled
2 slices of bacon, browned
2 tbsp sour cream

Instructions:
Heat up the waffle maker.
Add all the ingredients to a small mixing bowl and combine well.
Pour half of the batter into the waffle maker and cook for 4 minutes until brown. Repeat with the rest of the batter to make another chaffle.
Garnish the chaffle with bacon and asparagus.
Serve with a spoonful of sour cream and enjoy!

Cheese Chaffle

Prep Time: 5 minutes
Cook Time: 5 minutes
Servings: 2 chaffles

Ingredients:
1 egg
½ cup Monterey Jack Cheese
1 tbsp almond flour
2 tbsp butter

Instructions:
Heat up the waffle maker.
Mix the egg, almond flour and Monterey Jack Cheese in a small mixing bowl.
Pour half of the batter into the waffle maker and cook for 4-5 minutes. Then cook the rest of the batter to make another chaffle.
In a small pan melt 2 tablespoons of butter. Add the chaffles and cook on each side for 2-3 minutes until crispy. Set aside for 2 minutes.
Serve and enjoy!

Bacon and Jalapenos Chaffle

Prep Time: 4 minutes
Cook Time: 8 minutes
Servings: 2 chaffles

Ingredients:
2 tbsp cream cheese
1 egg, beaten
½ cup cheddar cheese
2 tbsp bacon bits
½ tbsp jalapenos
¼ tsp baking powder

Instructions:
Heat up the waffle maker.
In a pan cook bacon bits until brown and crispy.
Mix egg and vanilla extract in a small mixing bowl.
Add baking powder, jalapenos and bacon bites and mix well.
Add the cheese and stir until well combined.
Pour half of the batter into the waffle maker and cook for 4 minutes until golden brown. Repeat with the rest of the batter to make another chaffle.
Serve and enjoy!

Chili Taco Chaffle Shell

Prep Time: 4 minutes
Cook Time: 8 minutes
Servings: 2 chaffles

Ingredients:
1 egg white
¼ cup shredded Monterey jack cheese

¼ cup shredded cheddar cheese
1 tsp water
1 tsp coconut flour
¼ tsp baking powder
¼ tsp chili powder

Instructions:
Heat up the mini waffle maker.
Add all the ingredients to a small mixing bowl and stir until well combined.
Add half of batter to the waffle maker and cook chaffle for approx. 4 minutes until brown.
Remove the chaffle from the waffle maker and drape over the side of a bowl.
Continue making chaffles until you are out of batter.
Fill your taco shells with your favorite toppings.
Serve and enjoy!

Bacon & Egg Chaffle

Prep Time: 5 minutes
Cook Time: 8 minutes
Servings: 2 chaffles

Ingredients:
1 egg
½ cup shredded cheddar cheese
Ingredients for topping:
2 slices of bacon, cooked
1 small boiled egg, sliced

Instructions:
Heat up the waffle maker.
Add egg and shredded cheese to a small mixing bowl and combine well.
Pour half of the batter into the waffle maker and cook for 4 minutes until golden brown. Repeat with the rest of the batter to make another chaffle.
Top the chaffle with a slice of bacon and a slice of boiled egg.
Serve with sour cream and enjoy!

Ham & Zucchini Chaffle

Prep Time: 10 minutes
Cook Time: 8 minutes
Servings: 2 chaffles

Ingredients:
1 egg, beaten
1 cup grated zucchini
½ cup parmesan cheese, shredded
¼ cup cheddar cheese, shredded
1 tbsp ham, diced
A pinch of salt and pepper

Instructions:
Heat up the waffle maker.
Add all the ingredients except for parmesan cheese to a small mixing bowl and combine well.
Pour half of the batter into the waffle maker, sprinkle with 1-2 tbsp of shredded parmesan cheese and cook for 4 minutes. Repeat with the rest of the batter to make another chaffle.
Let cool for 3 minutes to let chaffles get crispy.
Serve and enjoy!

Spinach & Mushroom Chaffle

Prep Time: 10 minutes
Cook Time: 8 minutes
Servings: 2 chaffles

Ingredients:
1 egg, beaten
½ cup spinach, boiled and chopped
½ cup white mushrooms, boiled and chopped
¼ cup parmesan cheese, shredded
½ cup mozzarella cheese, shredded
A pinch of salt and pepper

Instructions:
Heat up the waffle maker.
Add all the ingredients except for parmesan cheese to a small mixing bowl and combine well.
Pour half of the batter into the waffle maker, sprinkle with 1-2 tbsp of shredded parmesan cheese and cook for 4 minutes. Repeat with the rest of the batter to make another chaffle.
Serve immediately and enjoy!

Sausage Crispy Chaffle

Prep Time: 5 minutes
Cook Time: 8 minutes

Servings: 2 chaffles

Ingredients for the chaffles:
½ tsp baking powder
¼ egg white
½ cup cheddar cheese, grated
2 tsp pumpkin spice

Ingredients for the filling:
1 egg
2 chicken sausages
2 slices bacon
A pinch of salt and pepper
1 tsp olive oil

Instructions for the topping:
In a large pan over medium heat fry the egg in the olive oil and remove once cooked.
In the same pot, fry bacon and sausage until cooked. Set aside.

Instructions for chaffles:
Heat up the mini waffle maker.
Add all the ingredients for the chaffles to a small mixing bowl and combine well.
Pour half of the batter into the waffle maker and cook for 4 minutes. Repeat with the rest of the batter to make another chaffle.
Serve the chaffle with the fried egg, sausage and bacon. Enjoy!

Feta, Tomato and Olives Chaffle

Prep Time: 5 minutes
Cook Time: 5 minutes
Servings: 1 chaffle

Ingredients for chaffle:
1 white egg
¼ cup mozzarella cheese, shredded
2 tbsp almond flour
1 tsp Cajun seasoning

Ingredients for topping:
1 thin slice Feta cheese
1 tomato, sliced
1 tbsp black olives, pitted and chopped
1 tsp dried oregano

Instructions:
Heat up the waffle maker.

Add all the ingredients for the chaffle to a small mixing bowl and stir until well combined.
Pour the batter into the waffle maker and cook for 4 minutes until golden brown.
Let cool for 3 minutes to let chaffle get crispy.
Top the chaffle with a slice of feta cheese, a slice of tomato and sprinkle with chopped olives.
Season with dried oregano.
Serve and enjoy!

Chaffle Burger

Prep Time: 10 minutes
Cook Time: 25 minutes
Servings: 2 chaffles

Ingredients for burger:
6 oz. ground beef burger
A pinch of salt and pepper

Ingredients for chaffles:
½ cup mozzarella cheese, grated
1 egg
A pinch of salt and pepper
Garlic powder to taste
Oregano to taste

Ingredients for 1 burger sauce:
½ egg yolks
1 tsp of linseed oil
1 tsp olive oil
1 tbsp cream cheese
½ tsp sugar-free mustard
½ tsp lemon juice
A pinch of salt and pepper
1 tbsp red onion, finely chopped

Ingredients for filling:
2 tbsp low-carb ketchup
2 slices of tomatoes, diced
2 slices of onion, diced
4 slices of cucumber, diced
1 large sheet of lettuce

Instructions for burger sauce:
Put the egg yolk and all the other ingredients in a tall container and puree with the blender until a firm emulsion has formed. Season with salt, pepper, and lemon juice.

Instructions for burger:

In a saucepan over medium heat add the ground beef burger and cook it for about 10 minutes.

Once cooked, remove from heat, and add salt and pepper to taste.

Instructions for chaffles:

Heat up the waffle maker.

Add all the chaffles ingredients to a small mixing bowl and stir until well combined.

Pour half of the batter into the waffle maker and cook for 4 minutes. Repeat with the rest of the batter to make another chaffle.

Let cool for 3 minutes to let chaffles get crispy.

Top chaffle with burger, sauce, and all other filling ingredients.

Serve immediately and enjoy!

Creamy Veggie Chaffle

Prep Time: 5 minutes
Cook Time: 8 minutes
Servings: 2 chaffles

Ingredients:

1 egg
½ cup zucchini, grated
½ cup mozzarella cheese, shredded
½ tbsp onion, minced
½ tbsp tomato, diced
1 garlic clove, minced
Fresh dill, chopped
A pinch of salt
2 tbsp softened cream cheese for topping

Instructions:

Heat up the waffle maker.

Whisk eggs in bowl and stir in zucchini, onions, garlic, herbs, tomatoes and most of the cheese. You can reserve some of the cheese to make the crispy coating.

Pour half of the batter into the waffle maker and cook for 4 minutes until brown. Repeat with the rest of the batter to make another chaffle.

Let cool for 3 minutes to let chaffles get crispy.

Spread the chaffle with softened cream cheese.

Serve and enjoy!

Tasty Scallion Chaffle

Prep Time: 5 minutes
Cook Time: 8 minutes
Servings: 2 chaffles

Ingredients for chaffles:

1 large egg, beaten
½ cup of mozzarella cheese, shredded
2 tbsp almond flour
¼ tsp baking powder
1 tbsp scallion browned and chopped
1 tsp fresh basil
A pinch of salt

Ingredients for topping:

2 slices Gruyère cheese
2 slices deli ham

Instructions for chaffles:

Heat up the waffle maker.

Add all the ingredients to a small mixing bowl and combine well.

Pour half of the batter into the waffle maker and cook for 4 minutes until brown. Repeat with the rest of the batter to make another chaffle.

Let cool for 3 minutes to let chaffles get crispy.

Top each chaffle with a slice of Gruyère and a slice of deli ham.

Serve and enjoy!

Mayo and Vegetables Chaffle

Prep Time: 5 minutes
Cook Time: 16 minutes
Servings: 4 chaffles

Ingredients for chaffles:

2 large eggs, beaten
2 tbsp keto mayonnaise
1 tbsp almond flour
¼ tsp baking powder
1 tbsp cream cheese
A pinch of salt and pepper

Ingredients for topping:

Lettuce leaves
1 tomato sliced
1 onion, sliced and browned

4-6 slices of grilled zucchini
4 slices of grilled eggplant

Instructions:
Heat up the waffle maker.
Add all the ingredients to a small mixing bowl and stir until well combined.
Pour ¼ of the batter into the waffle maker and cook for 4 minutes until brown. Repeat with the rest of the batter to make the other chaffles.
Let cool for 3 minutes to let chaffles get crispy.
Garnish the chaffles with lettuce, tomato, onions, zucchini and eggplant slices.
Serve warm and enjoy!

Eggplant & Bacon Chaffle

Prep Time: 5 minutes
Cook Time: 8 minutes
Servings: 2 chaffles

Ingredients for chaffles:
1 egg, beaten
½ cup shredded mozzarella cheese
2 tbsp bacon bits
A pinch of salt
Ingredients for topping:
2-4 slices of grilled eggplants, very thin
2 tbsp keto mayonnaise
Fresh parsley to taste

Instructions:
Heat up the waffle maker.
Add all the ingredients to a small mixing bowl and combine well.
Pour half of the batter into the waffle maker and cook for 4 minutes until brown. Repeat with the rest of the batter to make another chaffle.
Spread the chaffle with mayonnaise, top with a slice of grilled eggplant and season with fresh minced parsley.
Serve and enjoy!

Creamy Turnip Chaffle

Prep Time: 5 minutes
Cook Time: 8 minutes

Servings: 2 chaffles

Ingredients for chaffles:
1 egg, beaten
½ cup Monterey Jack cheese, shredded
1 turnip, cooked and mashed
2 tbsp ham diced
Ingredients for topping:
2 tbsp softened cream cheese
1 tbsp fresh basil, chopped

Instructions:
Heat up the waffle maker.
Add all the chaffles ingredients to a small mixing bowl and stir until well combined.
Pour half of the batter into the waffle maker and cook for 4 minutes until golden brown. Repeat with the rest of the batter to make another chaffle.
Spread the chaffle with cream cheese and season with fresh basil.
Serve and enjoy!

Ground Beef Chaffle

Prep Time: 4 minutes
Cook Time: 20 minutes
Servings: 2 chaffles

Ingredients for chaffles:
1 egg, beaten
½ cup shredded cheddar cheese
½ tbsp fresh basil, finely chopped
A pinch of salt
Ingredients for beef:
1 tsp olive oil
2 cups ground beef
½ tsp garlic powder
1 scallion, chopped
2 tsp butter for topping
2-3 spinach leaves for topping

Instructions for chaffles:
Heat up the waffle maker.
Add egg, shredded cheddar cheese, a pinch of salt and basil to a small mixing bowl and combine well.
Pour half of the batter into the waffle maker and cook for 4 minutes until brown. Repeat with the rest of the batter to make another chaffle.

Instructions for beef:
In a saucepan over medium heat cook the ground beef in olive oil. Season with salt and pepper if needed and add scallion. Stir occasionally and cook until the meat is browned.
Instruction for topping:
Spread the chaffle with butter, garnish with spinach leaves and beef.
Serve and enjoy!

Parsley and Hard-Boiled Egg Chaffle

Prep Time: 4 minutes
Cook Time: 8 minutes
Servings: 2 chaffles

Ingredients for chaffles:
1 large egg, beaten
½ cup of mozzarella cheese, shredded
2 tbsp almond flour
¼ tsp baking powder
Ingredients for topping:
1 tbsp chopped fresh parsley
2 tbsp keto mayonnaise
1 hard-boiled egg, thin sliced

Instructions:
Heat up the waffle maker.
Add all the chaffles ingredients in a small mixing bowl and combine well.
Pour half of the batter into the waffle maker and cook for 4 minutes until brown. Repeat with the rest of the batter to make another chaffle.
Let cool for 3 minutes to let chaffles get crispy.
Spread the chaffle with mayonnaise, garnish with a few slices of hard-boiled egg and sprinkle with parsley.
Serve and enjoy!

Parmesan Garlic Chaffle

Prep Time: 5 minutes
Cook Time: 8 minutes
Servings: 2 chaffles
Ingredients:
1 large egg, beaten
½ cup parmesan cheese, finely grated

A pinch of black pepper
1 tsp garlic powder

Instructions:
Heat up the waffle maker.
Add all the ingredients to a small mixing bowl and combine well.
Pour half of the batter into the waffle maker and cook for 4 minutes until golden brown. Repeat with the rest of the batter to make another chaffle.
Let cool for 3 minutes to let chaffles get crispy.
Serve and enjoy!

Broccoli Chaffle with Sausage

Prep Time: 5 minutes
Cook Time: 18 minutes
Servings: 2 chaffles

Ingredients for chaffles:
1 large egg, beaten
½ cup boiled, chopped broccoli
½ cup parmesan cheese, finely grated
A pinch of black pepper
Ingredients for topping:
½ cup chicken sausage, browned and chopped
2 slices of Brie cheese

Instructions:
Heat up the waffle maker.
Add all the chaffles ingredients to a small mixing bowl and combine well.
Pour half of the batter into the waffle maker and cook for 4 minutes until golden brown. Repeat with the rest of the batter to make another chaffle.
Top the chaffle with warm sausage and a slice of brie cheese. Season with black pepper if desired.
Serve immediately and enjoy!

Radishes Chaffle

Prep Time: 5 minutes
Cook Time: 8 minutes
Servings: 2 chaffles

Ingredients:
1 large egg, beaten
½ cup cheddar cheese, shredded

½ tsp baking powder
2 tbsp radishes, boiled and puree
A pinch of black pepper

Instructions:
Heat up the waffle maker.
Add all the ingredients to a small mixing bowl and stir until well combined.
Pour half of the batter into the waffle maker and cook for 4 minutes until golden brown. Repeat with the rest of the batter to make another chaffle.
Let cool for 3 minutes to let chaffles get crispy.
Serve with your favorite keto dressing and enjoy!

Savory Chaffle Sticks

Prep Time: 5 minutes
Cook Time: 8 minutes
Servings: 2 chaffles

Ingredients:
1 egg, beaten
½ cup shredded parmesan cheese
2 tbsp onion, browned and minced
½ tsp paprika powder

Instructions:
Heat up the waffle maker.
Add all the ingredients to a small mixing bowl and combine well.
Pour half of the batter into the waffle maker and cook for 4 minutes until golden brown. Repeat with the rest of the batter to make another chaffle.
Let cool for 3 minutes to let chaffles get crispy.
Cut the chaffles in sticks and dip into keto Tartar sauce.
Serve and enjoy!

Turkey in Lemon Sauce Chaffle

Prep Time: 5 minutes
Cook Time: 18 minutes
Servings: 2 chaffles

Ingredients for chaffles:
1 large egg, beaten
½ cup cheddar cheese, shredded
Ingredients for turkey:

½ cup of turkey breast, shredded
¼ tsp garlic powder
¼ tsp paprika powder
1 tsp lemon juice
A pinch of salt and black pepper
2 tbsp heavy cream
1 tbsp finely grated Parmesan cheese
½ tsp fresh thyme, minced
½ tsp fresh parsley, minced
1 tbsp unsalted butter
½ cup chicken broth

Instructions for turkey:
In a saucepan over medium heat, cook the turkey breast in the unsalted butter part by part, for approx. 10 minutes. Season with a pinch of salt, black pepper and paprika.
Set aside the meat.
In the same saucepan, add garlic powder, chicken broth, heavy cream, parmesan cheese, lemon juice and thyme. Bring to a boil and simmer until the sauce thickens. Add the turkey and mix well.

Instructions for chaffles:
Heat up the waffle maker.
Add all the chaffles ingredients to a small mixing bowl and stir until well combined.
Pour half of the batter into the waffle maker and cook for 4 minutes until golden brown. Repeat with the rest of the batter to make another chaffle.
Top the chaffle with lemon sauce turkey.
Serve warm and enjoy!

Gourmet Grilled Prawns Chaffle

Prep Time: 5 minutes
Cook Time: 8 minutes
Servings: 2 chaffles

Ingredients for chaffles:
1 large egg, beaten
½ cup mozzarella cheese, shredded
A pinch of salt
Ingredients for topping:
6-8 grilled prawns
2 tsp fresh parsley, minced
2 tbsp butter, unsalted
Lettuce leaves

1 small avocado, sliced
1 tomato, sliced

Instructions:
Heat up the waffle maker.
Add all the chaffles ingredients to a small mixing bowl and stir until well combined.
Pour half of the batter into the waffle maker and cook for 4 minutes until golden brown. Repeat with the rest of the batter to make another chaffle.
Spread the chaffles with butter. Top it with lettuce, tomato, slices of avocado and grilled prawns. Sprinkle with fresh parsley.
Serve immediately and enjoy!

Paprika & Scallion Chaffle

Prep Time: 5 minutes
Cook Time: 8 minutes
Servings: 2 chaffles

Ingredients for chaffles:
1 large egg, beaten
½ cup cheddar cheese, shredded
½ tbsp paprika powder
1 tbsp scallion, browned and thinly sliced

Instructions:
Heat up the waffle maker.
Add all the chaffles ingredients to a small mixing bowl and stir until well combined.
Pour half of the batter into the waffle maker and cook for 4 minutes, until brown. Repeat with the rest of the batter to make another chaffle.
Let cool for 3 minutes to let chaffles get crispy.
Serve and enjoy!

Anchovies Chaffle

Prep Time: 5 minutes
Cook Time: 8 minutes
Servings: 2 chaffles

Ingredients for chaffles:
1 large egg, beaten
½ cup shredded mozzarella cheese
4 filets anchovies, canned
A pinch of black pepper

Instructions for chaffles:
Heat up the waffle maker.
Add all the chaffles ingredients to a small mixing bowl and stir until well combined.
Pour half of the batter into the waffle maker and cook for 4 minutes until golden brown. Repeat with the rest of the batter to make another chaffle.
Serve and enjoy!

Keto Chaffle with Scallion Cream

Prep Time: 5 minutes
Cook Time: 8 minutes
Servings: 2 chaffles

Ingredients for chaffles:
1 large egg, beaten
½ cup of mozzarella cheese, shredded
2 tbsp almond flour
¼ tsp baking powder
Ingredients for scallion cream:
2 tbsp cream cheese, softened
2 tbsp scallion, browned and chopped

Instructions for cream:
In a small bowl, whisk cream cheese and scallion until smoothy. Set aside.
Instructions for chaffles:
Heat up the mini waffle maker.
Add all the chaffles ingredients to a small mixing bowl and combine well.
Pour half of the batter into the waffle maker and cook for 4 minutes until brown. Repeat with the rest of the batter to make another chaffle.
Let cool for 3 minutes to let chaffles get crispy.
Spread the chaffle with scallion cream.
Serve with cucumber pickles and enjoy!

Ground Pork Savory Chaffle

Prep Time: 5 minutes
Cook Time: 20 minutes
Servings: 2 chaffles

Ingredients for chaffles:
1 egg, beaten
½ cup shredded mozzarella cheese

½ tbsp fresh basil, finely chopped
A pinch of salt

Ingredients for pork:
1 tsp olive oil, extra virgin
2 cups ground pork
1 small red onion, chopped
1 tsp fresh parsley, minced
A pinch of salt and black pepper

Ingredients for topping:
1 tbsp keto mayonnaise
1 slice of cheddar cheese

Instructions for pork:
In a saucepan over low heat brown the onion in olive oil. Season with salt and pepper if needed. Add the ground pork and the fresh parsley. Stir occasionally and cook until the meat is browned.

Instructions for chaffles:
Heat up the waffle maker.
Add egg, shredded cheddar cheese, a pinch of salt and basil in a small mixing bowl and combine well.
Pour half of the batter into the waffle maker and cook for 4 minutes until brown. Repeat with the rest of the batter to make another chaffle.
Spread the chaffle with mayonnaise and garnish with ground pork. Add a slice of cheddar cheese.
Serve immediately and enjoy!

Dill Butter and Vegetables Chaffle

Prep Time: 5 minutes
Cook Time: 8 minutes
Servings: 2 chaffles

Ingredients for chaffles:
1 egg, beaten
½ tbsp spinach, boiled and chopped
½ cup mozzarella cheese, shredded
1 tsp onion, minced, browned
½ tbsp broccoli, boiled and chopped
A pinch of salt and pepper

Ingredients for dill butter:
½ tbsp cream cheese, softened
1 tbsp butter, softened
1 tbsp fresh dill, minced
1 tsp lemon juice
A pinch of salt and pepper

Instructions for dill butter:
Mix all the ingredients in a blender and whisk until creamy.

Instructions for chaffles:
Heat up the waffle maker.
Add all the chaffles ingredients to a small mixing bowl and stir until well combined.
Pour half of the batter into the waffle maker and cook for 4 minutes until brown. Repeat with the rest of the batter to make another chaffle.
Let cool for 3 minutes to let chaffles get crispy.
Serve with dill butter and enjoy!

Blue Cheese Butter Chaffle

Prep Time: 5 minutes
Cook Time: 8 minutes
Servings: 2 chaffles

Ingredients for chaffles:
1 large egg, beaten
½ cup of mozzarella cheese, shredded
2 tbsp almond flour
¼ tsp baking powder

Ingredients for Blue cheese butter:
1 tbsp butter, softened
2 tbsp Blue cheese, shredded
1 tsp fresh basil, chopped
A pinch of salt and black pepper

Instructions for Blue cheese butter:
In a small mixing bowl, combine all the ingredients and stir well. Set aside.

Instructions for chaffles:
Heat up the waffle maker.
Add all the chaffles ingredients to a small mixing bowl and combine well.
Pour half of the batter into the waffle maker and cook for 4 minutes until brown. Repeat with the rest of the batter to make another chaffle.
Let cool for 3 minutes to let chaffles get crispy.
Spread the chaffle with Blue cheese butter.
Serve and enjoy!

Gourmet Chicken Salad Chaffle

Prep Time: 5 minutes
Cook Time: 8 minutes
Servings: 2 chaffles

Ingredients for chaffles:
1 large egg, beaten
½ cup shredded cheddar cheese
Ingredients for chicken salad:
½ cup chicken, cooked and shredded
1 tbsp fresh celery, chopped
1 tsp scallion, browned and minced
2 tbsp avocado pulp, smashed
1 tsp fresh basil, minced
2 tbsp keto mayonnaise
1 tsp keto mustard
1 tsp lemon juice
A pinch of salt and pepper
Ingredients for filling:
Spinach leaves
1 small hard-boiled egg, sliced
1 small tomato, sliced
1-2 pickled cucumbers, sliced

Instructions for chicken salad:
Combine all the ingredients in a mixing bowl and stir well. Set aside.
Instructions for chaffles:
Heat up the waffle maker.
Add egg and shredded cheese to a small mixing bowl and combine well.
Pour half of the batter into the waffle maker and cook for 4 minutes until golden brown. Repeat with the rest of the batter to make another chaffle.
Garnish the chaffle with spinach leaves, chicken salad and 1 or 2 slices of hard-boiled egg. Add tomato and cucumbers.
Serve and enjoy!

Corned Beef Chaffle

Prep Time: 5 minutes
Cook Time: 8 minutes
Servings: 2 chaffles

Ingredients for chaffles:
1 large egg, beaten
½ cup of cheddar cheese, shredded
1 tbsp almond flour
¼ tsp baking powder
Ingredients for topping:
2 slices of corned beef
2 tbsp keto mayonnaise
A pinch of salt and black pepper

Instructions:
Heat up the waffle maker.
Add all the chaffles ingredients to a small mixing bowl and stir until well combined.
Pour half of the batter into the waffle maker and cook for 4 minutes until golden brown. Repeat with the rest of the batter to make another chaffle.
Let cool for 3 minutes to let chaffles get crispy.
Spread the chaffle with mayonnaise and top it with corned beef. Season with salt and pepper.
Serve and enjoy!

CHAPTER 5: PIZZA CHAFFLE RECIPES

Pizza Chaffle

Prep Time: 5 minutes
Cook Time: 13 minutes
Servings: 2 chaffles

Ingredients:
½ cup shredded mozzarella cheese
1 tbsp almond flour
½ tsp baking powder
1 egg
¼ tsp garlic powder
¼ tsp basil
2 tbsp low carb pasta sauce
2 tbsp mozzarella cheese

Instructions:
Heat up the waffle maker.
Add mozzarella cheese, baking powder, garlic, basil, egg, and almond flour to a medium mixing bowl and combine well.
Pour half of the batter into the waffle maker and cook for about 4 minutes. Repeat with the rest of the batter to make another chaffle.
Once both pizza chaffles are cooked, place them on the baking sheet of the toaster oven.
Put 1 tablespoon of low carb pasta sauce on top of each pizza chaffle.

Sprinkle 1 tablespoon of shredded mozzarella cheese on top of each one.

Bake at 350° in the toaster oven for about 5 minutes, until the cheese is melted.

Serve and enjoy!

Italian Pizza Chaffle

Prep Time: 5 minutes
Cook Time: 10 minutes
Servings: 2 pizza chaffles

Ingredients:
1 tsp coconut flour
1 egg white
½ cup shredded mozzarella cheese
1 tsp softened cream cheese
¼ tsp baking powder
1/8 tsp Italian seasoning
1/8 tsp garlic powder
A pinch of salt
3 tsp low carb tomato sauce
½ cup mozzarella cheese
1 tbsp shredded parmesan cheese
¼ tsp basil

Instructions:
Heat up the waffle maker and preheat oven to 400°F.
Mix coconut flour, egg white, mozzarella cheese, softened cream cheese, baking powder, garlic powder, Italian seasonings, and a pinch of salt in a small mixing bowl.
Pour half of the batter in the waffle maker and cook for about 4 minutes. Repeat with the rest of the batter to make another chaffle.
Top each chaffle with tomato sauce, mozzarella cheese, and parmesan cheese.
Place in the oven on a baking sheet and broil pizza for approx. 2 minutes so that cheese begins to bubble and brown.
Remove from oven, sprinkle basil on top.
Serve and enjoy!

Ham and Olives Pizza Chaffle

Prep Time: 5 minutes
Cook Time: 13 minutes

Servings: 2 chaffles

Ingredients for chaffles:
½ cup shredded mozzarella cheese
1 tbsp almond flour
½ tsp baking powder
1 egg, beaten
A pinch of salt

Ingredients for topping:
2 tbsp low carb pasta sauce
2 tbsp mozzarella cheese, shredded
2 slices of ham
2 tsp olives, pitted and chopped

Instructions:
Heat up the waffle maker.
Add all the chaffle ingredients to a small mixing bowl and combine well.
Pour half of the batter into the waffle maker and cook for about 4 minutes until golden brown. Repeat with the rest of the batter to make another chaffle.
Once both chaffles are cooked, place them on the baking sheet of the toaster oven.
Put 1 tablespoon of low carb pasta sauce on top of each chaffle.
Sprinkle 1 tablespoon of shredded mozzarella cheese on top of each one.
Top with a slice of ham and sprinkle with olives.
Bake at 350° in the toaster oven for about 5 minutes, until the cheese is melted.
Serve and enjoy!

Pepperoni Pizza Chaffle

Prep Time: 5 minutes
Cook Time: 10 minutes
Servings: 2 pizza chaffles

Ingredients for chaffles:
1 egg
½ cup shredded mozzarella cheese
½ tsp Italian seasoning
A pinch of garlic powder
Ingredients for Pizza Toppings:
2 tbsp tomato sauce
½ cup shredded mozzarella cheese
6 slices of pepperoni salami

Instructions:
Heat up the waffle maker and preheat oven to 400° F.
Mix egg, cheese, garlic, and herbs in a small mixing bowl. Stir until well combined.
Pour 1/2 of the batter in the waffle maker and cook for about 4 minutes. Repeat with the rest of the batter to make another chaffle.
Top the chaffle with tomato sauce, cheese, and pepperoni. Place in the oven on a baking sheet for 2 minutes.
Serve and enjoy!

Chicken Pizza Chaffle

Prep Time: 5 minutes
Cook Time: 10 minutes
Servings: 2 pizza chaffles

Ingredients:
1/3 cup chicken, cooked
1 egg
1/3 cup mozzarella cheese
¼ tsp basil
¼ tsp garlic powder
2 tbsp tomato sauce
2 tbsp mozzarella cheese

Instructions:
Heat up the mini waffle maker and preheat oven to 400°.
Add the egg, chicken, basil, garlic, and mozzarella cheese to a small mixing bowl and combine well.
Pour 1/2 of the batter in the waffle maker and cook for about 4 minutes. Repeat with the rest of the batter to make another chaffle.
Top each chaffle with tomato sauce and mozzarella cheese.
Place in the oven on a baking sheet and broil pizza for approx. 2 minutes so that cheese begins to bubble and brown.
Remove from oven, sprinkle basil on top.
Serve and enjoy!

Mushroom & Bacon Pizza Chaffle

Prep Time: 5 minutes

Cook Time: 13 minutes
Servings: 2 pizza chaffles

Ingredients for chaffles:
½ cup shredded mozzarella cheese
1 tbsp almond flour
½ tsp baking powder
1 egg
¼ tsp garlic powder
¼ tsp basil

Ingredients for topping:
2 tbsp low carb pasta sauce
2 tbsp mozzarella cheese
2 slices of bacon
2 tbsp of mushrooms, chopped

Instructions:
Heat up the waffle maker.
Add mozzarella cheese, baking powder, garlic, basil, egg, and almond flour to a medium mixing bowl and combine well.
Pour half of the batter into the waffle maker and cook for about 4 minutes. Repeat with the rest of the batter to make another chaffle.
Once both chaffles are cooked, place them on the baking sheet of the toaster oven.
Put 1 tablespoon of low carb pasta sauce on top of each chaffle.
Sprinkle 1 tablespoon of shredded mozzarella cheese on top of each one.
Top with a slice of bacon and 1 tbsp of mushrooms. Bake at 350° in the toaster oven for about 5 minutes, until the cheese is melted.
Serve and enjoy!

Turkey Pizza Chaffle

Prep Time: 5 minutes
Cook Time: 10 minutes
Servings: 2 pizza chaffles

Ingredients:
½ cup turkey breast, cooked and chopped
1 egg, beaten
½ cup mozzarella cheese, shredded
¼ tsp basil
2 tbsp tomato sauce
2 tbsp mozzarella cheese

Instructions:

Heat up the mini waffle maker and preheat oven to 400°.

Add the egg, turkey, basil, and mozzarella cheese to a small mixing bowl and combine well.

Pour half of the batter in the waffle maker and cook for about 4 minutes. Repeat with the rest of the batter to make another chaffle.

Top each chaffle with tomato sauce and mozzarella cheese.

Place in the oven on a baking sheet and broil pizza for approx. 2 min so that cheese begins to bubble and brown.

Remove from oven, sprinkle basil on top.

Serve and enjoy!

Tuna Pizza Chaffle

Prep Time: 5 minutes
Cook Time: 10 minutes
Servings: 2 chaffles

Ingredients for chaffles:
½ cup shredded mozzarella cheese
1 tbsp almond flour
½ tsp baking powder
1 egg, beaten
A pinch of salt
Ingredients for topping:
2 tbsp low carb pasta sauce
2 tbsp mozzarella cheese, shredded
1 can tuna, drained
1 tsp dried oregano

Instructions:

Heat up the waffle maker.

Add all the chaffle ingredients to a small mixing bowl and combine well.

Pour half of the batter into the waffle maker and cook for about 4 minutes until golden brown. Repeat with the rest of the batter to make another chaffle.

Once both chaffles are cooked, place them on the baking sheet of the toaster oven.

Put 1 tablespoon of low carb pasta sauce on top of each chaffle.

Sprinkle 1 tablespoon of shredded mozzarella cheese on top of each one.

Top with tuna and sprinkle with oregano.

Bake at 350° in the toaster oven for about 2 minutes, until the cheese is melted.

Serve and enjoy!

Ham Pizza Chaffle

Prep Time: 5 minutes
Cook Time: 10 minutes
Servings: 2 chaffles

Ingredients for chaffles:
½ cup shredded mozzarella cheese
1 tbsp almond flour
½ tsp baking powder
1 egg, beaten
A pinch of salt
Ingredients for topping:
2 tbsp low carb pasta sauce
2 tbsp mozzarella cheese, shredded
2 slices of ham
1 tsp dried oregano

Instructions:

Heat up the waffle maker.

Add all the chaffle ingredients to a small mixing bowl and combine well.

Pour half of the batter into the waffle maker and cook for about 4 minutes until golden brown. Repeat with the rest of the batter to make another chaffle.

Once both chaffles are cooked, place them on the baking sheet of the toaster oven.

Put 1 tablespoon of low carb pasta sauce on top of each chaffle.

Sprinkle 1 tablespoon of shredded mozzarella cheese on top of each one.

Top with a slice of ham and sprinkle with oregano.

Bake at 350° in the toaster oven for about 2 minutes, until the cheese is melted.

Serve and enjoy!

Bacon Pizza Chaffle

Prep Time: 5 minutes
Cook Time: 10 minutes
Servings: 2 chaffles

Ingredients for chaffles:
½ cup shredded mozzarella cheese
1 tbsp almond flour
½ tsp baking powder
1 egg, beaten
A pinch of salt

Ingredients for topping:
2 tbsp low carb pasta sauce
2 tbsp mozzarella cheese, shredded
2 tbsp bacon bits

Instructions:
Heat up the waffle maker.

Add all the chaffle ingredients to a small mixing bowl and combine well.

Pour half of the batter into the waffle maker and cook for about 4 minutes until golden brown. Repeat with the rest of the batter to make another chaffle.

Once both chaffles are cooked, place them on the baking sheet of the toaster oven.

Put 1 tablespoon of low carb pasta sauce on top of each chaffle.

Sprinkle 1 tablespoon of shredded mozzarella cheese on top of each one.

Top with bacon bits.

Bake at 350° in the toaster oven for about 2 minutes, until the cheese is melted.

Serve and enjoy!

Zucchini and Brie Pizza Chaffle

Prep Time: 5 minutes
Cook Time: 10 minutes
Servings: 2 pizza chaffles

Ingredients:
1 egg
1/3 cup mozzarella cheese
¼ tsp garlic powder
½ cup of zucchini, grated
2 tbsp tomato sauce
2 tbsp mozzarella cheese
2 tsp Brie cheese

Instructions:
Heat up the mini waffle maker and preheat oven to 400°.

Add the egg, garlic, zucchini and mozzarella cheese to a small mixing bowl and combine well.

Pour 1/2 of the batter in the waffle maker and cook for about 4 minutes until golden brown. Repeat with the rest of the batter to make another chaffle.

Top each chaffle with tomato sauce, mozzarella cheese and Brie cheese.

Place in the oven on a baking sheet and broil pizza for approx. 2 min so that cheese begins to bubble and brown.

Remove from oven.

Serve and enjoy!

Mushrooms Pizza Chaffle

Prep Time: 5 minutes
Cook Time: 10 minutes
Servings: 2 chaffles

Ingredients for chaffles:
½ cup shredded mozzarella cheese
1 tbsp almond flour
½ tsp baking powder
1 egg, beaten
A pinch of salt

Ingredients for topping:
2 tbsp low carb pasta sauce
2 tbsp mozzarella cheese, shredded
1 can mushrooms, drained
1 tsp dried oregano

Instructions:
Heat up the waffle maker.

Add all the chaffle ingredients to a small mixing bowl and combine well.

Pour half of the batter into the waffle maker and cook for about 4 minutes until golden brown. Repeat with the rest of the batter to make another chaffle.

Once both chaffles are cooked, place them on the baking sheet of the toaster oven.

Put 1 tablespoon of low carb pasta sauce on top of each chaffle.

Sprinkle 1 tablespoon of shredded mozzarella cheese on top of each one.

Top with mushrooms and sprinkle with oregano.

Bake at 350° in the toaster oven for about 2 minutes, until the cheese is melted.

Serve and enjoy!

Tuna and Olives Pizza Chaffle

Prep Time: 5 minutes
Cook Time: 10 minutes
Servings: 2 pizza chaffles

Ingredients:
1 egg
½ cup mozzarella cheese
¼ tsp garlic powder
1 can of tuna, drained
1 tbsp black olives, pitted
2 tbsp tomato sauce
2 tbsp mozzarella cheese

Instructions:
Heat up the waffle maker and preheat oven to 400°.
Add the egg, garlic, and mozzarella cheese to a small mixing bowl and combine well.
Pour 1/2 of the batter in the waffle maker and cook for about 4 minutes until golden brown. Repeat with the rest of the batter to make another chaffle.
Top each chaffle with tomato sauce, mozzarella cheese, tuna and a few black olives.
Place in the oven on a baking sheet and broil pizza for approx. 2 min so that cheese begins to bubble and brown.
Remove from oven.
Serve and enjoy!

Parmesan Pizza Chaffle

Prep Time: 5 minutes
Cook Time: 13 minutes
Servings: 2 chaffles

Ingredients:
½ cup shredded mozzarella cheese
1 tbsp almond flour
½ tsp baking powder
1 egg, beaten
¼ tsp garlic powder
A pinch of salt and pepper
Ingredients for pizza topping:
2 tbsp low carb pasta sauce
2 tbsp mozzarella cheese, shredded
1 tbsp parmesan cheese, shredded
¼ tsp fresh basil

Instructions:
Heat up the waffle maker.
Add all the chaffle ingredients to a small mixing bowl and combine well.
Pour half of the batter into the waffle maker and cook for about 4 minutes until golden brown. Repeat with the rest of the batter to make another chaffle.
Once both chaffles are cooked, place them on the baking sheet of the toaster oven.
Put 1 tablespoon of low carb pasta sauce on top of each chaffle.
Sprinkle 1 tbsp of shredded mozzarella and 1 tbsp of shredded parmesan on top of each one. Season with fresh basil.
Bake at 350° in the toaster oven for about 5 minutes, until the cheese is melted.
Serve and enjoy!

Bacon and Zucchini Pizza Chaffle

Prep Time: 5 minutes
Cook Time: 10 minutes
Servings: 2 chaffles

Ingredients for chaffles:
½ cup shredded mozzarella cheese
1 tbsp almond flour
½ tsp baking powder
1 egg, beaten
A pinch of salt
Ingredients for topping:
2 tbsp low carb pasta sauce
2 tbsp mozzarella cheese, shredded
2 tbsp bacon bits
2 tbsp zucchinis, grated

Instructions:
Heat up the waffle maker.
Add all the chaffle ingredients to a small mixing bowl and combine well.
Pour half of the batter into the waffle maker and cook for about 4 minutes until golden brown. Repeat with the rest of the batter to make another chaffle.

Once both chaffles are cooked, place them on the baking sheet of the toaster oven.

Put 1 tablespoon of low carb pasta sauce on top of each chaffle.

Sprinkle 1 tablespoon of shredded mozzarella cheese on top of each one.

Top with bacon bits and zucchinis.

Bake at 350° in the toaster oven for about 2 minutes, until the cheese is melted.

Serve and enjoy!

Tuna and Onion Pizza Chaffle

Prep Time: 5 minutes
Cook Time: 13 minutes
Servings: 2 chaffles

Ingredients for chaffles:

1 egg, beaten
½ cup mozzarella cheese, shredded
A pinch of salt

Ingredients for pizza topping:

2 tbsp tomato sauce
2 tbsp mozzarella cheese, shredded
1 can of tuna, drained
1 tbsp onion, browned and chopped
1 tsp dried oregano

Instructions:

Heat up the waffle maker and preheat oven to 400°.

Add all the chaffle ingredients to a small mixing bowl and stir until well combined.

Pour ½ of the batter in the waffle maker and cook for about 4 minutes until golden brown. Repeat with the rest of the batter to make another chaffle.

Top each chaffle with tomato sauce, mozzarella cheese, tuna and onions. Season with oregano.

Place in the oven on a baking sheet and broil pizza for approx. 2 minutes so that cheese begins to bubble.

Serve and enjoy!

Ham and Parmesan Pizza Chaffle

Prep Time: 5 minutes
Cook Time: 13 minutes
Servings: 2 pizza chaffles

Ingredients for chaffles:

½ cup shredded mozzarella cheese
1 tbsp almond flour
½ tsp baking powder
1 egg, beaten

Ingredients for topping:

2 tbsp low carb pasta sauce
2 tbsp mozzarella cheese
1 tbsp parmesan cheese
2 slices of ham

Instructions:

Heat up the waffle maker.

Add mozzarella cheese, baking powder, egg, and almond flour to a medium mixing bowl and combine well.

Pour half of the batter into the waffle maker and cook for about 4 minutes. Repeat with the rest of the batter to make another chaffle.

Once both chaffles are cooked, place them on the baking sheet of the toaster oven.

Put 1 tablespoon of low carb pasta sauce on top of each pizza chaffle.

Sprinkle 1 tablespoon of shredded mozzarella cheese on top of each one.

Top with a slice of ham and sprinkle with parmesan cheese.

Bake at 350° in the toaster oven for about 5 minutes, until the cheese is melted.

Serve and enjoy!

Broccoli Pizza Chaffle

Prep Time: 5 minutes
Cook Time: 10 minutes
Servings: 2 chaffles

Ingredients for chaffles:

½ cup shredded mozzarella cheese
1 tbsp almond flour
½ tsp baking powder
1 egg, beaten
½ tsp garlic powder
A pinch of salt

Ingredients for topping:

2 tbsp low carb pasta sauce
2 tbsp mozzarella cheese, shredded

2 tbsp broccoli, boiled and chopped

Instructions:
Heat up the waffle maker.
Add all the chaffle ingredients to a small mixing bowl and combine well.
Pour half of the batter into the waffle maker and cook for about 4 minutes until golden brown. Repeat with the rest of the batter to make another chaffle.
Once both chaffles are cooked, place them on the baking sheet of the toaster oven.
Put 1 tablespoon of low carb pasta sauce on top of each chaffle.
Sprinkle 1 tablespoon of shredded mozzarella cheese on top of each one.
Top with broccoli.
Bake at 350° in the toaster oven for about 2 minutes, until the cheese is melted.
Serve and enjoy!

Veggie Pizza Chaffle

Prep Time: 5 minutes
Cook Time: 13 minutes
Servings: 2 chaffles

Ingredients:
½ cup shredded mozzarella cheese
1 tbsp almond flour
½ tsp baking powder
1 egg, beaten
¼ tsp garlic powder
A pinch of salt and pepper
Ingredients for pizza topping:
2 tbsp low carb pasta sauce
2 tbsp mozzarella cheese, shredded
½ tbsp onion, browned and chopped
½ tbsp mushrooms, chopped
½ tbsp zucchini, grated
¼ tsp fresh basil

Instructions:
Heat up the waffle maker.
Add all the chaffle ingredients to a small mixing bowl and combine well.
Pour half of the batter into the waffle maker and cook for about 4 minutes until golden brown. Repeat with the rest of the batter to make another chaffle.

Once both chaffles are cooked, place them on the baking sheet of the toaster oven.
Put 1 tablespoon of low carb pasta sauce on top of each chaffle.
Sprinkle 1 tbsp of shredded mozzarella on top of each one. Season with fresh basil.
Top the chaffle with onions, zucchinis and mushrooms.
Bake at 350° in the toaster oven for about 5 minutes, until the cheese is melted.
Serve and enjoy!

Ham and Zucchini Pizza Chaffle

Prep Time: 5 minutes
Cook Time: 10 minutes
Servings: 2 chaffles

Ingredients for chaffles:
½ cup shredded mozzarella cheese
1 tbsp almond flour
½ tsp baking powder
1 egg, beaten
A pinch of salt
Ingredients for topping:
2 tbsp low carb pasta sauce
2 tbsp mozzarella cheese, shredded
2 slices of ham
2 tbsp zucchini, grated

Instructions:
Heat up the waffle maker.
Add all the chaffle ingredients to a small mixing bowl and combine well.
Pour half of the batter into the waffle maker and cook for about 4 minutes until golden brown. Repeat with the rest of the batter to make another chaffle.
Once both chaffles are cooked, place them on the baking sheet of the toaster oven.
Put 1 tablespoon of low carb pasta sauce on top of each chaffle.
Sprinkle 1 tablespoon of shredded mozzarella cheese on top of each one.
Top with a slice of ham and zucchinis.
Bake at 350° in the toaster oven for about 2 minutes, until the cheese is melted.
Serve and enjoy!

Spicy Pizza Chaffle

Prep Time: 5 minutes
Cook Time: 10 minutes
Servings: 2 chaffles

Ingredients for chaffles:
½ cup shredded mozzarella cheese
1 tbsp almond flour
½ tsp baking powder
1 egg, beaten
½ tsp hot pepper powder
A pinch of salt

Ingredients for topping:
2 tbsp low carb pasta sauce
2 tbsp mozzarella cheese, shredded
1 tsp fresh parsley

Instructions:
Heat up the waffle maker.
Add all the chaffle ingredients to a small mixing bowl and combine well.
Pour half of the batter into the waffle maker and cook for about 4 minutes until golden brown. Repeat with the rest of the batter to make another chaffle.
Once both chaffles are cooked, place them on the baking sheet of the toaster oven.
Put 1 tablespoon of low carb pasta sauce on top of each chaffle.
Sprinkle 1 tablespoon of shredded mozzarella cheese on top of each one. Season with parsley.
Bake at 350° in the toaster oven for about 2 minutes, until the cheese is melted.
Serve and enjoy!

Broccoli & Provolone Pizza Chaffle

Prep Time: 5 minutes
Cook Time: 10 minutes
Servings: 2 chaffles

Ingredients for chaffles:
½ cup shredded mozzarella cheese
1 tbsp almond flour
½ tsp baking powder
1 egg, beaten
½ tsp garlic powder
A pinch of salt

Ingredients for topping:
2 tbsp low carb pasta sauce
2 tbsp mozzarella cheese, shredded
2 tbsp broccoli, boiled and chopped
2 tbsp Provolone cheese, finely grated

Instructions:
Heat up the waffle maker.
Add all the chaffle ingredients to a small mixing bowl and combine well.
Pour half of the batter into the waffle maker and cook for about 4 minutes until golden brown. Repeat with the rest of the batter to make another chaffle.
Once both chaffles are cooked, place them on the baking sheet of the toaster oven.
Put 1 tablespoon of low carb pasta sauce on top of each chaffle.
Sprinkle 1 tablespoon of shredded mozzarella cheese on top of each one.
Top with broccoli and sprinkle with Provolone cheese.
Bake at 350° in the toaster oven for about 2 minutes, until the cheese is melted.
Serve and enjoy!

Mascarpone & Pecans Pizza Chaffle

Prep Time: 5 minutes
Cook Time: 13 minutes
Servings: 2 pizza chaffles

Ingredients for chaffles:
½ cup shredded mozzarella cheese
1 tbsp almond flour
½ tsp baking powder
1 egg, beaten

Ingredients for topping:
2 tbsp low carb pasta sauce
2 tbsp mozzarella cheese
1 tbsp Mascarpone cheese, softened
½ tbsp pecans, minced

Instructions:
Heat up the waffle maker.
Add mozzarella cheese, baking powder, egg, and almond flour to a medium mixing bowl and combine well.

Pour half of the batter into the waffle maker and cook for about 4 minutes. Repeat with the rest of the batter to make another chaffle.

Once both chaffles are cooked, place them on the baking sheet of the toaster oven.

Put 1 tablespoon of low carb pasta sauce on top of each chaffle.

Sprinkle 1 tablespoon of shredded mozzarella cheese on top of each one.

Top with Mascarpone cheese and chopped pecans.

Bake at 350° in the toaster oven for about 5 minutes, until the cheese is melted.

Serve and enjoy!

Pumpkin Pizza Chaffle

Prep Time: 5 minutes
Cook Time: 13 minutes
Servings: 2 chaffles

Ingredients for chaffles:
½ cup shredded mozzarella cheese
1 tbsp almond flour
½ tsp baking powder
1 egg, beaten
A pinch of salt and pepper

Ingredients for topping:
2 tbsp low carb pasta sauce
2 tbsp mozzarella cheese, shredded
1 tbsp baked pumpkin, diced
1 tsp dried or fresh rosemary

Instructions:
Heat up the waffle maker.

Add all the chaffle ingredients to a small mixing bowl and combine well.

Pour half of the batter into the waffle maker and cook for about 4 minutes until golden brown. Repeat with the rest of the batter to make another chaffle.

Once both chaffles are cooked, place them on the baking sheet of the toaster oven.

Put 1 tablespoon of low carb pasta sauce on top of each chaffle.

Sprinkle 1 tablespoon of shredded mozzarella cheese on top of each one.

Top with diced pumpkin and sprinkle with rosemary.

Bake at 350° in the toaster oven for about 2-3 minutes, until the cheese is melted.

Serve and enjoy!

Rosemary Bacon Pizza Chaffle

Prep Time: 5 minutes
Cook Time: 13 minutes
Servings: 2 chaffles

Ingredients for chaffles:
½ cup shredded mozzarella cheese
1 tbsp almond flour
½ tsp baking powder
1 egg, beaten
A pinch of salt and pepper

Ingredients for topping:
2 tbsp low carb pasta sauce
2 tbsp mozzarella cheese, shredded
1 tbsp bacon, diced
1 tsp dried or fresh rosemary

Instructions:
Heat up the waffle maker.

Add all the chaffle ingredients to a small mixing bowl and combine well.

Pour half of the batter into the waffle maker and cook for about 4 minutes until golden brown. Repeat with the rest of the batter to make another chaffle.

Once both chaffles are cooked, place them on the baking sheet of the toaster oven.

Put 1 tablespoon of low carb pasta sauce on top of each chaffle.

Sprinkle 1 tablespoon of shredded mozzarella cheese on top of each one.

Top with diced bacon and sprinkle with rosemary.

Bake at 350° in the toaster oven for about 2-3 minutes, until the cheese is melted.

Serve and enjoy!

Ham and Mushrooms Pizza Chaffle

Prep Time: 5 minutes
Cook Time: 10 minutes
Servings: 2 chaffles

Ingredients for chaffles:
½ cup shredded mozzarella cheese
1 tbsp almond flour
½ tsp baking powder
1 egg, beaten
A pinch of salt

Ingredients for topping:
2 tbsp low carb pasta sauce
2 tbsp mozzarella cheese, shredded
2 slices of ham
2 tsp mushrooms, minced
¼ tsp dried oregano

Instructions:
Heat up the waffle maker.

Add all the chaffle ingredients to a small mixing bowl and combine well.

Pour half of the batter into the waffle maker and cook for about 4 minutes until golden brown. Repeat with the rest of the batter to make another chaffle.

Once both chaffles are cooked, place them on the baking sheet of the toaster oven.

Put 1 tablespoon of low carb pasta sauce on top of each chaffle.

Sprinkle 1 tablespoon of shredded mozzarella cheese on top of each one.

Top with a slice of ham and mushrooms. Sprinkle with oregano.

Bake at 350° in the toaster oven for about 2 minutes, until the cheese is melted.

Serve and enjoy!

Cauliflower Pizza Chaffle

Prep Time: 5 minutes
Cook Time: 13 minutes
Servings: 2 pizza chaffles

Ingredients for chaffles:
½ cup shredded mozzarella cheese
1 tbsp almond flour
½ tsp baking powder
1 egg, beaten
1 tbsp grated cauliflower

Ingredients for topping:
2 tbsp low carb pasta sauce
2 tbsp mozzarella cheese, shredded
½ tbsp green bell pepper, thinly sliced
1 tsp dried oregano

Instructions:
Heat up the waffle maker.

Add all the chaffle ingredients to a small mixing bowl and combine well.

Pour half of the batter into the waffle maker and cook for about 4 minutes. Repeat with the rest of the batter to make another pizza chaffle.

Once both chaffles are cooked, place them on the baking sheet of the oven.

Put 1 tablespoon of low carb pasta sauce on top of each chaffle.

Sprinkle 1 tablespoon of shredded mozzarella cheese on top of each one.

Top chaffle with green bell peppers and oregano.

Bake at 350° in the oven for about 5 minutes, until the cheese is melted.

Serve and enjoy!

CHAPTER 6:   SWEET CHAFFLE ROLL RECIPES

Chaffle Roll with Cinnamon

Prep Time: 5 minutes
Cook Time: 8 minutes
Servings: 2 chaffles

Ingredients for the chaffles:
½ cup mozzarella cheese
2 tbsp almond flour
¼ tsp baking powder
1 egg
1 tsp cinnamon
1 tsp sweetener
Ingredients for the glaze:
1 tbsp butter

1 tbsp cream cheese
¼ tsp vanilla extract
2 tsp sweetener

Instructions for the chaffles:
Heat up the waffle maker.
Add all the chaffle ingredients to a small mixing bowl and stir until well combined.
Pour half of the batter into the waffle maker and cook for 4 minutes until golden brown. Repeat with the rest of the batter to make another chaffle.
Let cool for 3 minutes to let chaffle get crispy.
In the meantime, mix 1 tablespoon butter and 1 tablespoon of cream cheese in a small bowl. Heat in the microwave for 10-15 seconds until soft enough.

Add the vanilla extract and the sweetener to the butter and cream cheese and mix well using a whisk. Drizzle keto cream cheese glaze on top of chaffle. Roll it.

Serve and enjoy!

Cinnamon Chaffle Roll

Prep Time: 5 minutes
Cook Time: 12 minutes
Servings: 3 chaffles

Ingredients for the chaffles:
1/3 cup shredded mozzarella cheese
4 tbsp cream cheese, softened
1 egg
2 tbsp sweetener
1 tbsp coconut flour
¼ tsp baking powder
¼ tsp cinnamon
½ tsp vanilla extract

Ingredients for the icing:
1 tbsp heavy whipping cream
3 tbsp sweetener
¼ tsp cinnamon

Instructions for the chaffles:
Heat up the waffle maker.

Mix the mozzarella cheese and the cream cheese in a mixing bowl suitable for microwave.

Microwave for 30 seconds until they are melted.

Mix the coconut flour, baking powder, sweetener, cinnamon, and vanilla extract into the cheese mixture until well combined.

Place the dough into a mixing bowl with one egg and beat until smooth.

Add ⅓ of the batter to the waffle maker and cook for approx. 4 minutes until your desired level of doneness has been reached. Repeat with the remaining batter until three chaffles have been made.

Blend the heavy whipping cream and the sweetener until your desired consistency has been reached.

Drizzle the icing over the top of the chaffles and sprinkle with cinnamon. Roll them.

Serve and enjoy!

Blackberry Roll Chaffle

Prep Time: 5 minutes
Cook Time: 16 minutes
Servings: 4 chaffles

Ingredients for the chaffles:
1 egg
1 egg yolk
3 tbsp melted butter
1 tbsp swerve confectioner's sugar substitute
1 cup parmesan cheese, grated
2 tbsp mozzarella cheese, shredded

Ingredients for the cream:
½ cup ricotta cheese
2 tbsp swerve confectioner's sugar substitute
1 tsp vanilla extract
2 tbsp fresh blackberries, chopped

Instructions for the cream:
In a small mixing bowl stir ricotta cheese, vanilla extract and swerve confectioner's sugar substitute until creamy.

Add the blackberries and mix well.

Instructions for chaffles:
Heat up the waffle maker.

Add all the chaffle ingredients to a small mixing bowl and stir until well combined.

Pour 1/4 of the batter into the waffle maker and cook for 4 minutes until brown. Repeat with the rest of the batter to make the other chaffles.

Let cool for 3 minutes to let chaffle get crispy.

Spread some filling on each chaffle and wrap over. Serve and enjoy!

Lemon Icing Chaffle Roll

Prep Time: 5 minutes
Cook Time: 8 minutes
Servings: 2 chaffles

Ingredients for chaffles:
1 large egg, beaten
2 tbsp cream cheese, softened
2 tbsp almond flour
2 tsp sweetener
¼ tsp baking powder

Ingredients for lemon icing:
2 tbsp sweetener
4 tsp heavy cream
1 tsp lemon juice
Fresh lemon zest

Instructions:
Heat up the waffle maker.
Add all the chaffles ingredients to a small mixing bowl and stir until well combined.
Pour half of the batter into the waffle maker and cook for about 4 minutes, until golden brown.
Repeat with the rest of the batter to prepare another chaffle.
Combine in a mixing bowl the sweetener, heavy cream, lemon juice and lemon
zest. Pour over the chaffles and roll them.
Serve and enjoy!

Cherry Chocolate Chaffle Roll

Prep Time: 5 minutes
Cook Time: 8 minutes
Servings: 2 chaffles

Ingredients for chaffles:
½ cup shredded mozzarella cheese
1 tbsp almond flour
1 egg, beaten
¼ tsp cinnamon
½ tbsp sweetener
1 tbsp low carb chocolate chips
1 tbsp dark sweet cherries, halved

Ingredients for roll:
2 tbsp whipped heavy cream, unsweetened
2 tsp sweetener

Instructions:
Heat up the waffle maker.
Add all the ingredients to a small mixing bowl and stir until well combined.
Add half of the batter into the waffle maker and cook it for approx. 4-5 minutes. When the first one is completely done cooking, cook the second one.
Set aside for 1-2 minutes.
Spread the chaffles with whipped heavy cream and sprinkle with sweetener. Roll them.
Serve and enjoy!

Ricotta & Berries Chaffle Roll

Prep Time: 5 minutes
Cook Time: 8 minutes
Servings: 2 chaffles

Ingredients:
1 large egg, beaten
½ cup skim ricotta cheese
1 tbsp almond flour
½ tsp baking powder
1 tbsp fresh blackberries, chopped
1 tbsp fresh raspberries, chopped
2 tbsp sweetener for topping

Instructions:
Heat up the waffle maker.
Add all the ingredients to a small mixing bowl and stir until well combined.
Pour half of the batter into the waffle maker and cook for 4 minutes until golden brown. Repeat with the rest of the batter to make another chaffle.
Let cool for 3 minutes to let chaffle get crispy.
Sprinkle the chaffle with sweetener and roll it.
Serve with keto maple syrup and enjoy!

Peanut Butter Chaffle Roll

Prep Time: 5 minutes
Cook Time: 8 minutes
Servings: 2 chaffles

Ingredients:
1 large egg, beaten
½ cup shredded mozzarella cheese
2 tbsp almond flour
½ tsp baking powder
1 tbsp cream cheese, softened
2 tbsp keto peanut butter for topping

Instructions:
Heat up the waffle maker.
Add all the chaffle ingredients to a small mixing bowl and stir until well combined.
Pour half of the batter into the waffle maker and cook for 4 minutes until golden brown. Repeat with the rest of the batter to make another chaffle.
Spread the chaffle with peanut butter and roll it.

Serve and enjoy!

Buttercream Chaffle Roll

Prep Time: 5 minutes
Cook Time: 8 minutes
Servings: 2 chaffles

Ingredients for chaffles:
1 tbsp almond flour
½ cup mozzarella cheese
1 egg, beaten
1 tbsp sweetener
½ tsp vanilla extract
Ingredients for frosting:
2 tbsp butter, softened
2 tbsp sweetener
¼ tsp vanilla extract
Ingredients for roll:
2 tbsp fresh raspberries, minced
2 tsp cocoa powder, unsweetened

Instruction for frosting:
Mix all the frosting ingredients until the mixture is creamy. Set aside.
Instructions for chaffles:
Heat up the waffle maker.
Add all the chaffle ingredients to a small mixing bowl and combine well.
Pour ½ of the batter into your waffle maker and cook for 4 minutes. Then cook the remaining batter to make another chaffle.
Top the chaffle with buttercream frosting. Add raspberries, sprinkle with cocoa powder and roll it.
Serve and enjoy!

Custard Chaffle Roll

Prep Time: 5 minutes
Cook Time: 55 minutes
Servings: 2 chaffles

Ingredients for chaffles:
2 tbsp almond flour
½ cup mozzarella cheese
1 egg, beaten
1 tbsp sweetener
½ tsp vanilla extract
Ingredients for custard:
2 eggs
2 tbsp heavy cream
1 tbsp brown sugar substitute
½ tsp cinnamon powder
½ tsp vanilla extract
Ingredients for topping:
2 tsp of coconut flour

Instructions for custard:
Preheat the oven at 350°.
Place all ingredients in a small bowl and stir until well combined.
Pour the mixture in a baking tin and bake it for about 40-45 minutes.
Remove from heat and set aside to cool.
Instructions for chaffles:
Heat up the waffle maker.
Add all the chaffle ingredients to a small mixing bowl and combine well.
Pour ½ of the batter into your waffle maker and cook for 4 minutes until golden brown. Then cook the remaining batter to make another chaffle.
Top the chaffles with custard and sprinkle with coconut flour. Roll them.
Serve and enjoy!

CHAPTER 7:   SAVORY CHAFFLE ROLL RECIPES

Olives Chaffle Roll

Prep Time: 5 minutes
Cook Time: 8 minutes
Servings: 2 chaffles

Ingredients:
1 egg, beaten
½ cup of mozzarella cheese, shredded
1 tbsp almond flour
1 tbsp pitted black olives, finely chopped
A pinch of salt and pepper
2 tbsp cream cheese, softened for the roll

Instructions:
Heat up the mini waffle maker.
Add all the ingredients to a small mixing bowl and combine well.
Pour half of the batter into the waffle maker and cook for 4 minutes until brown. Repeat with the rest of the batter to make another chaffle.
Let cool for 3 minutes to let chaffles get crispy.
Spread the chaffle with softened cream cheese and roll it.
Serve with a slice of bacon and enjoy!

Vegetables Chaffle Roll

Prep Time: 5 minutes
Cook Time: 8 minutes
Servings: 2 chaffles

Ingredients:
1 egg
½ tbsp spinach, boiled and chopped
½ cup mozzarella cheese, shredded
1 tsp onion, minced and browned
½ tbsp broccoli, boiled and chopped
1 garlic clove, minced
A pinch of salt and pepper
2 tbsp softened cream cheese for the roll

Instructions:
Heat up the waffle maker.
Add all the ingredients to a small mixing bowl and stir until well combined.
Pour half of the batter into the waffle maker and cook for 4 minutes until brown. Repeat with the rest of the batter to make another chaffle.
Let cool for 3 minutes to let chaffles get crispy.
Spread the chaffle with softened cream cheese and roll it.
Serve with sliced tomato and enjoy!

Chives Chaffle Roll

Prep Time: 5 minutes
Cook Time: 8 minutes
Servings: 2 chaffles

Ingredients for chaffles:
1 large egg, beaten
½ cup of mozzarella cheese, shredded
Ingredients for topping:
1 tbsp chopped fresh chives
2 tbsp keto ketchup
1 hard-boiled egg, smashed

Instructions:
Heat up the waffle maker.
Add all the chaffle ingredients to a small mixing bowl and combine well.

Pour half of the batter into the waffle maker and cook for 4 minutes until brown. Repeat with the rest of the batter to make another chaffle.
Let cool for 3 minutes to let chaffles get crispy.
Spread the chaffle with ketchup, smashed egg and chives. Roll the chaffle.
Serve with sour cream and enjoy!

Basil Chaffle Roll

Prep Time: 5 minutes
Cook Time: 8 minutes
Servings: 2 chaffles

Ingredients for chaffles:
1 large egg, beaten
½ cup of mozzarella cheese, shredded
Ingredients for topping:
1 tbsp chopped fresh basil
2 tbsp keto ketchup
1 hard-boiled egg, smashed

Instructions:
Heat up the waffle maker.
Add all the chaffle ingredients to a small mixing bowl and combine well.
Pour half of the batter into the waffle maker and cook for 4 minutes until brown. Repeat with the rest of the batter to make another chaffle.
Let cool for 3 minutes to let chaffles get crispy.
Spread the chaffle with ketchup, smashed egg and basil. Roll the chaffle.
Serve with sour cream and enjoy!

Parsley Chaffle Roll

Prep Time: 5 minutes
Cook Time: 8 minutes
Servings: 2 chaffles

Ingredients for chaffles:
1 large egg, beaten
½ cup of mozzarella cheese, shredded
Ingredients for topping:
1 tbsp chopped fresh parsley
2 tbsp keto ketchup
1 hard-boiled egg, smashed

Instructions:

Heat up the waffle maker.

Add all the chaffle ingredients to a small mixing bowl and combine well.

Pour half of the batter into the waffle maker and cook for 4 minutes until brown. Repeat with the rest of the batter to make another chaffle.

Let cool for 3 minutes to let chaffles get crispy.

Spread the chaffle with ketchup, smashed egg and parsley. Roll the chaffle.

Serve and enjoy!

Asparagus Chaffle Roll

Prep Time: 10 minutes
Cook Time: 8 minutes
Servings: 2 chaffles

Ingredients for chaffles:

1 egg, beaten
2 asparagus, boiled and finely cut
½ cup parmesan cheese, shredded
¼ cup Provolone cheese, shredded
A pinch of salt and black pepper

Ingredients for roll:

1 large egg, hard-boiled and smashed
1 tbsp of fresh parsley, chopped
2 tbsp of keto mayonnaise

Instructions for chaffle:

Heat up the waffle maker.

Add all the ingredients except for parmesan cheese to a small mixing bowl and combine well.

Pour half of the batter into the waffle maker, sprinkle with 1-2 tbsp of shredded parmesan cheese and cook for 4 minutes. Repeat with the rest of the batter to make another chaffle.

Spread the chaffle with mayonnaise, top with smashed egg and sprinkle with fresh parsley. Roll it. Serve warm and enjoy!

Crabmeat Chaffle Roll

Prep Time: 5 minutes
Cook Time: 8 minutes
Servings: 2 chaffles

Ingredients for chaffles:

1 large egg, beaten
½ cup of mozzarella cheese, shredded
2 tbsp almond flour
¼ tsp baking powder
¼ tsp garlic powder

Ingredients for topping:

¾ cup crabmeat
2 tbsp keto mayonnaise
1 tsp lemon juice

Instructions:

Heat up the waffle maker.

Add all the chaffle ingredients to a small mixing bowl and combine well.

Pour half of the batter into the waffle maker and cook for 4 minutes until brown. Repeat with the rest of the batter to make another chaffle.

In a small bowl mix the crabmeat with mayonnaise and lemon juice.

Top the chaffle with the crabmeat mixture and roll it.

Serve and enjoy!

Peppers Chaffle Roll

Prep Time: 5 minutes
Cook Time: 8 minutes
Servings: 2 chaffles

Ingredients:

1 large egg, beaten
½ cup of mozzarella cheese, shredded
2 tbsp almond flour
¼ tsp baking powder
1 tbsp red bell pepper, minced
1 tbsp yellow bell pepper, minced
1 tsp fresh parsley, minced
2 tbsp cream cheese, softened for topping

Instructions:

Heat up the waffle maker.

Add all the chaffle ingredients to a small mixing bowl and combine well.

Pour half of the batter into the waffle maker and cook for 4 minutes until brown. Repeat with the rest of the batter to make another chaffle.

Let cool for 3 minutes to let chaffles get crispy.

Spread the chaffle with cream cheese and roll it.
Serve and enjoy!

Cauliflower Chaffle Roll

Prep Time: 5 minutes
Cook Time: 8 minutes
Servings: 2 chaffles

Ingredients for chaffles:
1 egg, beaten
½ cup steamed cauliflower mash
¼ cup parmesan cheese, shredded
½ cup mozzarella cheese, shredded
A pinch of salt and black pepper
2 tbsp cream cheese, softened, for topping

Instructions:
Heat up the waffle maker.
Add all the chaffle ingredients except for parmesan cheese to a small mixing bowl and combine well.
Pour half of the batter into the waffle maker, sprinkle with 1-2 tbsp of shredded parmesan cheese and cook for 4 minutes until golden brown. Repeat with the rest of the batter/parmesan to make another chaffle.
Let cool for 3 minutes to let chaffles get crispy.
Spread the chaffle with cream cheese and roll it.
Serve and enjoy!

Paprika & Ham Chaffle Roll

Prep Time: 5 minutes
Cook Time: 8 minutes
Servings: 2 chaffles

Ingredients for chaffles:
1 large egg, beaten
½ cup cheddar cheese, shredded
½ tbsp paprika powder
Ingredients for roll:
2 slices of ham
2 tbsp butter, unsalted
2 tsp fresh basil, minced

Instructions:
Heat up the waffle maker.
Add all the chaffles ingredients to a small mixing bowl and stir until well combined.

Pour half of the batter into the waffle maker and cook for 4 minutes, until brown. Repeat with the rest of the batter to make another chaffle.
Let cool for 3 minutes to let chaffles get crispy.
Spread the chaffle with butter and top with ham. Sprinkle with fresh basil and roll it.
Serve and enjoy!

Fontina Chaffle Roll

Prep Time: 5 minutes
Cook Time: 8 minutes
Servings: 2 chaffles

Ingredients for chaffles:
1 large egg, beaten
½ cup of Fontina cheese, shredded
Ingredients for roll:
2 slices of thin Deli Ham
1 tsp fresh chives, minced
2 tbsp unsalted butter

Instructions:
Heat up the waffle maker.
Add all the chaffle ingredients to a small mixing bowl and combine well.
Pour half of the batter into the waffle maker and cook for 4 minutes until golden brown. Repeat with the rest of the batter to make another chaffle.
Let cool for 3 minutes to let chaffles get crispy.
Spread the chaffle with butter and top with a slice of deli ham. Sprinkle with fresh chives and roll it.
Serve and enjoy!

Egg Salad Chaffle Wrap

Prep Time: 5 minutes
Cook Time: 8 minutes
Servings: 2 chaffles

Ingredients for chaffles:
1 large egg, beaten
½ cup mozzarella cheese, shredded
Ingredients for egg salad:
1 hard-boiled egg, smashed
2 tsp avocado pulp, smashed
2 tsp keto mayonnaise

A pinch of salt and black pepper
Ingredients for wrap:
2 slices of bacon, cooked
1 small tomato, sliced

Instructions for egg salad:
Combine all the salad ingredients in a bowl and mix well.
Instructions for chaffles:
Heat up the waffle maker.
Add all the chaffle ingredients to a small mixing bowl and stir until well combined.
Pour half of the batter into the waffle maker and cook for 4 minutes until golden brown. Repeat with the rest of the batter to make another chaffle.
Let cool for 3 minutes to let chaffles get crispy.
Spread the chaffle with egg salad. Top with bacon and tomato slices. Wrap it.
Serve and enjoy!

Chaffle Tasty Wrap

Prep Time: 5 minutes
Cook Time: 8 minutes
Servings: 2 chaffles

Ingredients:
1 large egg, beaten
½ cup mozzarella cheese, shredded
Ingredients for wrap:
Iceland lettuce leaves
2 slices of cheddar cheese
2 slices of turkey
2 slices of ham
2 slices of pepperoni
1 tsp dried oregano

Instructions:
Heat up the waffle maker.
Add all the chaffle ingredients to a small mixing bowl and stir until well combined.
Pour half of the batter into the waffle maker and cook for 4 minutes until golden brown. Repeat with the rest of the batter to make another chaffle.
Let cool for 3 minutes to let chaffles get crispy.
Top the chaffle with lettuce, a slice of cheddar cheese, a slice of turkey, a slice of ham, a slice of

pepperoni. Sprinkle with dried oregano and wrap the chaffle.
Serve with sour cream and enjoy!

Peppers Sauce Wrap

Prep Time: 5 minutes
Cook Time: 8 minutes
Servings: 2 chaffles

Ingredients:
1 large egg, beaten
½ cup mozzarella cheese, shredded
Ingredients for roasted pepper sauce:
2 tbsp roasted yellow peppers
2 tbsp mayonnaise
¼ tsp garlic powder
1 tbsp olive oil
¼ tsp red hot pepper powder
1 tbs capers

Instructions for sauce:
Mix in a blender all the sauce ingredients and set aside.
Instructions for chaffles:
Heat up the waffle maker.
Add all the chaffle ingredients to a small mixing bowl and stir until well combined.
Pour half of the batter into the waffle maker and cook for 4 minutes until golden brown. Repeat with the rest of the batter to make another chaffle.
Let cool for 3 minutes to let chaffles get crispy.
Spread the chaffle with the peppers cream. Roll it.
Serve with sour cream and enjoy!

Provolone Chaffle Wrap

Prep Time: 5 minutes
Cook Time: 8 minutes
Servings: 2 chaffles

Ingredients for chaffles:
1 large egg, beaten
½ cup of Provolone cheese, shredded
Ingredients for roll:
2 slices of Ham
1 tsp fresh basil, minced

2 tbsp unsalted butter

Instructions:

Heat up the waffle maker.

Add all the chaffle ingredients to a small mixing bowl and combine well.

Pour half of the batter into the waffle maker and cook for 4 minutes until golden brown. Repeat with the rest of the batter to make another chaffle.

Let cool for 3 minutes to let chaffles get crispy.

Spread the chaffle with butter and top with a slice of ham. Sprinkle with fresh basil and roll it.

Serve and enjoy!

Garlic Bacon Chaffle Roll

Prep Time: 5 minutes
Cook Time: 8 minutes
Servings: 2 chaffles

Ingredients for chaffles:

1 egg, beaten
½ cup shredded mozzarella cheese
¼ tsp garlic powder

Ingredients for roll:

2 tbsp cream cheese, softened
2-4 slices of bacon, cooked

Instructions:

Heat up the waffle maker.

Add egg, shredded mozzarella cheese and garlic powder to a small mixing bowl and combine well.

Pour half of the batter into the waffle maker and cook for 4 minutes. Repeat with the rest of the batter to make another chaffle.

Let cool for 3 minutes to let chaffles get crispy.

Spread the chaffle with cream cheese and top with bacon. Roll it.

Serve with keto BBQ sauce and enjoy!

Chaffle Wrap with Herbs Cream

Prep Time: 5 minutes
Cook Time: 8 minutes
Servings: 2 chaffles

Ingredients for chaffles:

1 egg, beaten
½ cup shredded cheddar cheese
A pinch of salt

Ingredients for herbs cream:

2 tbsp cream cheese, softened
1 tsp fresh basil, chopped
½ tsp dried oregano
½ tsp dried thyme
½ tsp fresh coriander, chopped

Instructions for cream:

In a small bowl, whisk cream cheese and herbs until smoothy. Set aside.

Instructions for chaffles:

Heat up the waffle maker.

Add all the chaffle ingredients to a small mixing bowl and combine well.

Pour half of the batter into the waffle maker and cook for 4 minutes until golden brown. Repeat with the rest of the batter to make another chaffle.

Let cool for 3 minutes to let chaffles get crispy.

Spread the chaffle with herbs cream. Roll it.

Serve with sliced cucumber and enjoy!

Swiss Cheese Pumpkin Chaffle Wrap

Prep Time: 5 minutes
Cook Time: 8 minutes
Servings: 2 chaffles

Ingredients:

1 large egg, beaten
½ cup grated mozzarella cheese
1 tbsp pumpkin puree
½ tsp pumpkin spice
½ tbsp almond flour
A pinch of salt and black pepper
2 slices of Swiss cheese for wrap

Instructions:

Heat up the waffle maker.

Add all the ingredients to a large mixing bowl and stir until well combined.

Pour half of the batter into the waffle maker and cook for 4 minutes until golden brown. Repeat with the rest of the batter to make another chaffle.

Top the chaffle with a slice of Swiss cheese. Season with salt and pepper to taste. Roll it.

Serve and enjoy!

Tuna Salad Chaffle Roll

Prep Time: 5 minutes
Cook Time: 8 minutes
Servings: 2 chaffles

Ingredients for chaffles:
1 large egg, beaten
½ cup mozzarella cheese, shredded
Ingredients for tuna salad:
1 can tuna, drained
1 tbsp keto mayonnaise
2 tbsp cream cheese, softened
1 tsp capers
½ tsp paprika powder
A pinch of salt and black pepper
Ingredients for wrap:
Lettuce leaves
2 tsp fresh parsley, minced

Instructions for tuna salad:
Combine all the salad ingredients in a bowl and mix well.
Instructions for chaffles:
Heat up the waffle maker.
Add all the chaffle ingredients to a small mixing bowl and stir until well combined.
Pour half of the batter into the waffle maker and cook for 4 minutes until golden brown. Repeat with the rest of the batter to make another chaffle.
Let cool for 3 minutes to let chaffles get crispy.
Top the chaffle with lettuce and tuna salad. Sprinkle with fresh parsley. Roll it.
Serve and enjoy!

Chicken and Bacon Butter Chaffle Roll

Prep Time: 5 minutes
Cook Time: 8 minutes
Servings: 2 chaffles

Ingredients for chaffle:
1 large egg, beaten
½ cup of mozzarella cheese, shredded
½ cup cooked chicken, chopped
2 tbsp almond flour
¼ tsp baking powder
Ingredients for bacon butter:
2 tbsp butter, softened
1 tbsp scallion, browned and chopped
1 tbsp bacon, browned and chopped
1 tsp basil, minced
½ tsp tomato paste
A pinch of salt and black pepper

Instructions for bacon butter:
In a small mixing bowl, combine all the ingredients and stir well. Set aside.
Instructions for chaffles:
Heat up the waffle maker.
Add all the chaffle ingredients to a small mixing bowl and combine well.
Pour half of the batter into the waffle maker and cook for 4 minutes until brown. Repeat with the rest of the batter to make another chaffle.
Let cool for 3 minutes to let chaffles get crispy.
Spread the chaffle with bacon butter and roll it.
Serve and enjoy!

Blue Cheese Butter & Bacon Chaffle Wrap

Prep Time: 5 minutes
Cook Time: 8 minutes
Servings: 2 chaffles

Ingredients for chaffles:
1 large egg, beaten
½ cup of mozzarella cheese, shredded
2 tbsp almond flour
¼ tsp baking powder
Ingredients for Blue cheese butter:
1 tbsp butter, softened
2 tbsp Blue cheese, shredded
1 tsp fresh basil, chopped
A pinch of salt and black pepper
Ingredients for topping:
2 slices of bacon, browned
Lettuce leaves

Instructions for Blue cheese butter:
In a small mixing bowl, combine all the ingredients and stir well. Set aside.
Instructions for chaffles:

Heat up the waffle maker.

Add all the chaffle ingredients to a small mixing bowl and combine well.

Pour half of the batter into the waffle maker and cook for 4 minutes until brown. Repeat with the rest of the batter to make another chaffle.

Let cool for 3 minutes to let chaffles get crispy.

Spread the chaffle with Blue cheese butter. Top with lettuce and bacon. Wrap it.

Serve and enjoy!

Curry Chaffle Wrap

Prep Time: 5 minutes
Cook Time: 8 minutes
Servings: 2 chaffles

Ingredients for chaffles:

1 egg, beaten
½ cup shredded mozzarella cheese
¼ tsp curry powder
½ tbsp fresh basil, finely chopped
A pinch of salt and pepper

Ingredients for wrap:

2 tbsp cream cheese
Lettuce leaves

Instructions:

Heat up the waffle maker.

Add egg, shredded mozzarella cheese, curry powder and basil to a small mixing bowl and combine well.

Pour half of the batter into the waffle maker and cook for 4 minutes until brown. Repeat with the rest of the batter to make another chaffle. Season with salt and pepper.

Spread the chaffle with cream cheese and top with lettuce. Wrap it.

Serve and enjoy!

CHAPTER 8:   CHAFFLES CAKE RECIPES

Mint Chaffles Cake

Prep Time: 5 minutes
Cook Time: 16 minutes
Servings: 4 chaffles

Ingredients for chaffles:
2 tbsp almond flour
1 cup mozzarella cheese, shredded
2 eggs, beaten
2 tbsp sweetener
1 tsp vanilla extract
8 chopped mint leaves
A pinch of salt

Ingredients for filling:
3 fresh chopped strawberries
½ tbsp sweetener
2 tbsp keto whipped cream

Instructions for filling:
Place the strawberries in a bowl and add ½ tablespoon of sweetener. Mix and set aside.

Instructions for chaffles:
Heat up the waffle maker.
Add all the ingredients to a small mixing bowl and combine well.

Pour ¼ of the batter into your waffle maker and cook for 4 minutes until golden brown. Then cook the remaining batter to prepare the other chaffles. Assemble the cake by placing whipped cream and strawberries on top of your mint chaffles. Then drizzle the juice that will also be in the bowl with the strawberries on top.
Serve and enjoy!

Coconut Chaffles Cake

Prep Time: 5 minutes
Cook Time: 16 minutes
Servings: 4 chaffles

Ingredients for chaffles:
8 tbsp cream cheese
4 eggs, beaten
4 tbsp coconut flour
1 tsp baking powder
1 tbsp butter, melted
2 tsp vanilla
1 tbsp sweetener
Ingredients for filling:
4 tbsp keto whipped cream
½ cup fresh blueberries
4 tsp sweetener

Instructions:
Heat up the waffle maker.
Add all the chaffles ingredients to a small mixing bowl and combine well.
Pour 1/4 of the batter into your waffle maker and cook for 4 minutes until golden brown. Then cook the remaining batter to make the other chaffles.
Top the chaffle with whipped cream and blueberries. Cover with another chaffle and repeat the procedure. Sprinkle the cake with sweetener.
Serve and enjoy!

Cocoa Chaffles Cake

Prep Time: 5 minutes
Cook Time: 8 minutes
Servings: 2 chaffles

Ingredients:
1 egg, beaten
½ cup of cheese
2 tbsp cocoa powder
2 tbsp sweetener
1 tbsp whipping cream
1 tbsp almond flour
½ tsp vanilla extract
¼ tsp baking powder
Ingredients for the cream frosting:
2 tbsp cream cheese, softened
2 tsp sweetener
1/8 tsp vanilla extract
1 tsp heavy cream

Instructions for chaffles:
Whisk cocoa powder, sweetener, almond flour, and baking powder in a medium mixing bowl.
Add in the vanilla extract and whipping cream. Mix well.
Add in the egg and cheese and mix well.
Set aside and heat up the mini waffle maker.
Add half of the mixture to the waffle maker and cook for about 4-5 minutes. Repeat with the rest of the batter to make the second chaffle.
Instructions for the cream frosting:
Add in the whipping cream, the cream cheese and the vanilla extract and mix well.
Add in the sweetener, mix well to fluffy the frosting.
To assemble the cake:
Place the first chaffle on a plate and top with a layer of cream frosting.
Put the second chaffle on top of the frosting layer and spread the rest of the frosting on top.
Serve and enjoy!

Orange Frosting Chaffles Cake

Prep Time: 5 minutes
Cook Time: 16 minutes
Servings: 4 chaffles

Ingredients for chaffles:
2 tbsp almond flour
1 cup mozzarella cheese
2 eggs, beaten
1 tsp vanilla extract

152

1 tsp sweetener

Ingredients for glaze:

1 tbsp unsalted butter, softened

1 tbsp sweetener

2 tbsp cream cheese, softened

¼ tsp orange extract

Ingredients for filling:

3-4 tbsp fresh blueberries

Instructions for glaze:

Add all the ingredients in a blender and whisk until creamy.

Instructions for chaffles:

Heat up the waffle maker.

Add all the chaffles ingredients to a small mixing bowl and combine well.

Pour ¼ of the batter into your waffle maker and cook for 4 minutes until brown. Then cook the remaining batter to make the other chaffles.

Spread the first chaffle with orange frosting and top it with blueberries. Cover with another chaffle and proceed with layers in the same way.

Serve and enjoy!

Strawberry Chaffles Cake

Prep Time: 5 minutes

Cook Time: 12 minutes

Servings: 3 chaffles

Ingredients for chaffles:

1 tbsp almond flour

½ cup mozzarella cheese

1 egg, beaten

1 tbsp sweetener

¼ tsp vanilla extract

Keto whipped cream

Ingredients for strawberry topping:

3 fresh chopped strawberries

½ tsp sweetener

Instructions:

Heat up the waffle maker.

Add the almond flour, egg, mozzarella cheese, sweetener, and vanilla extract to a small mixing bowl and combine well.

Pour 1/3 of the batter into your waffle maker and cook for 4 minutes. Then cook the remaining batter to make the other chaffles.

Place the strawberries in a bowl and add ½ tablespoon of sweetener. Mix and set aside.

Make your keto whipped cream if you do not have any on hand.

Assemble the cake by placing whipped cream and strawberries on top of your sweet chaffle. Then drizzle the juice that will also be in the bowl with the strawberries on top.

Serve and enjoy!

Sweet Chaffles Cake

Prep Time: 5 minutes

Cook Time: 16 minutes

Servings: 4 chaffles

Ingredients for chaffles:

2eggs, beaten

1 cup mozzarella cheese, shredded

2 tbsp cocoa powder, unsweetened

4 tbsp almond flour

Ingredients for cake:

2 tbsp whipped cream, unsweetened

2 tbsp fresh raspberries

2 tsp coconut flour

Instructions:

Heat up the waffle maker.

Add all the chaffles ingredients to a small mixing bowl and stir until well combined.

Pour ¼ of the batter into the waffle maker and cook for 4 minutes until golden brown. Repeat with the rest of the batter to make the other chaffles.

Spread the chaffle with whipped cream and raspberries. Sprinkle with coconut flour and cover with another chaffle. Repeat with the other chaffles/topping.

Serve and enjoy!

Raspberries Chaffles Cake

Prep Time: 5 minutes

Cook Time: 12 minutes

Servings: 3 chaffles

Ingredients for chaffles:
1 tbsp almond flour
½ cup mozzarella cheese
1 egg
1 tbsp sweetener
¼ tsp vanilla extract
Keto whipped cream
Ingredients for raspberries topping:
10 fresh chopped raspberries
½ tbsp sweetener

Instructions:
Heat up the waffle maker.
Add the almond flour, egg, mozzarella cheese, sweetener, and vanilla extract to a small mixing bowl and combine well.
Pour 1/3 of the batter into your waffle maker and cook for 4 minutes. Then cook the remaining batter to make the other chaffles.
Place the raspberries in a bowl and add 1/2 tablespoon of sweetener. Mix and set aside.
Make your keto whipped cream if you do not have any on hand.
Assemble the cake by placing whipped cream and raspberries on top of your sweet chaffle. Then drizzle the juice that will also be in the bowl with the raspberries on top.
Serve and enjoy!

Chocolate Chaffles Cake

Prep Time: 5 minutes
Cook Time: 16 minutes
Servings: 4 chaffles

Ingredients for chaffles:
2 eggs
1 tbsp butter, melted
1 tbsp softened cream cheese
2 tbsp unsweetened cocoa powder
2 tbsp almond flour
2 tsp coconut flour
2 tbsp sweetener
½ tsp baking powder
½ tsp instant coffee granules dissolved in 1 tablespoon hot water
½ tsp vanilla extract

A pinch of salt
Ingredients for chaffles filling:
1 egg yolk
¼ cup heavy cream
2 tbsp sweetener
1 tbsp butter
½ tsp caramel
¼ cup pecans, chopped
¼ cup unsweetened flaked coconut
1 teaspoon coconut flour

Instructions for chaffles:
Heat up the mini waffle maker.
Add all the chaffles ingredients to a small mixing bowl and mix well.
Pour ¼ of the batter into the waffle maker and cook for 4 minutes. Repeat with the rest of the batter to make 3 more chaffles.
Let cool for 3 minutes to let chaffles get crispy.
Instructions for chaffles filling:
Combine the egg yolk, heavy cream, butter, and sweetener in a pan over medium heat.
Simmer slowly for approx. 4 minutes.
Remove from heat and stir in extract, pecans, flaked coconut, and coconut flour.
Spread the filling between chaffles.
Serve and enjoy!

Peanut Butter Chaffles Cake

Prep Time: 5 minutes
Cook Time: 8 minutes
Servings: 2 chaffles

Ingredients for chaffles:
1 large egg, beaten
½ cup shredded mozzarella cheese
2 tbsp almond flour
½ tsp baking powder
1 tbsp cream cheese, softened
Ingredients for topping:
2 tbsp keto peanut butter
2 tsp sweetener
2 tbsp blackberries, chopped

Instructions:
Heat up the waffle maker.

Add all the chaffles ingredients to a small mixing bowl and stir until well combined.

Pour half of the batter into the waffle maker and cook for 4 minutes until golden brown. Repeat with the rest of the batter to make another chaffle.

Spread the chaffle with peanut butter and blackberries. Sprinkle with sweetener. Top with another chaffle and repeat the topping.

Serve with ice-cream and enjoy!

Lime Chaffles Cake

Prep Time: 5 minutes
Cook Time: 8 minutes
Servings: 2 chaffles

Ingredients for chaffles:
1 tbsp heavy whipping cream
1 tsp sweetener
¼ cup almond flour
1 egg
2 tsp cream cheese
½ tsp baking powder
½ tsp lime juice
½ tsp lime zest

Ingredients for icing:
4 tbsp cream cheese
4 tbsp butter
2 tsp sweetener
1 tsp lime juice

Instructions for icing:
In a small bowl, whisk all the icing ingredients until creamy.

Instructions for chaffles:
Heat up the mini waffle maker.

Mix all the ingredients in a small mixing bowl and blend until creamy.

Pour half of the batter into the waffle maker and cook for about 4 minutes until brown. Repeat with the remaining batter to prepare another chaffle.

Spoon the chaffle with the lime frosting and cover with another chaffle.

Serve with sweetener and enjoy!

White Chocolate Chaffles Cake

Prep Time: 5 minutes
Cook Time: 16 minutes
Servings: 4 chaffles

Ingredients for chaffles:
2 eggs
1 tbsp butter, melted
1 tbsp softened cream cheese
2 tbsp unsweetened white chocolate chips
2 tbsp almond flour
2 tsp coconut flour
2 tbsp sweetener
½ tsp baking powder
½ tsp instant coffee granules dissolved in 1 tablespoon hot water
½ tsp vanilla extract
A pinch of salt

Ingredients for chaffles filling:
1 egg yolk
¼ cup heavy cream
2 tbsp sweetener
1 tbsp butter
½ tsp caramel
¼ cup pecans, chopped
¼ cup unsweetened flaked coconut
1 tsp coconut flour

Instructions for chaffles:
Heat up the mini waffle maker.

Add all the chaffles ingredients to a small mixing bowl and mix well.

Pour 1/4 of the batter into the waffle maker and cook for 4 minutes. Repeat with the rest of the batter to make 3 more chaffles.

Let cool for 3 minutes to let chaffles get crispy.

Instructions for chaffles filling:
Combine the egg yolk, heavy cream, butter and sweetener in a pan over medium heat.

Simmer slowly for approx. 4 minutes.

Remove from heat and stir in caramel, pecans, flaked coconut, and coconut flour.

Spread the filling between chaffles.

Serve and enjoy!

Caramel Chaffles Cake

Prep Time: 4 minutes
Cook Time: 16 minutes
Servings: 4 chaffles

Ingredients for chaffles:
2 eggs, beaten
1 cup mozzarella cheese, grated
2 tsp coconut flour
2 tsp water
½ tsp baking powder

Ingredients for filling:
4 tbsp keto caramel sauce
4 tbsp coconut whipped cream
1 tsp coconut flakes

Instructions:
Heat up the waffle maker.
Add all the chaffles ingredients to a small mixing bowl and combine well.
Pour 1/4 of the batter into the waffle maker and cook for 4 minutes until brown. Repeat with the rest of the batter to prepare the other chaffles.
Let cool for 3 minutes to let chaffles get crispy.
Top the chaffle with caramel sauce and whipped cream. Cover with another chaffle and repeat the procedure.
Serve with coconut flakes and enjoy!

Pumpkin Chaffles Cake

Prep Time: 5 minutes
Cook Time: 8 minutes
Servings: 2 chaffles

Ingredients for chaffles:
1 egg, beaten
½ cup mozzarella cheese, shredded
1 tbsp almond flour
½ tsp baking powder
¼ cup pumpkin puree
1 tbsp heavy cream
1 tsp cream cheese
½ tsp vanilla extract

Ingredients for filling cake:
2 tbsp cream cheese, softened

1 tbsp sweetener
½ tsp vanilla extract
1 tsp keto maple syrup

Instructions for cake filling:
Whisk all the ingredients until creamy.

Instructions for chaffles:
Heat up the waffle maker.
Add all the chaffles ingredients to a small mixing bowl and stir until well combined.
Pour half of the batter into the waffle maker and cook for 4 minutes until golden brown. Repeat with the rest of the batter to make another chaffle.
Let cool for 3 minutes to let chaffles get crispy.
Spread the chaffle with cream and cover with another chaffle. Sprinkle with sweetener or cocoa powder.
Serve and enjoy!

Strawberry Chaffles Cake with Frosting

Prep Time: 5 minutes
Cook Time: 12 minutes
Servings: 3 chaffles

Ingredients for chaffles:
½ cup mozzarella cheese
1 egg, beaten
1 tbsp cream cheese
¼ tsp baking powder
2 fresh strawberries, sliced
1 tsp strawberry extract

Ingredients for frosting:
¼ tbsp strawberry extract
1 tbsp cream cheese
1 tbsp sweetener

Ingredients for the whipped cream:
1 tsp vanilla
1 tbsp sweetener
1 cup heavy whipping cream

Instructions:
Heat up the waffle maker.
Add all the ingredients to a small mixing bowl and combine well.
Pour 1/3 of the batter into your waffle maker and cook for 4 minutes until golden brown. Then cook the remaining batter to make the other chaffles.

156

In a small mixing bowl whisk the ingredients for the whipped cream until fluffy.

Prepare the frosting by mixing the whipping cream with vanilla and the sweetener.

Assemble the cake by placing whipped cream and strawberries on top of your sweet chaffle. Then drizzle the juice that will also be in the bowl with the strawberries on top.

Serve and enjoy!

CHAPTER 9: CHAFFLES SANDWICH RECIPES

Ham and Cheese Chaffles Sandwich

Prep Time: 5 minutes
Cook Time: 8 minutes
Servings: 2 chaffles

Ingredients for chaffles:
1 egg
½ cup shredded mozzarella cheese
Fresh basil to taste
A pinch of salt and pepper
Ingredients for filling:
1 slice of ham
1 slice American cheese
1 tomato, sliced
1 lettuce leaf
1 tbsp keto butter

Instructions:
Heat up the waffle maker.
Add all the chaffles ingredients to a small mixing bowl and combine well.
Pour half of the batter into the waffle maker and cook for 4 minutes until brown. Repeat with the rest of the batter to make another chaffle.
Spread butter over the chaffle; top with a slice of ham, lettuce, tomato and American cheese. Cover with another chaffle.

Serve and enjoy!

Turkey Patties & Vegetables Chaffles Sandwich

Prep Time: 10 minutes
Cook Time: 30 minutes
Servings: 4 chaffles

Ingredients for chaffles:
2 eggs, beaten
1 cup cheddar cheese, shredded
A pinch of salt and pepper
Ingredients for patties and filling:
2 cups ground turkey
Lettuce leaves
1 tomato, sliced
1 onion, sliced and browned
1 sliced grilled zucchini
Keto BBQ sauce
1 tbsp olive oil
A pinch of salt and pepper

Instructions for the chaffles:
Heat up the waffle maker.
Add all the chaffles ingredients to a small mixing bowl and stir until well combined.
Pour ¼ of the batter into the waffle maker and cook for 4 minutes until golden brown. Repeat with the rest of the batter to prepare the other chaffles.
Let cool for 3 minutes to let chaffles get crispy.
Instructions for the patties:
In a small bowl, season the ground turkey with salt and pepper.
Create small patties.
In a saucepan over low heat, cook the turkey patties in olive oil until completely cooked and brown.
Instructions for topping:
Spread each chaffle with Keto BBQ sauce. Garnish with lettuce, tomato, onion, zucchini and the patty.
Cover with another chaffle.
Serve and enjoy!

Gourmet Chaffles Sandwich

Prep Time: 5 minutes

Cook Time: 8 minutes
Servings: 2 chaffles

Ingredients for the chaffles:
1 egg
½ cup shredded Cheddar cheese
Ingredients for the sandwich:
2 strips bacon
1-2 slices tomato
1-2 lettuce leaves
1 tbsp mayonnaise
Instructions:
Heat up the waffle maker.
Mix egg and shredded cheese in a small mixing bowl. Pour half of the batter into the waffle maker and cook for 4 minutes. Repeat with the rest of the batter to make another chaffle.
Let cool for 3 minutes to let chaffles get crispy.
In a pan over medium heat, cook the bacon until crispy.
Assemble the sandwich topping the chaffle with bacon, lettuce, tomato, and mayonnaise.
Serve and enjoy!

U.S.A. Chaffles Sandwich

Prep Time: 5 minutes
Cook Time: 8 minutes
Servings: 2 chaffles

Ingredients for the chaffles:
1 egg
½ cup shredded Cheddar cheese
Ingredients for the sandwich:
2 strips bacon
1 egg
1-2 slices tomato
1 slice American cheese

Instructions:
Heat up the waffle maker.
Mix egg and shredded cheese in a small mixing bowl. Pour half of the batter into the waffle maker and cook for 4 minutes. Repeat with the rest of the batter to make another chaffle.
Let cool for 3 minutes to let chaffles get crispy.
In a pan over medium heat, cook the bacon until crispy.

In the same skillet, in 1 tbsp of reserved bacon drippings, fry the egg over medium heat.

Assemble the sandwich, serve and enjoy!

Big Chaffles Burger

Prep Time: 9 minutes
Cook Time: 20 minutes
Servings: 4 chaffles

Ingredients for the chaffles:
2 eggs
1 cup shredded mozzarella cheese
¼ tsp garlic powder
Ingredients for the cheeseburgers:
½ cup ground beef
½ tsp garlic powder
2 slices American cheese
Ingredients for the sauce:
2 tsp mayonnaise
1 tsp ketchup
1 tsp dill pickle relish
Ingredients to assemble:
1-2 lettuce leaves, shredded
2 dill pickles
1 tsp onion, minced

Instructions to make the burgers:
Heat a griddle over medium heat.
Divide the ground beef into 2 balls and place each on the griddle. Let cook for 1 minute.
Flatten the meat and sprinkle it with garlic powder.
Cook 2 minutes or until halfway cooked through.
Flip the burgers carefully and sprinkle with remaining garlic powder. Continue cooking until cooked through.
Place one slice of cheese over each burger and then stack the burgers and set aside.
Instructions to make the chaffles and assemble the burger:
Heat up the waffle maker.
Mix the egg, cheese, and garlic powder in a small mixing bowl.
Pour ¼ of the batter into the waffle maker and cook for 4 minutes. Repeat with the rest of the batter to make the other chaffles.

Prepare the sauce whisking together all the ingredients.
Top one chaffle with the stacked burger patties, shredded lettuce, pickles, and onions. Cover with another chaffle.
Serve with the sauce and enjoy!

Tuna Chaffles Sandwich

Prep Time: 10 minutes
Cook Time: 8 minutes
Servings: 2 chaffles

Ingredients for chaffles:
1 egg, beaten
1 cup tomatoes, chopped
¼ cup parmesan cheese, shredded
½ cup swiss cheese, shredded
1 tsp fresh basil
A pinch of salt and pepper
Ingredients for filling:
A can of drained tuna
Lettuce leaf
1 tbsp keto mayonnaise

Instructions:
Heat up the waffle maker.
Add all the chaffles ingredients except for parmesan cheese to a small mixing bowl and combine well.
Pour half of the batter into the waffle maker, sprinkle with 1-2 tbsp of shredded parmesan cheese and cook for 4 minutes. Repeat with the rest of the batter to make another chaffle.
Let cool for 3 minutes to let chaffles get crispy.
Spread the chaffle with keto mayonnaise, top with drained tuna, a lettuce leaf and cover with the other chaffle.
Serve and enjoy!

Philadelphia Chaffles Sandwich

Prep Time: 5 minutes
Cook Time: 30 minutes
Servings: 8 chaffles

Ingredients for the chaffles:
8 tbsp cheesesteak meat

½ onion, sliced
½ bell pepper, sliced
1 tsp Worcestershire sauce
1 tbsp mozzarella cheese
Ingredients for the chaffles:
2 cups mozzarella cheese, shredded
4 eggs, beaten
¼ tsp garlic powder

Instructions:
Heat up the mini waffle maker.
Add all the chaffles ingredients to a small mixing bowl and whisk well to combine.
Pour 1/8 of the batter into the waffle maker and cook for 4 minutes. Repeat with the rest of the batter to make 7 more chaffles.
Let cool for 3 minutes to let chaffles get crispy.
On a pan over medium heat cook the cheesesteak meat until browned. Remove.
Cook the onions and peppers in the same saucepan until tendered.
Return the meat to the pan with the vegetables, stir in the Worcestershire sauce.
Top the chaffles with a serving of meat mixture, add mozzarella cheese and top with an additional chaffle to form a sandwich.
Serve and enjoy!

Mexican Chaffles Sandwich

Prep Time: 15 minutes
Cook Time: 8 minutes
Servings: 2 chaffles

Ingredients for the chaffles:
1 cup mozzarella cheese, grated
2 eggs
A pinch of salt
Spices to taste
2 slices chorizo for the filling, very thin
Ingredients for the avocado cream:
1 small avocado pulp, mashed
1 tbsp cherry tomatoes, diced
1 tsp onions, sliced
2 tbsp olive oil
1 tbsp lemon juice
A pinch of salt and pepper

A pinch of Chili powder
Instructions for the avocado cream:
In a small bowl, add the olive oil and lemon juice to the avocado and stir.
Add onions, and tomatoes, mix well and season with salt, pepper, and chili to taste.
Instructions for the chaffles:
Heat up the waffle maker.
Add all the chaffles ingredients except chorizo to a small mixing bowl. Stir until well combined.
Pour half of the batter into the waffle maker and cook for 4 minutes. Repeat with the rest of the batter to make another chaffle.
Let cool for 3 minutes to let chaffles get crispy.
Spread avocado cream on a chaffle and cover with chorizo, then put another chaffle on top.
Serve and enjoy!

Avocado Chaffles Toast

Prep Time: 5 minutes
Cook Time: 16 minutes
Servings: 4 chaffles

Ingredients for chaffles:
2 eggs
1 cup cheese, shredded
4 tbsp avocado, pulp
1 tsp lemon juice
A pinch of salt and pepper
Ingredients for topping:
2 eggs
½ avocado, sliced
1 tomato, sliced

Instructions:
Combine the avocado pulp with lemon juice, salt and pepper in a small mixing bowl.
Beat the eggs with the avocado cream.
Heat up the waffle maker.
Pour ¼ of the batter into the waffle maker and cook for 4 minutes until golden brown. Repeat with the rest of the batter to make the other chaffles.
Let cool for 3 minutes to let chaffles get crispy.
In the meantime, in a small saucepan fry the eggs.
Top every chaffle with fried egg, tomatoes and avocado slices. Cover with another chaffle.
Serve and enjoy!

Shrimps Green Chaffles Sandwich

Prep Time: 15 minutes
Cook Time: 24 minutes
Servings: 8 chaffles

Ingredients for chaffles:
4 eggs, beaten
2 cups mozzarella cheese, shredded
1 tsp your favorite spices

Ingredients for filling:
4 tbsp shrimps, deveined and cooked
4 slices bacon cooked
1 avocado, sliced
¼ cup onion, sliced
A pinch of salt and pepper

Instructions for chaffles:
Heat up the mini waffle maker.
Add all the chaffles ingredients to a small mixing bowl and stir until well combined.
Pour 1/8 of the batter into the waffle maker and cook for 4 minutes. Repeat with the rest of the batter to make the other chaffles.
Let cool for 3 minutes to let chaffles get crispy.

Instructions to assemble the sandwich:
Top the chaffle with a slice of bacon, shrimps, avocado and onion. Add salt, pepper and your favorite spices to taste. Cover with another chaffle. Serve with keto mayonnaise or sour cream and enjoy!

Salmon Chaffles Sandwich

Prep Time: 5 minutes
Cook Time: 16 minutes
Servings: 4 chaffles

Ingredients for chaffles:
2 cans of salmon, drained
1 cup almond flour
2 eggs
1 jalapeño, diced
A pinch of salt
1 cup onion, diced
1 pepper, diced
1 tsp garlic powder
1 tsp lemon juice

Ingredients for filling:
2 tbsp keto mayonnaise
1 cup carrots, matchstick cut
1 tbsp Greek yogurt
2 lettuce leaves

Instructions for chaffles:
Heat up the waffle maker.
Add all the chaffles ingredients to a small mixing bowl and stir until well combined.
Pour ¼ of the batter into the waffle maker and cook for 4 minutes until brown. Repeat with the rest of the batter to prepare the other chaffles.
Let cool for 3 minutes to let chaffles get crispy.

Instructions to assemble the sandwich:
Top a chaffle with lettuce, carrots, Greek yogurt, keto mayonnaise, and cover with another chaffle. Serve and enjoy!

Fish and Cajun Slaw Chaffles Sandwich

Prep Time: 12 minutes
Cook Time: 26 minutes
Servings: 4 chaffles

Ingredients for chaffles:
2 eggs, beaten
2 tbsp almond flour
2 tbsp full-fat plain Greek yogurt
¼ tsp baking powder
1 cup shredded cheddar cheese

Ingredients for Cajun slaw:
1 cup coleslaw
3 tbsp keto mayonnaise
1 tbsp Greek yogurt
1 tsp Tabasco sauce
½ tsp Cajun seasoning

Ingredients for fish:
¼ cup avocado oil
2 small flounder
¼ cup heavy cream
½ tsp lemon juice
1/3 cup shredded parmesan cheese
1/3 cup pork rind crumbs
½ tsp garlic powder
A pinch of black pepper

Instructions for chaffles:
Heat up the mini waffle maker.
Mix all the chaffles ingredients to a small mixing bowl and stir until well combined.
Pour ¼ of the batter into the waffle maker and cook for 4 minutes. Repeat with the rest of the batter to make the other chaffles.
Let cool for 3 minutes to let chaffles get crispy.
Instructions for Cajun slaw:
Add all the ingredients to a small bowl and mix well.
Instructions for fish:
In a saucepan heat oil over medium-high heat.
Mix the heavy cream and lemon juice in a small bowl until it thickens.
In a separate bowl, combine the parmesan cheese, pork rind crumbs, garlic powder, and pepper until mixed.
Dip the fish filet in the cream mixture, then sprinkle with crumbs.
Place it into the oil and repeat with the remaining fish filet. Cook for about 5 minutes, until golden brown.
Instructions to assemble the chaffles sandwich:
Top the chaffle with a fish filet, the slaw, and then top with another chaffle.
Serve and enjoy!

Tex Chaffles Sandwich

Prep Time: 5 minutes
Cook Time: 40 minutes
Servings: 10 chaffles

Ingredients for the chaffles:
4 eggs, beaten
¼ cup almond flour
4 tbsp cream cheese
½ tsp baking powder
2 tsp yellow flax seed meal
2 cups mozzarella cheese, shredded
Ingredients for the sandwich:
5 hard-boiled eggs, sliced
5 slices bacon
5 slices American cheese

Instructions:
Heat up the mini waffle maker.

Combine the raw eggs with the almond flour, cream cheese, baking powder and blend until smoothy.
Sprinkle 1/10 teaspoon of the flax seed meal and 1 tablespoon of mozzarella onto the waffle maker. Add two tablespoons of egg mixture and cook for 4 minutes. Repeat with the rest of the batter to prepare the other chaffles.
Let cool for 3 minutes to let chaffles get crispy.
Top the chaffle with bacon, a few slices of hard-boiled egg, American cheese and cover with another chaffle.
Serve and enjoy!

Italian Chaffles Sandwich

Prep Time: 5 minutes
Cook Time: 16 minutes
Servings: 4 chaffles

Ingredients for the chaffles:
2 large eggs, beaten
1 cup shredded cheddar cheese
Ingredients for the filling:
1 tomato, sliced
2 lettuce leaves
1 cup mozzarella cheese, shredded
2 tbsp keto mayonnaise
1 tsp of dried oregano

Instructions for the chaffles:
Heat up the waffle maker.
Add egg and shredded cheese to a small mixing bowl and combine well.
Pour ¼ of the batter into the waffle maker and cook for 4 minutes. Repeat with the rest of the batter to prepare the remaining chaffles.
Let cool for 3 minutes to let chaffles get crispy.
Spread the chaffle with keto mayo. Top with a slice of tomato, a lettuce leaf, and sprinkle with dried oregano and mozzarella cheese. Cover with another chaffle.
Serve and enjoy!

Roast Beef Chaffles Sandwich

Prep Time: 5 minutes
Cook Time: 16 minutes

Servings: 4 chaffles

Ingredients for the chaffles:
2 large eggs
1 cup shredded cheddar cheese
A pinch of salt
Ingredients for the filling:
1 tomato, sliced
2 lettuce leaves
2 thin slices of Roast beef
2 tbsp keto mayonnaise

Instructions for the chaffles:
Heat up the waffle maker.
Add eggs, shredded cheese and salt to a small mixing bowl and combine well.
Pour ¼ of the batter into the waffle maker and cook for 4 minutes. Repeat with the rest of the batter to prepare the remaining chaffles.
Let cool for 3 minutes to let chaffles get crispy.
Spread the chaffle with keto mayo. Top with a slice of tomato, lettuce leave and roast beef. Cover with another chaffle.
Serve and enjoy!

Turkey Chaffles Sandwich with Brie and Cranberry Jam

Prep Time: 4 minutes
Cook Time: 8 minutes
Servings: 2 chaffles
Ingredients for the chaffles:
1 large egg, beaten
½ cup mozzarella cheese, shredded
2 tbsp almond flour
Ingredients for the filling:
1 slice of turkey
1 slice of Brie cheese
1 tbsp chia cranberry jam

Instructions for the chaffles:
Heat up the waffle maker.
Add all the chaffles ingredients to a small mixing bowl and combine well.
Pour half of the batter into the waffle maker and cook for 4 minutes until golden brown. Repeat with the rest of the batter to prepare the remaining chaffle.
Let cool for 3 minutes to let chaffles get crispy.
Spread the chaffle with chia cranberry jam and top with a slice of brie and of turkey.
Add spices if desired. Cover with another chaffle.
Serve and enjoy!

Egg and Bacon Chaffles Sandwich

Prep Time: 4 minutes
Cook Time: 16 minutes
Servings: 4 chaffles

Ingredients for the chaffles:
2 large eggs
1 cup shredded cheddar cheese
A pinch of salt
Ingredients for the filling:
2 hard-boiled eggs, sliced
2 lettuce leaves
4 slices of bacon, fried
2 tbsp keto mayonnaise or keto ketchup

Instructions for the chaffles:
Heat up the waffle maker.
Add eggs, shredded cheese and salt to a small mixing bowl and combine well.
Pour ¼ of the batter into the waffle maker and cook for 4 minutes until brown. Repeat with the rest of the batter to prepare the remaining chaffles.
Let cool for 3 minutes to let chaffles get crispy.
Spread the chaffle with keto mayo or keto ketchup. Top with lettuce leave, bacon, hard-boiled egg and add spices if desired. Cover with another chaffle.
Serve and enjoy!

Tasty Shrimps Chaffles Sandwich

Prep Time: 5 minutes
Cook Time: 16 minutes
Servings: 4 chaffles

Ingredients for shrimps:
1 tsp olive oil
2 tbsp shrimps, peeled and deveined
1 tbsp Creole seasoning

2 tbsp hot sauce
3 tbsp butter
A pinch of salt
Ingredients for the chaffles:
2 eggs, beaten
1 cup Monterey Jack cheese, shredded
Ingredients for filling:
1 tomato, sliced
2 tbsp keto mayonnaise

Instructions for shrimps:
In a small saucepan over medium heat, heat the olive oil and cook the shrimps for approx. 3-4 minutes.
Season the shrimps with Creole seasoning.
Pour in the butter and the hot sauce. Mix well.

Instructions for the chaffles:
Heat up the waffle maker.
Add all the chaffles ingredients to a small mixing bowl and stir until well combined.
Pour ¼ of the batter into the waffle maker and cook for 4 minutes until golden brown. Repeat with the rest of the batter to make the other chaffles.
Let cool for 3 minutes to let chaffles get crispy.
Spread the chaffle with keto mayonnaise, a slice of tomato and the shrimps. Cover with another chaffle.
Serve and enjoy!

Chaffles Sandwich with Sausage Patty

Prep Time: 10 minutes
Cook Time: 16 minutes
Servings: 4 chaffles

Ingredients for the chaffles:
2 large eggs, beaten
1 cup mozzarella cheese, shredded
2 tbsp coconut flour
2 tbsp keto mayonnaise
½ tsp baking powder
Ingredients for the filling:
2 sausage patties, cooked
2 slices of cheddar cheese
A pinch of salt and pepper

Instructions for chaffles:
Heat up the waffle maker.

Add all the ingredients for the chaffles to a small mixing bowl and combine well.
Pour ¼ of the batter into the waffle maker and cook for 4 minutes until golden brown. Repeat with the rest of the batter to prepare other chaffles.
Top each chaffle with a slice of cheddar cheese, a sausage patty and a pinch of salt and pepper. Cover with the other chaffle.
Serve and enjoy!

Worcestershire Beef Chaffles Sandwich

Prep Time: 10 minutes
Cook Time: 8 minutes
Servings: 2 chaffles

Ingredients for beef:
½ cup beef broth
4 oz roast beef, very thin
Ingredients for chaffles:
1 large egg, beaten
1 tsp coconut flour
¼ tsp baking powder
½ cup cheese, shredded
Ingredients for sauce:
1 tbsp keto ketchup
¼ tsp Worcestershire sauce
A pinch of pepper

Instructions for beef:
In a big pan bring to a boil the beef broth.
Cook the beef on the broth over low heat for approx. 5 minutes.
Set aside.
Instructions for sauce:
Combine all the sauce ingredients in a small mixing bowl.
Instructions for chaffles:
Heat up the waffle maker.
Add all the chaffles ingredients to a small mixing bowl and stir until well combined.
Pour half of the batter into the waffle maker and cook for 4 minutes until brown. Repeat with the rest of the batter to make another chaffle.
Spread the chaffle with the sauce and top with the beef. Cover with another chaffle.
Serve and enjoy!

Delicious Bread Turkey Chaffles Sandwich

Prep Time: 5 minutes
Cook Time: 8 minutes
Servings: 2 chaffles

Ingredients for chaffles:
2 eggs white, beaten
2 tbsp almond flour
1 tbsp mayonnaise
¼ tsp baking powder
1 tsp water
Salt to taste
Ingredients for the filling:
1 tbsp keto mayonnaise
1 slice deli ham
1 slice deli turkey
1 slice cheddar cheese
1 lettuce leaf
1 tomato, sliced

Instructions:
Heat up the waffle maker.
Add all the ingredients to a small mixing bowl and stir until well combined.
Pour half of the batter into the waffle maker and cook for 4 minutes until golden brown. Repeat with the rest of the batter to make another chaffle.
Spread each chaffle with mayonnaise, top with tomato slice, the lettuce leaf, a slice of cheddar cheese, ham and turkey. Cover with another chaffle. Serve immediately and enjoy!

Trinidad Chaffles Sandwich

Prep Time: 5 minutes
Cook Time: 8 minutes
Servings: 2 chaffles

Ingredients for chaffles:
1 egg, beaten
1 tbsp almond flour
1 tbsp Greek yogurt
1/8 tsp baking powder
¼ cup swiss cheese, shredded
Ingredients for filling:

3 ounces roast pork
1 slice deli ham
1 slice swiss cheese
4 pickles, minced
1 tsp keto mustard

Instructions:
Heat up the waffle maker.
Add all the chaffles ingredients to a small mixing bowl and stir until well combined.
Pour half of the batter into the waffle maker and cook for 4 minutes until golden brown. Repeat with the rest of the batter to make another chaffle.
Let cool for 3 minutes to let chaffles get crispy.
Spread the chaffle with mustard and top with ingredients in this order: roast pork, swiss cheese, deli ham, pickles. Cover with another chaffle.
Microwave the chaffles for 20 seconds and serve immediately. Enjoy!

Veggie Chaffles Sandwich

Prep Time: 5 minutes
Cook Time: 8 minutes
Servings: 2 chaffles

Ingredients for chaffles:
1 egg
½ cup mozzarella cheese, shredded
½ cup zucchini, grated
½ tbsp onion, minced
½ tbsp tomato, diced
1 garlic clove, minced
Fresh dill, chopped
A pinch of salt
Ingredients for filling:
Lettuce leaves
1 tbsp keto mayonnaise
1 slice cheddar cheese

Instructions:
Heat up the waffle maker.
Whisk eggs in bowl and stir in zucchini, onions, garlic, herbs, tomatoes and most of the cheese. You can reserve some of the cheese to make the crispy coating.

Pour half of the batter into the waffle maker and cook for 4 minutes until brown. Repeat with the rest of the batter to make another chaffle.

Let cool for 3 minutes to let chaffles get crispy.

Spread the chaffle with keto mayonnaise and top with lettuce and cheddar cheese. Cover with another chaffle.

Serve and enjoy!

Chaffles Sandwich with Turkey Patties

Prep Time: 10 minutes
Cook Time: 30 minutes
Servings: 4 chaffles

Ingredients for chaffles:
2 eggs, beaten
1 cup cheddar cheese, shredded
A pinch of salt and pepper
Ingredients for patties and filling:
2 cups ground turkey
Lettuce leaves
1 tomato, sliced
Keto Ketchup & Keto Mayonnaise
1 tbsp olive oil
A pinch of salt and pepper

Instructions for the chaffles:
Heat up the waffle maker.
Add all the chaffles ingredients to a small mixing bowl and stir until well combined.
Pour ¼ of the batter into the waffle maker and cook for 4 minutes until golden brown. Repeat with the rest of the batter to prepare the other chaffles.
Let cool for 3 minutes to let chaffles get crispy.
Instructions for the patties:
In a small bowl, season the ground turkey with salt and pepper.
Create small patties.
In a saucepan over low heat, cook the turkey patties in olive oil until completely cooked and brown.
Instructions for topping:
Top each chaffle with Keto mayo or Keto Ketchup according to your taste. Garnish with lettuce, tomato and the patty. Cover with another chaffle.
Serve and enjoy!

Mayonnaise and Ham Chaffles Sandwich

Prep Time: 5 minutes
Cook Time: 16 minutes
Servings: 4 chaffles

Ingredients for chaffles:

2 large eggs, beaten
2 tbsp keto mayonnaise
½ tbsp almond flour
1 tbsp cream cheese
A pinch of salt and pepper
Ingredients for filling:
Lettuce leaves
1 tomato sliced
2 slices of ham
1 scallion, sliced and browned
Keto Ketchup
Instructions:
Heat up the waffle maker.
Add all the ingredients to a small mixing bowl and stir until well combined.
Pour ¼ of the batter into the waffle maker and cook for 4 minutes until brown. Repeat with the rest of the batter to make the other chaffles.
Let cool for 3 minutes to let chaffles get crispy.
Spread the chaffle with keto ketchup. Garnish with lettuce, tomato, ham and onions. Cover with another chaffle.
Serve warm and enjoy!

Blue Cheese Chaffles Sandwich

Prep Time: 5 minutes
Cook Time: 8 minutes
Servings: 2 chaffles

Ingredients for chaffles:
1 large egg, beaten
½ cup mozzarella cheese, shredded
¼ cup blue cheese, shredded
1 tsp sweetener
Ingredients for filling:
1 tbsp raspberries jam
Lettuce leaves
1-2 slices of deli ham

Instructions for chaffles:

Heat up the waffle maker.

Add all the ingredients to a small mixing bowl and stir until well combined.

Pour half of the batter into the waffle maker and cook for 4 minutes until golden brown. Repeat with the rest of the batter to make another chaffle.

Let cool for 3 minutes to let chaffles get crispy.

Spread the chaffle with raspberries jam. Garnish with a lettuce leaf and a slice of deli ham.

Cover with another chaffle.

Serve and enjoy!

Ground Beef and Mushrooms Chaffles Sandwich

Prep Time: 5 minutes
Cook Time: 20 minutes
Servings: 2 chaffles

Ingredients for chaffles:

1 egg, beaten
½ cup shredded cheddar cheese
½ tbsp fresh basil, finely chopped
A pinch of salt

Ingredients for beef:

1 tsp olive oil
2 cups ground beef
½ tsp garlic powder
1 onion, chopped
2 tbsp white mushrooms, chopped
1 tsp butter for topping

Instructions for chaffles:

Heat up the waffle maker.

Add egg, shredded cheddar cheese, a pinch of salt and basil to a small mixing bowl and combine well.

Pour half of the batter into the waffle maker and cook for 4 minutes until brown. Repeat with the rest of the batter to make another chaffle.

Instructions for beef:

In a saucepan over medium heat cook the ground beef in olive oil. Season with salt and pepper if needed and add mushrooms and onion. Stir occasionally and cook until the meat is browned.

Instruction for topping:

Spread the chaffle with butter and garnish with beef and mushrooms. Cover with another chaffle.

Serve immediately and enjoy!

Butter, Spinach and Bacon Chaffles Sandwich

Prep Time: 5 minutes
Cook Time: 8 minutes
Servings: 2 chaffles

Ingredients for chaffles:

1 large egg, beaten
½ cup of mozzarella cheese, shredded
2 tbsp almond flour
¼ tsp baking powder
A pinch of salt

Ingredients for topping:

2 fresh spinach leaves
1 tbsp butter
1 tsp parmesan cheese, flakes
1 slices of bacon, cooked

Instructions:

Heat up the waffle maker.

Add all the ingredients to a small mixing bowl and combine well.

Pour half of the batter into the waffle maker and cook for 4 minutes until brown. Repeat with the rest of the batter to make another chaffle.

Let cool for 3 minutes to let chaffles get crispy.

Spread the chaffle with butter. Garnish with spinach leaves and bacon. Sprinkle with parmesan flakes. Cover with another chaffle.

Serve and enjoy!

Avocado & Turkey Breast Chaffles Sandwich

Prep Time: 15 minutes
Cook Time: 8 minutes
Servings: 2 chaffles

Ingredients for the chaffles:

1 cup mozzarella cheese, grated
2 eggs, beaten

A pinch of salt
Spices to taste
1 slice turkey breast for the filling, very thin
1 tsp keto mayonnaise for the filling

Ingredients for the avocado cream:
1 small avocado pulp, mashed
1 tbsp cherry tomatoes, diced
1 tsp onions, sliced
2 tbsp olive oil
1 tbsp lemon juice
A pinch of salt and pepper
A pinch of Chili powder

Instructions for the avocado cream:
In a small bowl, add the olive oil and lemon juice to the avocado and stir.
Add onions, and tomatoes, mix well and season with salt, pepper, and chili to taste.

Instructions for the chaffles:
Heat up the waffle maker.
Add all the chaffles ingredients except turkey breast and mayonnaise to a small mixing bowl. Stir until well combined.
Pour half of the batter into the waffle maker and cook for 4 minutes. Repeat with the rest of the batter to make another chaffle.
Let cool for 3 minutes to let chaffles get crispy.
Spread avocado cream on a chaffle, fill with turkey breast. Spread keto mayonnaise on the other chaffle and close the sandwich.
Serve and enjoy!

Radishes Chaffles Toast

Prep Time: 5 minutes
Cook Time: 8 minutes
Servings: 2 chaffles

Ingredients for chaffles:
1 large egg, beaten
½ cup mozzarella cheese, shredded
½ tsp baking powder
2 tbsp radishes, boiled and puree
A pinch of black pepper
Ingredients for topping:
1 tbsp butter
1 slice of bacon, browned
2 fresh spinach leaves

1 tsp parmesan cheese, shredded

Instructions:
Heat up the waffle maker.
Add all the chaffles ingredients to a small mixing bowl and stir until well combined.
Pour half of the batter into the waffle maker and cook for 4 minutes until golden brown. Repeat with the rest of the batter to make another chaffle.
Let cool for 3 minutes to let chaffles get crispy.
Spread the chaffle with butter, top with bacon, spinach leaves and sprinkle with parmesan cheese. Cover with another chaffle.
Serve and enjoy!

Ranch Chaffles Sandwich

Prep Time: 5 minutes
Cook Time: 8 minutes
Servings: 2 chaffles

Ingredients for chaffles:
1 egg, beaten
½ cup cheddar cheese, shredded
¼ cup chicken cooked, shredded
1 tbsp bacon bits, browned
1 tsp Ranch seasoning
Ingredients for filling:
Lettuce leaves
1 small tomato, sliced
1 tsp dried oregano
1 slice of American cheese

Instructions:
Heat up the waffle maker.
Add all the chaffles ingredients to a small mixing bowl and stir until well combined.
Pour half of the batter into the waffle maker and cook for 4 minutes until golden brown. Repeat with the rest of the batter to make another chaffle.
Top the chaffle with lettuce, tomato slices, oregano and a slice of American cheese. Cover with another chaffle.
Serve warm and enjoy!

Chicken & Radishes Chaffles Sandwich

Prep Time: 5 minutes
Cook Time: 8 minutes
Servings: 2 chaffles

Ingredients for chaffles:
1 egg, beaten
½ cup cheddar cheese, shredded
Ingredients for filling:
Lettuce leaves
¼ cup chicken cooked, shredded
1 tbsp radishes, grilled and thin sliced
1 tbsp cream cheese, softened

Instructions:
Heat up the waffle maker.
Add all the chaffles ingredients to a small mixing bowl and stir until well combined.
Pour half of the batter into the waffle maker and cook for 4 minutes until golden brown. Repeat with the rest of the batter to make another chaffle.
Spread the chaffle with cream cheese. Top with lettuce, chicken and grilled radishes. Cover with another chaffle.
Serve warm and enjoy!

Cabbage & Tuna Chaffles Sandwich

Prep Time: 5 minutes
Cook Time: 8 minutes
Servings: 2 chaffles

Ingredients for chaffles:
1 large egg, beaten
½ cup of cheddar cheese, shredded
2 tbsp almond flour
¼ tsp baking powder
Ingredients for topping:
½ cup fresh cabbage, shredded
1 tbsp keto mustard
1 tbsp tuna, drained
A pinch of salt and pepper

Instructions:
Heat up the waffle maker.
Add all the chaffles ingredients to a small mixing bowl and stir until well combined.

Pour half of the batter into the waffle maker and cook for 4 minutes until golden brown. Repeat with the rest of the batter to make another chaffle.
Let cool for 3 minutes to let chaffles get crispy.
Spread the chaffle with mustard and top it with cabbage and tuna. Season with salt and pepper. Cover with another chaffle.
Serve and enjoy!

Crabmeat Chaffles Sandwich

Prep Time: 5 minutes
Cook Time: 8 minutes
Servings: 2 chaffles

Ingredients for chaffles:
1 large egg, beaten
½ cup of mozzarella cheese, shredded
2 tbsp almond flour
¼ tsp baking powder
¼ tsp garlic powder
Ingredients for filling:
¾ cup crabmeat
1 tbsp keto mayonnaise
1 tsp lemon juice
Lettuce leaves
1 tomato, sliced

Instructions:
Heat up the waffle maker.
Add all the chaffles ingredients to a small mixing bowl and combine well.
Pour half of the batter into the waffle maker and cook for 4 minutes until brown. Repeat with the rest of the batter to make another chaffle.
In a small bowl mix the crabmeat with mayonnaise and lemon juice.
Top the chaffle with lettuce, tomato and the crabmeat mixture. Cover with another chaffle.
Serve and enjoy!

Grilled Chaffles Sandwich & Vegetables

Prep Time: 5 minutes
Cook Time: 12 minutes
Servings: 2 chaffles

Ingredients for chaffles:
1 large egg, beaten
½ cup of cheddar cheese, shredded
¼ tsp dried oregano
Ingredients for filling:
1 tbsp butter
1 slice of American cheese
2 slices of grilled onions
2 slices of grilled zucchinis

Instructions:
Heat up the waffle maker.
Add all the chaffles ingredients to a small mixing bowl and stir until well combined.
Pour half of the batter into the waffle maker and cook for 4 minutes until golden brown. Repeat with the rest of the batter to make another chaffle.
Top the chaffle with a slice of American cheese, onions and zucchinis. Cover with another chaffle.
In a small saucepan over low heat melt the butter and cook the chaffle part by part for about 2 minutes or until the filling is melt.
Serve and enjoy!

Lemon Sauce Chicken Chaffles Sandwich

Prep Time: 5 minutes
Cook Time: 18 minutes
Servings: 2 chaffles

Ingredients for chaffles:
1 large egg, beaten
½ cup cheddar cheese, shredded
Ingredients for chicken:
½ cup of chicken breast, shredded
¼ tsp garlic powder
¼ tsp paprika powder
1 tsp lemon juice
A pinch of salt and black pepper
2 tbsp heavy cream
1 tbsp finely grated Parmesan cheese
½ tsp fresh thyme, minced
½ tsp fresh parsley, minced
1 tbsp unsalted butter
½ cup chicken broth
Ingredients for filling:
Fresh spinach leaves

1 small tomato, sliced

Instructions for chicken:
In a saucepan over medium heat, cook the chicken breast in the unsalted butter part by part, for approx. 10 minutes. Season with a pinch of salt, black pepper and paprika.
Set aside the meat.
In the same saucepan, add garlic powder, chicken broth, heavy cream, parmesan cheese, lemon juice and thyme. Bring to a boil and simmer until the sauce thickens. Add the chicken and mix well.
Instructions for chaffles:
Heat up the waffle maker.
Add all the chaffles ingredients to a small mixing bowl and stir until well combined.
Pour half of the batter into the waffle maker and cook for 4 minutes until golden brown. Repeat with the rest of the batter to make another chaffle.
Top the chaffle with spinach leaves, tomato, and lemon sauce chicken. Cover with another chaffle.
Serve warm and enjoy!

Sliced Beef Chaffles Sandwich

Prep Time: 5 minutes
Cook Time: 8 minutes
Servings: 2 chaffles

Ingredients for chaffles:
1 large egg, beaten
½ cup mozzarella cheese, shredded
Ingredients for filling:
1 slice of beef (seared in butter)
1 tbsp of keto mustard
A pinch of black pepper
2 slices of grilled bell peppers
½ tbsp scallion, browned and chopped

Instructions for chaffles:
Heat up the waffle maker.
Add all the chaffles ingredients to a small mixing bowl and stir until well combined.
Pour half of the batter into the waffle maker and cook for 4 minutes until golden brown. Repeat with the rest of the batter to make another chaffle.
Spread the chaffle with keto mustard, top with sliced beef, bell peppers and scallion.

Season with black pepper according to your taste.
Cover with another chaffle.
Serve immediately and enjoy!

Fried Fish & Peppers Chaffles Sandwich

Prep Time: 5 minutes
Cook Time: 8 minutes
Servings: 2 chaffles

Ingredients for chaffles:
1 large egg, beaten
½ cup of mozzarella cheese, shredded
2 tbsp almond flour
¼ tsp baking powder
1 tbsp red bell pepper, minced
1 tbsp yellow bell pepper, minced
1 tsp fresh parsley, minced
Ingredients for filling:
Lettuce leaves
1 tbsp keto ketchup
1 fried white fish cutlet

Instructions:
Heat up the waffle maker.
Add all the chaffles ingredients to a small mixing bowl and combine well.
Pour half of the batter into the waffle maker and cook for 4 minutes until brown. Repeat with the rest of the batter to make another chaffle.
Spread the chaffle with ketchup and top it with lettuce and fried fish cutlet. Cover with another chaffle.
Serve warm and enjoy!

Cheese Peppers Chaffles Sandwich

Prep Time: 5 minutes
Cook Time: 8 minutes
Servings: 2 chaffles

Ingredients for chaffles:
1 large egg, beaten
½ cup of mozzarella cheese, shredded
2 tbsp almond flour
¼ tsp baking powder
1 tsp fresh parsley, minced

Ingredients for filling:
1 tbsp keto mayonnaise
½ tbsp red bell pepper, grilled and thinly sliced
½ tbsp yellow bell pepper, grilled and thinly sliced
Fresh spinach leaves
1 slice cheddar cheese
Instructions:

Heat up the waffle maker.
Add all the chaffles ingredients to a small mixing bowl and combine well.
Pour half of the batter into the waffle maker and cook for 4 minutes until brown. Repeat with the rest of the batter to make another chaffle.
Spread the chaffle with mayonnaise and top it with spinach leaves, cheddar cheese and peppers. Cover with another chaffle.
Serve warm and enjoy!

Chaffles Sandwich Ham & Guacamole

Prep Time: 15 minutes
Cook Time: 8 minutes
Servings: 2 chaffles

Ingredients for the chaffles:
1 cup cheddar cheese, grated
2 eggs, beaten
A pinch of salt
1 slice ham for the filling
Ingredients for Guacamole sauce:
1 small avocado pulp, mashed
1 tbsp cherry tomatoes, diced
1 tsp onions, sliced
2 tbsp olive oil
1 tbsp lemon juice
A pinch of salt and pepper
A pinch of Chili powder

Instructions for Guacamole sauce:
In a small bowl, add the olive oil and lemon juice to the avocado and stir.
Add onions, and tomatoes, mix well and season with salt, pepper, and chili to taste.
Instructions for the chaffles:
Heat up the waffle maker.
Add all the chaffles ingredients except ham to a small mixing bowl. Stir until well combined.

Pour half of the batter into the waffle maker and cook for 4 minutes. Repeat with the rest of the batter to make another chaffle.
Spread the guacamole on a chaffle and cover with ham, then put another chaffle on top.
Serve and enjoy!

Cauliflower Chaffles Sandwich

Prep Time: 5 minutes
Cook Time: 8 minutes
Servings: 2 chaffles

Ingredients for chaffles:
1 egg, beaten
½ cup steamed cauliflower mash
¼ cup parmesan cheese, shredded
½ cup mozzarella cheese, shredded
A pinch of salt and black pepper
Ingredients for filling:
1 tbsp keto mayonnaise
1-2 slices of ham
1 slice cheddar cheese
1 small tomato, sliced

Instructions:
Heat up the waffle maker.
Add all the chaffles ingredients except for parmesan cheese to a small mixing bowl and combine well.
Pour half of the batter into the waffle maker, sprinkle with 1-2 tbsp of shredded parmesan cheese and cook for 4 minutes until golden brown. Repeat with the rest of the batter/parmesan to make another chaffle.
Let cool for 3 minutes to let chaffles get crispy.
Spread the chaffles with mayonnaise. Top with ham, tomato slices and cheddar cheese. Cover with another chaffle.
Serve and enjoy!

Artichoke Chaffles Sandwich

Prep Time: 5 minutes
Cook Time: 8 minutes
Servings: 2 chaffles

Ingredients for chaffles:
1 large egg, beaten
½ cup mozzarella cheese, shredded
¼ tsp garlic powder
1/3 cup artichoke hearts marinated, minced
A pinch of salt and pepper
Ingredients for filling:
1 tbsp of keto mayonnaise
1 slice of cheddar cheese
2 slices of bacon, browned

Instructions:
Heat up the waffle maker.
Add all the chaffles ingredients to a small mixing bowl and stir until well combined.
Pour half of the batter into the waffle maker and cook for 4 minutes until golden brown. Repeat with the rest of the batter to make another chaffle.
Spread the chaffle with mayonnaise and top with bacon and cheddar cheese. Cover with another chaffle.
Serve warm and enjoy!

Sardine's Pate Chaffles Sandwich

Prep Time: 5 minutes
Cook Time: 8 minutes
Servings: 2 chaffles

Ingredients for chaffles:
1 large egg, beaten
½ cup shredded mozzarella cheese
Ingredients for Sardine's Pate:
½ can sardines in extra virgin olive oil
½ tbsp pickled capers
1 filet anchovies, canned
1 tbsp butter
½ tbsp keto mayonnaise
A pinch of black pepper
Ingredients for filling:
1 tbsp pickled cucumbers, sliced
1 tsp paprika powder
1 small tomato, sliced

Instructions for pate:
Add all the pate ingredients to a blender and mix until smoothy.
Instructions for chaffles:
Heat up the waffle maker.

Add all the chaffles ingredients to a small mixing bowl and stir until well combined.

Pour half of the batter into the waffle maker and cook for 4 minutes until golden brown. Repeat with the rest of the batter to make another chaffle.

Top the chaffle with sardine's pate, tomato slices and pickled cucumbers. Season with paprika powder to taste. Cover with another chaffle.

Serve and enjoy!

Club Sandwich Chaffles

Prep Time: 4 minutes
Cook Time: 16 minutes
Servings: 4 chaffles

Ingredients for chaffles:
2 eggs, beaten
1 cup shredded cheddar cheese
Ingredients for club sandwich:
2 Iceberg lettuce leaves
2 tsp keto mayonnaise
2 slices of deli ham
2 slices deli turkey
2 sliced cheddar cheese
1 small tomato, sliced
2 slices of bacon, cooked

Instructions:
Heat up the waffle maker.
Add egg and shredded cheese to a small mixing bowl and combine well.
Pour ¼ of the batter into the waffle maker and cook for 4 minutes until golden brown. Repeat with the rest of the batter to prepare the other chaffles.
Let cool for 3 minutes to let chaffles get crispy. You need 3 chaffles for this sandwich.
Spread the chaffle with keto mayonnaise. Top with lettuce leaves, 1 slice of deli ham, 1 slice of deli turkey, 1 slice of cheddar cheese, 1 slice of tomato, 1 slice of bacon. Cover with another chaffle and repeat the procedure. Cover with the 3rd chaffle.
Serve and enjoy!

Chaffles Sandwich Deli Ham, Brie & Avocado

Prep Time: 5 minutes
Cook Time: 8 minutes
Servings: 2 chaffles

Ingredients for the chaffles:
½ cup cheddar cheese, grated
1 large egg, beaten
A pinch of salt
Ingredients for filling:
1 slice of deli ham
1 small avocado, thinly sliced
1 slice of Brie cheese, very thin
1 tsp sesame seeds
1 tbsp keto mayonnaise

Instructions for the chaffles:
Heat up the waffle maker.
Add all the chaffles ingredients to a mixing bowl. Stir until well combined.
Pour half of the batter into the waffle maker and cook for 4 minutes until golden brown. Repeat with the rest of the batter to make another chaffle.
Spread the chaffle with mayonnaise; top with a slice of deli ham, a slice of Brie, a few slices of avocado. Sprinkle with sesame seeds. Cover with another chaffle.
Serve and enjoy!

Vegetables Chaffles Sandwich

Prep Time: 5 minutes
Cook Time: 8 minutes
Servings: 2 chaffles

Ingredients for chaffles:
1 large egg, beaten
½ cup of mozzarella cheese, shredded
Ingredients for filling:
1 tbsp butter, unsalted
1 slice of Fontina cheese
2 slices of grilled onions
2 slices of grilled zucchinis
1 slice of grilled bell pepper

Instructions:

Heat up the waffle maker.

Add all the chaffles ingredients to a small mixing bowl and stir until well combined.

Pour half of the batter into the waffle maker and cook for 4 minutes until golden brown. Repeat with the rest of the batter to make another chaffle.

Spread the butter on the chaffle. Top it with a slice of Fontina cheese, onions, zucchinis and bell peppers. Cover with another chaffle.

Serve and enjoy!

Pork Tenderloin Chaffles Sandwich

Prep Time: 5 minutes
Cook Time: 8 minutes
Servings: 2 chaffles

Ingredients for chaffles:

1 large egg, beaten
½ cup of Mozzarella cheese, shredded

Ingredients for filling:

1 thin slice of cooked pork tenderloin
Lettuce leaves
1 small tomato, sliced
1 tbsp keto mayonnaise
A pinch of black pepper

Instructions:

Heat up the waffle maker.

Add all the chaffles ingredients to a small mixing bowl and combine well.

Pour half of the batter into the waffle maker and cook for 4 minutes until golden brown. Repeat with the rest of the batter to make another chaffle.

Spread the chaffle with mayonnaise and top with a slice of pork tenderloin, tomato and lettuce. Season with black pepper to taste. Cover with another chaffle.

Serve warm and enjoy!

Egg Salad Chicken Chaffles Sandwich

Prep Time: 5 minutes
Cook Time: 8 minutes
Servings: 2 chaffles

Ingredients for chaffles:

1 large egg, beaten
½ cup mozzarella cheese, shredded

Ingredients for egg salad:

1 hard-boiled egg, smashed
2 tsp avocado pulp, smashed
2 tsp keto mayonnaise
A pinch of salt and black pepper

Ingredients for filling:

½ cup of cooked chicken, shredded
1 small tomato, sliced

Instructions for egg salad:

Combine all the salad ingredients in a bowl and mix well.

Instructions for chaffles:

Heat up the waffle maker.

Add all the chaffles ingredients to a small mixing bowl and stir until well combined.

Pour half of the batter into the waffle maker and cook for 4 minutes until golden brown. Repeat with the rest of the batter to make another chaffle.

Spread the chaffle with egg salad. Top with tomato slices and chicken. Cover with another chaffle.

Serve and enjoy!

Arugula & Tuna Chaffles Sandwich

Prep Time: 5 minutes
Cook Time: 8 minutes
Servings: 2 chaffles

Ingredients for chaffles:

1 large egg, beaten
½ cup mozzarella cheese, shredded

Ingredients for filling:

1 tsp keto mustard
1 tbsp fresh arugula
1 can of tuna, drained

Instructions:

Heat up the waffle maker.

Add all the chaffles ingredients to a small mixing bowl and stir until well combined.

Pour half of the batter into the waffle maker and cook for 4 minutes until golden brown. Repeat with the rest of the batter to make another chaffle.

Let cool for 3 minutes to let chaffles get crispy.

Spread the chaffle with mustard. Top with arugula and tuna. Cover with another chaffle.
Serve and enjoy!

Roasted Peppers & Bacon Chaffles Sandwich

Prep Time: 5 minutes
Cook Time: 8 minutes
Servings: 2 chaffles

Ingredients for chaffles:
1 large egg, beaten
½ cup mozzarella cheese, shredded
Ingredients for roasted pepper sauce:
2 tbsp roasted yellow peppers
2 tbsp mayonnaise
¼ tsp garlic powder
1 tbsp olive oil
A pinch of salt and black pepper
Ingredients for filling:
1-2 slices of bacon, cooked
Fresh spinach leaves
1 slice of cheddar cheese

Instructions for sauce:
Mix in a blender all the sauce ingredients and set aside.
Instructions for chaffles:
Heat up the waffle maker.
Add all the chaffles ingredients to a small mixing bowl and stir until well combined.
Pour half of the batter into the waffle maker and cook for 4 minutes until golden brown. Repeat with the rest of the batter to make another chaffle.
Let cool for 3 minutes to let chaffles get crispy.
Spread the chaffle with pepper cream. Top with spinach leaves, bacon and cheddar cheese. Cover with another chaffle.
Serve and enjoy!

Swiss Cheese and Salami Chaffles Sandwich

Prep Time: 5 minutes
Cook Time: 8 minutes
Servings: 2 chaffles

Ingredients for chaffles:
1 large egg, beaten
½ cup of Swiss cheese, shredded
Ingredients for filling:
1-2 slices of Salami
1 tbsp keto Ranch dressing
Lettuce leaves

Instructions:
Heat up the waffle maker.
Add all the chaffles ingredients to a small mixing bowl and combine well.
Pour half of the batter into the waffle maker and cook for 4 minutes until golden brown. Repeat with the rest of the batter to make another chaffle.
Let cool for 3 minutes to let chaffles get crispy.
Spread the chaffle with Ranch dressing. Top the chaffle with lettuce and a slice of Salami. Cover with another chaffle.
Serve and enjoy!

Bread Chaffles Sandwich

Prep Time: 5 minutes
Cook Time: 8 minutes
Servings: 2 chaffles

Ingredients for chaffles:
1 egg, beaten
3 tbsp almond flour
1 tbsp mayonnaise
¼ tsp baking powder
1 tsp water
Ingredients for filling:
Lettuce leaves
1 small tomato, sliced
1 tsp dried oregano
1 slice of Cheddar cheese
Instructions:
Heat up the waffle maker.
Add all the chaffles ingredients to a small mixing bowl and stir until well combined.
Pour half of the batter into the waffle maker and cook for 4 minutes until golden brown. Repeat with the rest of the batter to make another chaffle.

Top the chaffle with lettuce, tomato slices, oregano and a slice of Cheddar cheese. Cover with another chaffle.
Serve warm and enjoy!

Ragù Chaffles Sandwich

Prep Time: 5 minutes
Cook Time: 20-25 minutes
Servings: 2 chaffles
Ingredients for chaffles:
1 egg, beaten
½ cup cheddar cheese, shredded
A pinch of salt

Ingredients for beef:
1 tsp olive oil, extra virgin
2 cups ground beef
½ tsp basil, minced
1 scallion, chopped
2 tbsp tomato sauce
A pinch of salt and pepper
Ingredients for filling:
1 tbsp Parmesan cheese, shredded
1 tsp fresh basil, minced
Lettuce leaves

Instructions for beef:
In a saucepan over medium heat brown the scallion in olive oil. Add the ground beef, season with salt and pepper and cook for 5-6 minutes. Add basil and tomato sauce. Stir occasionally and cook until the meat is browned.
Instructions for chaffles:
Heat up the waffle maker.
Add egg, shredded cheddar cheese, a pinch of salt to a small mixing bowl and combine well.
Pour half of the batter into the waffle maker and cook for 4 minutes until brown. Repeat with the rest of the batter to make another chaffle.
Top the chaffle with lettuce leaves and ground beef ragù. Sprinkle with parmesan cheese. Cover with another chaffle.
Serve immediately and enjoy!

Ground Pork Chaffles Sandwich

Prep Time: 5 minutes
Cook Time: 20 minutes
Servings: 2 chaffles

Ingredients for chaffles:
1 egg, beaten
½ cup shredded mozzarella cheese
½ tbsp fresh basil, finely chopped
A pinch of salt
Ingredients for pork:
1 tsp olive oil, extra virgin
2 cups ground pork
1 small red onion, chopped
1 tsp fresh parsley, minced
A pinch of salt and black pepper
Ingredients for topping:
1 tbsp keto mayonnaise
1 slice of cheddar cheese
1 lettuce leaf
1-2 slices of tomato
Instructions for pork:
In a saucepan over low heat brown the onion in olive oil. Season with salt and pepper if needed. Add the ground pork and the fresh parsley. Stir occasionally and cook until the meat is browned.
Instructions for chaffles:
Heat up the waffle maker.
Add egg, shredded cheddar cheese, a pinch of salt and basil in a small mixing bowl and combine well.
Pour half of the batter into the waffle maker and cook for 4 minutes until brown. Repeat with the rest of the batter to make another chaffle.
Spread the chaffle with mayonnaise. Top with lettuce, tomato, cheddar cheese and ground pork. Cover with another chaffle.
Serve immediately and enjoy!

Tuna Salad Chaffles Sandwich

Prep Time: 5 minutes
Cook Time: 8 minutes
Servings: 2 chaffles

Ingredients for chaffles:
1 large egg, beaten

½ cup mozzarella cheese, shredded

Ingredients for tuna salad:

1 can tuna, drained

1 tbsp keto mayonnaise

2 tbsp cream cheese, softened

1 tsp capers

½ tsp paprika powder

A pinch of salt and black pepper

Ingredients for filling:

Lettuce leaves

1 small hard-boiled egg, sliced

1 small tomato, sliced

Instructions for tuna salad:

Combine all the salad ingredients in a bowl and mix well.

Instructions for chaffles:

Heat up the waffle maker.

Add all the chaffles ingredients to a small mixing bowl and stir until well combined.

Pour half of the batter into the waffle maker and cook for 4 minutes until golden brown. Repeat with the rest of the batter to make another chaffle.

Let cool for 3 minutes to let chaffles get crispy.

Top the chaffle with lettuce, tomato, egg and tuna salad. Cover with another chaffle.

Serve and enjoy!

Parmesan Butter Chaffles Sandwich

Prep Time: 5 minutes

Cook Time: 8 minutes

Servings: 2 chaffles

Ingredients for chaffles:

1 large egg, beaten

½ cup of mozzarella cheese, shredded

2 tbsp almond flour

¼ tsp baking powder

Ingredients for Parmesan butter:

2 tbsp butter, softened

2 tbsp Parmesan cheese, shredded

A pinch of salt and black pepper

Ingredients for filling:

1 slice of ham

Spinach leaves

1 tbsp scallion, browned and chopped

Instructions for Parmesan butter:

In a small mixing bowl, combine all the ingredients and stir well. Set aside.

Instructions for chaffles:

Heat up the waffle maker.

Add all the chaffles ingredients to a small mixing bowl and combine well.

Pour half of the batter into the waffle maker and cook for 4 minutes until brown. Repeat with the rest of the batter to make another chaffle.

Let cool for 3 minutes to let chaffles get crispy.

Spread the chaffle with Parmesan butter. Top with spinach leaves, ham and scallions.

Serve and enjoy!

Curry Chaffles Sandwich

Prep Time: 5 minutes

Cook Time: 8 minutes

Servings: 2 chaffles

Ingredients for chaffles:

1 egg, beaten

½ cup shredded mozzarella cheese

¼ tsp curry powder

½ tbsp fresh basil, finely chopped

A pinch of salt and pepper

Ingredients for filling:

1 tbsp mayonnaise

1 small avocado, sliced

1 slice of turkey breast, very thin

Instructions:

Heat up the waffle maker.

Add egg, shredded mozzarella cheese, curry powder and basil to a small mixing bowl and combine well.

Pour half of the batter into the waffle maker and cook for 4 minutes until brown. Repeat with the rest of the batter to make another chaffle. Season with salt and pepper.

Spread the chaffle with mayonnaise. Top with avocado slices and turkey breast. Cover with another chaffle.

Serve and enjoy!

Chicken Salad Chaffles Sandwich

Prep Time: 5 minutes
Cook Time: 8 minutes
Servings: 2 chaffles

Ingredients for chaffles:
1 large egg, beaten
½ cup shredded cheddar cheese
Ingredients for chicken salad:
½ cup chicken, cooked and shredded
1 tbsp fresh celery, chopped
1 tsp scallion, browned and minced
2 tbsp avocado pulp, smashed
1 tsp fresh basil, minced
2 tbsp keto mayonnaise
1 tsp keto mustard
1 tsp lemon juice
A pinch of salt and pepper
Ingredients for filling:
Lettuce leaves
1 small hard-boiled egg, sliced

Instructions for chicken salad:
Combine all the ingredients in a mixing bowl and stir well. Set aside.

Instructions for chaffles:
Heat up the waffle maker.
Add egg and shredded cheese to a small mixing bowl and combine well.
Pour half of the batter into the waffle maker and cook for 4 minutes until golden brown. Repeat with the rest of the batter to make another chaffle.
Let cool for 3 minutes to let chaffles get crispy.
Garnish the chaffle with lettuce, chicken salad and 1 or 2 slices of hard-boiled egg. Cover with another chaffle.
Serve and enjoy!

Avocado & Roast Beef Chaffles Sandwich

Prep Time: 15 minutes
Cook Time: 8 minutes
Servings: 2 chaffles

Ingredients for the chaffles:
1 cup mozzarella cheese, grated

2 eggs, beaten
A pinch of salt
Spices to taste
1 slice roast beef for the filling, very thin
1 tsp keto mayonnaise for the filling
Ingredients for the avocado cream:
1 small avocado pulp, mashed
1 tbsp cherry tomatoes, diced
1 tsp onions, sliced
2 tbsp olive oil
1 tbsp lemon juice
A pinch of salt and pepper
A pinch of Chili powder

Instructions for the avocado cream:
In a small bowl, add the olive oil and lemon juice to the avocado and stir.
Add onions, and tomatoes, mix well and season with salt, pepper, and chili to taste.
Instructions for the chaffles:
Heat up the waffle maker.
Add all the chaffles ingredients except turkey breast and mayonnaise to a small mixing bowl. Stir until well combined.
Pour half of the batter into the waffle maker and cook for 4 minutes. Repeat with the rest of the batter to make another chaffle.
Let cool for 3 minutes to let chaffles get crispy.
Spread avocado cream on a chaffle, fill with roast beef. Spread keto mayonnaise on the other chaffle and close the sandwich.
Serve and enjoy!

Turkey Breast Chaffles Sandwich

Prep Time: 4 minutes
Cook Time: 16 minutes
Servings: 4 chaffles

Ingredients for the chaffles:
2 large eggs
1 cup shredded cheddar cheese
A pinch of salt
Ingredients for the filling:
1 tomato, sliced
2 lettuce leaves
2 slices turkey breast for the filling, very thin

2 tbsp keto mayonnaise

Instructions for the chaffles:
Heat up the waffle maker.
Add eggs, shredded cheese and salt to a small mixing bowl and combine well.
Pour ¼ of the batter into the waffle maker and cook for 4 minutes. Repeat with the rest of the batter to prepare the remaining chaffles.
Let cool for 3 minutes to let chaffles get crispy.
Spread the chaffle with keto mayo. Top with a slice of tomato, lettuce leave and turkey breast.
Add spices if desired. Cover with another chaffle.
Serve and enjoy!

Guacamole Turkey Patties Chaffles Sandwich

Prep Time: 10 minutes
Cook Time: 30 minutes
Servings: 4 chaffles

Ingredients for chaffles:
2 eggs, beaten
1 cup cheddar cheese, shredded
A pinch of salt and pepper
Ingredients for patties and filling:
2 cups ground turkey
1 tomato, sliced
4 pickles, sliced
Guacamole Sauce
Keto Ketchup
1 tbsp olive oil
A pinch of salt and pepper

Instructions for the chaffles:
Heat up the waffle maker.
Add all the chaffles ingredients in a small mixing bowl and stir until well combined.
Pour ¼ of the batter into the waffle maker and cook for 4 minutes until golden brown. Repeat with the rest of the batter to prepare the other chaffles.
Let cool for 3 minutes to let chaffles get crispy.
Instructions for the patties:
In a small bowl, season the ground turkey with salt and pepper.
Create small patties.

In a saucepan over low heat, cook the turkey patties in olive oil until completely cooked and brown.
Instructions for topping:
Spread each chaffle with Guacamole sauce. Garnish with tomato, pickles and the patty. Add keto ketchup if desired. Cover with another chaffle.
Serve and enjoy!

Mexican Ground Beef Chaffles Sandwich

Prep Time: 5 minutes
Cook Time: 20 minutes
Servings: 2 chaffles

Ingredients for chaffles:
1 egg, beaten
½ cup shredded cheddar cheese
½ tbsp fresh basil, finely chopped
A pinch of salt
Ingredients for beef:
1 tsp olive oil
2 cups ground beef
½ tsp garlic powder
1 onion, chopped
1 tbsp mushrooms, chopped
1 small red bell pepper, sliced
1 tbsp black olives, pitted and chopped
½ tsp red hot chili powder

Instructions for chaffles:
Heat up the waffle maker.
Add egg, shredded cheddar cheese, a pinch of salt and basil to a small mixing bowl and combine well.
Pour half of the batter into the waffle maker and cook for 4 minutes until brown. Repeat with the rest of the batter to make another chaffle.
Instructions for beef:
In a saucepan over medium heat cook the ground beef in olive oil. Season with salt and pepper if needed and add all the other ingredients. Stir occasionally and cook until the meat is browned.
Instruction for topping:
Garnish the chaffle with beef and cover with another chaffle.
Serve with sour cream and enjoy!

Savory Fried Radishes Chaffles Sandwich

Prep Time: 5 minutes
Cook Time: 8 minutes
Servings: 2 chaffles

Ingredients for chaffles:
1 large egg, beaten
½ cup mozzarella cheese, shredded
½ tsp baking powder
A pinch of salt and black pepper

Ingredients for filling:
1 tbsp fresh radishes, thin sliced
1 tbsp olive oil
1 tbsp keto mayonnaise
1 lettuce leaf
1 slice smoked salmon

Instructions:
Heat up the waffle maker.
Add all the chaffles ingredients to a small mixing bowl and stir until well combined.
Pour half of the batter into the waffle maker and cook for 4 minutes until golden brown. Repeat with the rest of the batter to make another chaffle.
In a small saucepan over medium heat, cook the radishes in olive oil until crispy.
Spread the chaffle with mayonnaise. Top with lettuce, fried radishes and a slice of smoked salmon.
Cover with another chaffle.
Serve and enjoy!

Cabbage Savory Chaffles Sandwich

Prep Time: 5 minutes
Cook Time: 8 minutes
Servings: 2 chaffles

Ingredients for chaffles:
1 large egg, beaten
½ cup of cheddar cheese, shredded
2 tbsp almond flour
¼ tsp baking powder

Ingredients for topping:
½ cup fresh cabbage, shredded
1 tbsp sour cream
1 slice of bacon, browned

A pinch of salt and black pepper

Instructions:
Heat up the waffle maker.
Add all the chaffles ingredients to a small mixing bowl and stir until well combined.
Pour half of the batter into the waffle maker and cook for 4 minutes until golden brown. Repeat with the rest of the batter to make another chaffle.
Let cool for 3 minutes to let chaffles get crispy.
Spread the chaffle with sour cream and top it with cabbage and bacon. Season with salt and pepper.
Cover with another chaffle.
Serve and enjoy!

Turkey in Lemon Sauce Chaffles Sandwich

Prep Time: 5 minutes
Cook Time: 18 minutes
Servings: 2 chaffles

Ingredients for chaffles:
1 large egg, beaten
½ cup cheddar cheese, shredded

Ingredients for turkey:
½ cup of turkey breast, shredded
¼ tsp garlic powder
¼ tsp paprika powder
1 tsp lemon juice
A pinch of salt and black pepper
2 tbsp heavy cream
1 tbsp finely grated Parmesan cheese
½ tsp fresh thyme, minced
½ tsp fresh parsley, minced
1 tbsp unsalted butter
½ cup chicken broth

Ingredients for filling:
Fresh spinach leaves
1 small tomato, sliced

Instructions for turkey:
In a saucepan over medium heat, cook the turkey breast in the unsalted butter part by part, for approx. 10 minutes. Season with a pinch of salt, black pepper and paprika.
Set aside the meat.

In the same saucepan, add garlic powder, chicken broth, heavy cream, parmesan cheese, lemon juice and thyme. Bring to a boil and simmer until the sauce thickens. Add the turkey and mix well.

Instructions for chaffles:

Heat up the waffle maker.

Add all the chaffles ingredients to a small mixing bowl and stir until well combined.

Pour half of the batter into the waffle maker and cook for 4 minutes until golden brown. Repeat with the rest of the batter to make another chaffle.

Top the chaffle with spinach leaves, tomato, and lemon sauce turkey. Cover with another chaffle.

Serve warm and enjoy!

Bacon and Cheese Chaffles Sandwich

Prep Time: 5 minutes
Cook Time: 8 minutes
Servings: 2 chaffles

Ingredients for chaffles:

1 egg
½ cup shredded mozzarella cheese
¼ cup almond flour
¼ tsp baking powder, gluten-free
A pinch of salt and pepper

Ingredients for filling:

1 slice of bacon
1 slice American cheese
1 tomato, sliced
1 lettuce leaf
1 tbsp keto butter

Instructions:

Heat up the waffle maker.

Add all the chaffles ingredients to a small mixing bowl and combine well.

Pour half of the batter into the waffle maker and cook for 4 minutes until brown. Repeat with the rest of the batter to make another chaffle.

Spread butter over the chaffle; top with a slice of bacon, lettuce, tomato and American cheese. Cover with another chaffle.

Serve and enjoy!

CONCLUSION

Chaffles are a nourishment meal that has changed the eating way of almost all Ketogenic diet followers for their simplicity. They are very versatile and easy to make with ingredients usually on-hand.

Chaffles open a world of possibilities if you are on a Keto diet, as they satisfy your cravings without cheating!

Thank you for reading this book, I hope it has provided enough insight to get you going into the fantastic world of chaffles and it will help you in your new lifestyle.

Get your hands on this special recipe collection and start cooking in this new and healthy way.

Have a lot of fun and enjoy your Ketogenic diet with chaffles!

Made in the USA
Coppell, TX
12 June 2021